Played in Peoria

Jerry Klein

The Kickapoo Press
P. O. Box 1443
Peoria, Illinois 61655

Acknowledgments

The essays reprinted in *Played In Peoria*, with the single exception of "Wilderness Train," all appeared previously in The Peoria *Journal Star* or *The New York Times*, and are reprinted with their kind permission. "Grant's Galena: An Illinois Town That Time Forgot" (November 26, 1978), "Nauvoo, the Town the Mormons Left" (November 11, 1976), and "All Quiet On the Western Front" (originally "The Poppies. The Stillness," November 11, 1976) copyright (c) by The New York Times Company. Reprinted by permission. "This Old House" (Sept. 14, 1975), "No Kicks, No Regrets" (Aug. 14, 1977), "The Vanishing Prairie" (May 8, 1977), "20 Miles West of Peoria and There You Are: the Republic of Forgottonia" (Sept. 16, 1973), "Day Breaks Gently on the Illinois" (July 4, 1976), "Along the Spoon" (Oct. 13, 1968), "The Other End of the Spoon" (July 17, 1977), "A Winter Day in Vermont, Illinois" (Jan. 19, 1975), "Elmwood: the Train Hardly Ever Stops Here Any More" (June 9, 1974), "Here's Looking at Toluca" (Feb. 16, 1975), "Goofy Ridge, Where the Living Is Easy" (March 16, 1975), "Welcome to Washburn" (May 23, 1976), "Princeton, a Page from the Past" (Aug. 17, 1975), "Lewistown" (May 9, 1976), "Grass May be Greener Beneath Eureka's Snow" (Jan. 23, 1977), "Spring Valley" (May 22, 1977), "Bath" (June 20, 1976), "Henry. Pop. 2600. Best Town by a Dam Site" (Aug. 25, 1974), "Fountain Green, Junkyard Town" (Oct. 24, 1976), "Havana: the Memories Linger On" (April 14, 1974), "Toulon: They're Still the Good Old Days" (Sept. 15, 1974), "Canton—the 30s Stay" (Aug. 5, 1973), "Oquawka" (Jan. 11, 1976), "A Touch of New England in Midwestern Monmouth" (Sept. 12, 1976), "Lacon . . . Where the Livin' Is Steady" (Aug. 22, 1976), "Beardstown" (June 17, 1973), "Minonk" (Nov. 12, 1978), "Colchester" (June 4, 1978), "There's No Rush in Rushville" (June 29, 1975), "Cherry Mine: 481 Went Down; 259 Never Came Back" (April 24, 1977), "Princeton: a Page from the Past" (Aug. 17, 1975), "There's Beauty Around the Bend" (Sept. 7, 1975), "Lake Superior Circle Route— Unspoiled, Unchanged" (Oct. 10, 1976), "Here Lie Custer's Men" (Aug. 5, 1979), "Mississagi Provincial Park, Ontario" (June 16, 1978), "New Orleans, Quick and Cheap" (March 20, 1977), Galesburg" (April 15, 1973), "Schaumburg" (April 8, 1979), "Abe Lincoln Sleeps Here" April 25, 1976), "St. Louis" (June 12, 1977), "The Best Place in Town" (March 27, 1977), "Las Vegas: A Desert Disneyland for Adults" (Sunday, March 4, 1979), "Chicago" (Feb. 22, 1976), "There's Still Something to Like in New York in June" (June 24, 1973), "Colonial New York" (May 11, 1975), and "Paris Anytime" (Nov. 2, 1975) from the Peoria *Journal Star*. Reprinted by permission.

ISBN 0-933180-14-4

Library of Congress Number 80-81454

Second Printing

To Mary, my family, and the members of that wider family herein, those who are still here, and those who have already gone.

Contents

Travels

Larger Places

End Piece

Introduction

Jerry Klein is a rarity in the world of contemporary literature, a serious author who reaches his audience through a newspaper. During the past decade or so, he has written a number of fine descriptive essays that have been presented as feature articles in the Peoria *Journal Star*, and others have appeared in the *New York Times*. As a result of these newspaper contributions, he is among the most well-known journalists in downstate Illinois. More importantly, he is gaining recognition as a very talented interpreter of midwestern culture.

Modern readers are not accustomed to finding literature of any kind in a newspaper—that is, writing that rises above the level of informative prose—but many years ago things were different. On the Illinois frontier, for example, newspaper editors such as James Hall, John Russell, and Thomas Gregg were among the most dedicated writers in the state, and they were dedicated to bringing literary experience to their readers, who usually had no other source of poems, short stories, and descriptive (travel) essays. Coincidentally, the most important early Illinois periodical for travel writing—a type of literature which is akin to Klein's essays—was a newspaper in Peoria, the *Register and North-Western Gazatteer*, edited by Samuel H. Davis.

After communication with the East Coast improved and libraries and literary magazines were founded in the Midwest, newspapers ceased to print much literature, except for humorous material. In the later nineteenth century, Chicago authors Eugene Field, George Ade, and Finley Peter Dunne received national acclaim for their humorous columns, and downstate Illinois produced Bob Burdette and George Fitch, the first of whom was raised in Peoria and began his newspaper career there while the second edited the Peoria *Herald Transcript* at the height of his career. Now, even humorous literature is seldom found in newspapers, and so, as a journalistic literary artist, Klein is an unusual figure in our time.

A native of Peoria, Klein was born on December 19, 1926 and grew up in the East Bluff area of the city. He attended St. Bernard's parochial school and Spalding Institute, graduating from the latter in 1945. However, he entered the navy in December, 1944—before receiving his secondary school diploma—and served as a radioman in the South Pacific during World War II. In 1950 he received his Bachelor of Music degree from Bradley University, which was followed by two years of graduate work in music at the University of Illinois.

He liked his home town well enough to want to stay in the area, but Peoria held few opportunities for a young concert pianist. After a one-year stint as a "rod man" and surveyor for the state highway department, he responded to a Peoria *Journal Star* ad for an editorial writer. That was September of 1953.

Fortunately, the managing editor, Gomer Bath, did not insist on much by way of experience—for Klein had none. Instead, he offered the tall young man a chance to prove he could fill the position. "Bring me in three editorials tomorrow," Bath said. Klein went home, looked at some editorials, wrote three of his own, and brought them in the next day. He got the job.

On June 4, 1955 he married Mary E. Dudas, who has also been raised in Washington, and in the years that followed, the Kleins had seven children. They currently live in Lourdes, about nine miles east of Peoria. Now in his fifties,

Klein is a modest, affable man who does not appear to take himself seriously as a writer—but he does.

His writing for the *Journal Star* during the past twenty-seven years falls roughly into three categories. Criticism of the performing arts in and around Peoria has been his main assignment. Also, for a few years he wrote a humorous column called "Once Over Lightly," which appeared in the newspaper's *Weekender* supplement. However, his literary achievement resides in the occasional feature articles that he has written during the past decade, most of which deal with the communities and countryside of west-central Illinois. Klein has also published articles and stories in *Redbook, Reader's Digest* and *Ford Times.*

Because he has remained in the region where he was raised and has chosen that locale for his primary subject matter, his writing displays a quality which many fine midwestern authors have sought: a sense of place. He has a deep sensitivity to the land and people of west-central Illinois, and he recognizes that there is something uniquely valuable about the life of the region, something that has resulted from the interaction of individuals with the places in which they reside. In the opening essay of this collection, for example, it is Klein's perception of the relationship between Leslie Ellenwood and his gas station on Route 81 that makes the character sketch effective. Likewise, in "Beardstown" he depicts Happy Jamison, Jr. as an old man who has thoroughly absorbed the Illinois River country near his home: "He talks about boats and the old days and the sharp memory keeps dredging up names and places— the barge *Pearl*, Treadway Lake, Mascoutin Bay, the Meredosia Bridge, Little Beardstown, Throckmorton's Button Factory, the *David Swain,* the Clendenin Slough, Little Field Spreads, and on and on."

As this characterization also suggests, in Klein's essays, places almost always have a temporal extension. A particular location is rich with meaning because it has a past. Beardstown, for instance, is described as "a sleepy river town that still has the melodious notes of the packet boat whistles ringing in its ears; the river forever rolling past, bankfull and treacherous in the spring, more lazy come July; memories of stage coaches clattering off to the east, to Springfield, and a tall, circuit-riding lawyer, boots thick with prairie dust, riding into town to defend Duff Armstrong . . . ." Sometimes it is Klein himself who is recalling earlier days, but more often it is people like Leslie Ellenwood or Happy Jamison, Jr.—or the old men on the square in Rushville, who cherish their collective memory of a different era: "The men in the square lament that Friday and Saturday nights are not what they used to be, when gay crowds of people surged along the streets and filled the grassy square, and when there was band music and a sense of the festive life." Of course, this emphasis on recollection lends a certain nostalgia to many of the essays, as "Canton," "Havana," and others indicate.

Klein's best prose pieces are also effective because they are carefully structured. "Rushville," for example, focuses on a summer day in the life of that community, developing a subtle contrast between the town's youngsters —hurrying to the circus, living thoroughly within the present moment, starting a summer that "will stretch away endlessly"—and the old men on the square, who measure the day's activity in relationship to the past and are concerned with making it to the fall. And in "This Old House" Klein evokes life in rural America decades ago by meditating on the abandoned farm houses that dot the Illinois countryside. The empty buildings, like some of the people that he characterizes, take on a certain dignity because they reflect the passage of time and the inevitable loss that comes with change.

Played in Peoria also includes essays based on Klein's travels—and among them"Armistice Day," a particularly fine achievement—but the book will be especially appealing to readers who are interested in locations that have a uniquely midwestern character. It is a collection of fine prose pieces by one of the most talented writers of the descriptive essay in the Midwest—a newspaperman who has raised journalistic prose to the level of significant literary art.

John E. Hallwas
Western Illinois University

The Feel of the Prairie

This Old House

They are empty now, these old houses, finished, like chapters of a book that has been read and put aside and no more will be taken down or opened. They dot the countryside, rising ghost-like at the edges of corn and soybean fields, windows gone, doors gaping, alive now only with the sounds of birds and the wind passing through with its ancient song. Sometimes the door bangs, a shutter bumps against the siding, a scrap of curtain waves and the haunting echoes and whispers stir again.

Once these doors slammed and children ran in. There were voices . . . "Don't forget to wipe your feet. And stop slamming that door . . ." There were babies crying on hot nights, then bouts of coughing and the doctor bending over the bed listening, listening, and alarm clocks going off in the gray dawns, coffee perking, bacon frying. Somebody celebrated Thanksgiving here and there were the Christmas mornings and children's eyes glowing with wonder.

Once there might have been birth and death, new sounds and new cries and the stiff and quiet bodies lying in wooden caskets in the parlors and banks of flowers, farmers mumbling their sympathies, gnarled hands clasping, and the women bringing in casseroles.

Once these houses were new and it was all promise. Excitement over the new curtains and shades, the men delivering the new stove, children gathered around the Arvin radio listening to the Kellogg Singing Lady and Eddie Cantor.

One time eyes watched through these now vacant windows and saw leaves falling in the autumn, the first snowflakes twisting out of a slate gray sky, the long dreary rains of spring, mudtime and seed-time. The children began to grow up and leave and the once-new linoleum grew thin and cracked. The cries began to fade. "Sara, your turn to do the dishes . . . Now don't be home late, George. Ten o'clock, you hear?" Orders from the catalog came in the mail, boots and overalls. There were the Watkins man and the veterinarian. Birth and death and sickness and good times and the summers turned to autumns and the calendars from the coal company and the implement yard came every winter.

And other times came when the people left the houses and moved off the farm, away from the wind, the long fields and the little schools. Lives passed and the echoes became softer. Curtains frayed, windows were broken, and poison ivy wound up the porch posts. The siding turned weathered, then gray and seamed, like the hands of the tough old men. The pump rusts, the wind blows and time passes. All things do.

The houses are empty now.

"No Kicks, No Regrets"

Outside, the incessant August rain turns the surface of Rt. 81 into a glistening black ribbon, like plastic electricians tape. Traffic whines past, tires hissing in the wetness. Not many cars stop here any more at Leslie Ellenwood's Phillips 66 station. "Sorry no gas" reads a sign out front, written in chalk. And inside, on the wall, are embossed plaques awarded by Phillips on the occasions of Ellenwood's 25th, 30th, 40th anniversaries as a dealer.

Forty-five years now since Ellenwood opened up his little wayside gas station out here between Kewanee and Cambridge. That was 1931-32 and when people ordered five gallons of regular, Ellenwood would pump gas up to the five gallon mark in the glass-topped pump and gravity did the rest. Sometime in the 30s a wind storm went through and broke off the glass tops and there have been electric pumps ever since. The pumps don't work any more and Ellenwood is afraid of the tanks, which are his originals.

"No, I don't sell gas any more," he says. "Not for a year or more. Just change oil, filters, do grease jobs, that kind of thing."

He is 76 now. He talks slowly, using the kind of economical, taciturn expressions country folk sometimes effect: "Sell the place? What for? Can't eat money." Three, four words to the sentence. A cigarette burns down to a nub between his second and third fingers and a long piece of ash falls to the floor. He sits on a swivel chair before a roll top desk, talking. All these years he has been the sole proprietor. "Only way to do it. Can't depend on anybody else."

There is a shelf stacked with Red Man, "America's Best Chew." There are boxes of White Owl Invincibles. Overhead a Country Air Fan drones away. An old refrigerator is plastered with humorous postcards. A fly strip hangs in the window, dotted with dead insects.

Not much has happened here. People broke in a couple of times, took cigarettes and the like. Ellenwood and his wife went to Miami and didn't like it. He doesn't like the summers here, or the winters, but doesn't think much of the southwest either. "Too hot." Besides, if you get cold in the winter here, you can go indoors.

There is a single car over the grease pit. The back room, once used as a repair shop, is empty now. A few tires. A grinder. The sound of crickets. "Cars used to be simple to work on. Not any more. It was easy to drop the motor out of a Model T. No trouble at all."

Ellenwood is still here every day, 7 to 5. If he wants to take off, he hangs up the closed sign. He has his television set. There is a table in the back room with wooden chairs. The old Kelvinator is full of soda. The place is full of memories. Flat tires in the night. People running out of gas. That daily, unspectacular interchange that marks a man's years in a business such as this.

"I've got no kicks against what we've done at all," Ellenwood says. "Wouldn't have done it any other way."

Noon. He puts the closed sign up in the window, bangs the door and walks through the rain to his house, right next door. No regrets. The road is still a glistening black ribbon. Another car passes, tires hissing in the wetness. Not many of them stop here any more.

The Vanishing Prairie

Who has seen the wind?
Neither you nor I:
But when the trees bow down their heads,
The wind is passing by.
　　　　　—Christina Georgina Rossetti

It does not seem likely that this incredibly rich Illinois prairie will ever blow away in the kind of situation that was known in the 30s as the dust bowl. But there are changes going on out there, some of them disturbing.

Nothing stays the same, of course, and the old family farm has pretty much vanished hereabouts. No longer that little cluster of buildings and trees, the long gravel lane leading up, past the pungent odors of pigs and cattle and chickens, to the house with its kitchen garden, the barns, the sheds. One still sees these old-time, all-purpose farms farther north or south, but out here on this rich, black prairie, the family farm houses from the earlier part of the century are empty, the barns abandoned, the pig lots deserted.

Other changes, too. The hedgerows and windbreaks are becoming rarer and rarer. Land, which was $700 to $800 an acre four years ago is now $4,000. It has become almost too precious to lie idle. One farmer said that you lose 10 rows of corn for every hedgerow.

And since so few of there farmers keep livestock, the fences are going, too. Some farmers have not bought a roll of barbed wire for more that 15 years. Miles of fences have been taken down to make it easier for the huge plows and planters to operate. Grass waterways are being tiled to give more room for crops. Little woods are cut down.

"Who has seen the wind?"

And with the windbreaks and fencerows going, so, too, are the songbirds, the quail, pheasant. Up above North Hampton, in that wide, black prairie above the river bluffs, the wind comes in an unbroken sweep from the west. Overalls on a farm line are stretched out almost horizontally in the wind. "With nothing to stop this wind," one farmer said, "something's going to happen."

In some places it has. Black dirt has drifted in the ditches along the remnants of a fence, piling up like winter's snow, rich, black, fertile and blowing, in some cases, clear across the road and into the opposite ditch. Here one sees the wind.

It is possible to drive for miles without seeing a chicken, a pig, a sheep, even a cow. There are horses, kept for riding, but milk cows and feeder cows do not make much money these days, if any. Nor do sheep. Wide, wide fields, endless, almost, as the sea, planted right up to the roadsides. The trees look lonely. Out in the distance a tractor pulling a planter raises a cloud of dust, which passes, like smoke.

In the tall grass of an abandoned farmhouse, the wind seems to rustle, like scurrying mice. It hurries through the windowless house, flapping across loose pieces of wallpaper and whistling through a thousand cracks. The heavy blue jeans on the farm line stretch out in their mad ballet. Dust, black and rich, sifts imperceptibly through the remains of an old fence, and across the road. Who has seen the wind?

20 Miles West of Peoria and There You Are: the Republic of Forgottonia

Drive 20 miles west of Peoria, and there you are, in that strange, wonderful, empty and neglected part of the world that has sprung into sudden prominence as Forgottonia, a microcosm of what happened when a government immerses itself in big problems and ignores the lesser ones.

It is an area of Henry Horner roads, all put down in the 20s and patched for 50 years. There are sleepy little towns, many of them with a ghostly sense of emptiness and decay. There is so much elbow room that anyone spending time here must inevitably ask himself, "What population explosion?" The people one runs across are in varying moods ranging from discontent to anger. Most of them support the idea of Forgottonia, not as an actuality, but as a shrewd attention-getting device.

One man seemed totally unaware of it at all. "Forgot who?" he said.

But much reaction was more volatile and less printable. "Them big pukes in Chicago don't pay taxes and they get everything," cried one man in a tavern at the eastern edge of the Republic. "All we get is ——!" A man on a nearby stool agreed. "That's right! They're even barging it back down the river for us."

The men in Post 17 American Legion Hall at Ipava say they're a hundred percent behind Neal Gamm's bizarre idea. Gamm is a member and was a captain in Vietnam. "People are pretty serious about it down here," said Roy Hallenbeck, vice commander of the post. "He's dead serious about highways and the way our taxes are being used." Another man said people were mad about Governor Walker promising all sorts of things and doing nothing.

Along Rt. 136 east of Macomb was hitchhiker Roy Rinehart of Astoria, standing beneath the incredibly wide skies. He was on his way home from Grants' Pass, Oregon. He said he had made pretty good time all the way— two days to Macomb—but was virtually stuck within shouting distance of home. He'd been dropped off at Macomb at 1 a.m. that day and hadn't gotten a ride yet. It was 12:40 p.m. when a car stopped and Roy hurried off and piled in with his gear.

There is a curiously pervasive air in the heart of Forgottonia, almost as if one is rambling around in some vast museum. In a grassy airfield near Macomb are two Hudson convertibles and a derelict U.S. Air Force training plane. The abandoned Standard School sits forlornly in a field of weeds along Rt. 100 near Duncan Mills, crickets sounding in the tall grass, wild grapes twining along the fence, the shouts of children long stilled. Near Adair is the Pine Cone Cafe, an early-day hamburger stand that sits empty in the wind.

Colchester has a boarded-up look, old buildings with tin roofs over the sidewalks, vacant windows and a feeling that somebody looking like John Wayne will canter into town at any moment. And Fandon, the capitol, is so small and insignificant that there are no signs to point the way or identify the location, save for that in front of the Fandon Christian Church ("U R Welcome"). The capitol is empty. A white dog peers through a glassless front window of the building that once was the Melvin D. Beck, General Merchandise firm, but it has been empty for years.

To the outsider there is something enormously appealing about all this.

For in various parts of Forgottonia he may rummage about through Edgar Lee Masters' country along the Spoon, into the Mormon past at Nauvoo, to Indian sites of Dickson Mounds, or through a hundred little towns that time seems to have passed, some along the river where steamboat whistles are still a bright memory, others in the middle of two bends in the hard road. It stands at the opposite extreme from rows of hamburger stands, gas stations, discount stores and neon lights winking in the night.

In the tiny post office at Summum where a sign limiting parking to 10 minutes rises from the foxgrass, Mrs. Lucille Cluts peered through the stamp window and admitted that Gamm is trying to bring attention to the area. "That's okay," she said. "We do need everything down here. They have left us out. But they won't do anything out here. They've always just let it go."

Nearby, John Onion stood behind the cash register in John's Jeneral Store in a pair of Key Imperial bib overalls, which he sells. Trucks rumbled past on Rt. 24. "We're a peaceful, agricultural community," he said. "I'd just as soon have it like it is now. We're getting enough traffic as it is." Another truck thundered past.

In Ken Moran's barber shop at Colchester, where haircuts are $2, Moran agreed that a lot of what Gamm says is true. "Only opposition I've heard is from farmers who are afraid they'll wreck their farms," he said. A customer, Marvin Kerber, said he came over from Iowa two years ago. "All they ever did in Iowa was gripe about the roads," he said. "I go back there now and ask them what they've got to gripe about. Boy, they haven't seen anything."

Other people talk about open manholes in the roads, or say that the state is going to stock some of the potholes and open them to fishermen.

They exaggerate, of course. Many of Forgottonia's roads have been widened from Model A width by the addition of two narrow bands of concrete along each side and then blacktopped. They have settled unevenly, cracked and sometimes tend to make cars uncontrollable. Some curves have been relocated. Most roads have at least partial blacktop, but they remain essentially unchanged since the big roadbuilding program of the 1920s, when Illinois had the best highway system in the nation. The only section of interstate in all of Forgottonia is that part of Rt. 74 which runs into the area around Brimfield and out near Alpha. Peoria to Macomb and Western Illinois University remains a 69-mile trip by a variety of roads and is a gruelling, 90-minute run under the best conditions.

But the Republic remains a marvel and for the tourist a rustic, quaint and inviting haven. Corn and beans stretch endlessly toward the far horizons. Small towns have old houses graced with ornate bric-a-brac around the front porches and stained glass window sections in the parlors. The Spoon rolls gently beneath its rusted iron bridges. The Burlington rumbles past and crickets momentarily cease their chirping. Farmers sit in small cafes, their hands wrapped around heavy coffee mugs, waiting, waiting for the rain to stop. Right outside of town the road makes a sharp bend to the left and down a ways is another bump, which has in its recesses half a century of tar. A sign on a bar says, "Mail Pouch" and in a farm yard are two old cars, a Hudson and a DeSoto, rusting side by side.

Galesburg, at the northeast corner, has a throbbing and metropolitan feeling that seems hardly to fit the notion of the tiny Republic, and it leads

17

speedily and comfortably, if somewhat jarringly, back to the present. As the sun sinks slowly into the west and our car arcs up the entrance ramp to interstate 74, we once again bid farewell to lovely Forgottonia, with its staggering vistas, its quaint towns and its colorful natives, who are growing understandably restless. Farewell, O farewell.

Day Breaks Gently on the Illinois

This is the fat lake, Pimiteoui. The upper Peoria Lake, one of Illinois' scenic wonders and recreational treasures, stretching in a broad reach from just south of Chillicothe to the narrows above the McCluggage Bridge, 20 miles in all and more than two miles wide at some points. Dotted with sailboats on summer weekends, bending under the long winds from the west and south, green water rolled into easy swells and the far shore so hazy in the distance that it is nearly lost from sight.

Once this was a wide, slow river that stretched from bluff to bluff. There were elk and bison along its banks, waterfowl beyond number. Ice and water and wind and the great flow shaped these hills and excavated these valleys, and this lake was finally confined by locks and dams into its present boundaries. Much of the wildlife is gone. No longer the great hauls of fish, the clams. Gone, too, are the sand beaches where children swam in scratchy woolen bathing suits, the ice houses, the rowboats and the amusement parks along its banks. A dead river, some say, strangled by pollution and siltation into a biological inertness, stripped of its seaweed beds and its duckweed and left with an impermeable mud bottom. But life goes on. The river goes on.

Morning. High above, a thin jet trail catches the first rays of the rising sun and traces a long streak of fire across the sky. Along the Woodford shore, the hills are gray and indistinct, rising in successive folds that fade toward the horizon. All rough-edged and jagged with summer trees.

Now the sun again. First a pale disc, oblong and watery. Then deepening, becoming the color of goldfish as it swims up through the haze, trailing a faint streak of red across the water. Water the color of slate, rough now and feathered by an early morning wind that sighs around the lonely buoys and flaps through the cottonwoods along the shore.

A great gray river barge noses through the Sante Fe Bridge, southward bound in the gloom. Huge, powerful creations, these, able to haul in a single barge more than a million gallons of oil, more than 85,000 bushels of grain. They have strong, muscular names, most of them, the Frank C. Rand, the Henry J. Gunderson, and they raise visions of firm-jawed men in sooty offices in Pittsburgh or Joliet. Coal. Steel. Oil. Grain.

Commerce and transportation, the reason why most of the world's great cities are on rivers. London. Paris. New York. Vienna. Leningrad. And recreation. There are sailboats at Paris, too. And the painters have always gone to the rivers, everybody from Monet to George Caleb Bingham, for there is beauty here, changing light, fascinating views, history, and life.

Here is a great blue heron rising like something out of Swan Lake, wings moving in smooth and almost lazy strokes until it soars high above the willows, In the gathering light, there is a small island that looks like a scene from a Japanese print, something from the Inland Sea, so serene and precisely composed that it seems unreal. Cool, green forests along the banks, hardly changed in some of the remote reaches of the lake from the time when Father Marquette came. Miles, too, of backwaters and swamps with sedge grass and scrub trees and a feel of the Deep South, of some endless swamp, like Okefenokee.

Now the wind is rolling up quick, choppy waves frosted with whitecaps. Most of the whole western shore of this big lake is lined with cottages resting on stilt legs or concrete, and it is a shoreline that could be from almost any middle class resort area. These are not the mansions of Milwaukee's north shore or the discreet estates along the Michigan side, but the modest summer homes and A-frames with their short rocky beaches and fishing boats. Higher up, along the western bluffs, are the greater mansions with staggering views of the long, wooded hills, the fat lake, the peaceful and fertile lands beyond.

And the lake is now filled with boats, cruising sailboats, speedboats with outboards large enough to propel a destroyer, houseboats, tiny sailboats with lateen rigs, catamarans and lavish cruisers. No longer is yachting restricted as it was when Commodore Vanderbilt is supposed to have quipped, "If you have to ask how much it costs, you can't afford it," for now the banks finance boats, fiberglass has replaced the old wooden boat and caulking compound and spar varnish type of yachting, and there are dozens of marinas. Boats of all sizes and and shapes. A whole new industry along the lake, boat sales, equipment, life jackets, nylon lines, slip rentals.

But much of the eastern shore of the big lake remains remote, unchanged, There are stretches of cottages, but also distant Tom Sawyer beaches where civilization seems years away. Cool forests with willows and cottonwoods near the shoreline, old trees with bare roots that grip the ground like spiders' feet. Farther inland are maples and an occasional sycamore. And one finds even now jetsam from the spring floods, the remains of a rowboat, a nun buoy that broke from its moorings, a soda bottle that looks with its moss and growth like a miniature terrarium. Steamboat captains used to nose ashore here to cut wood. Flatboats before that, and the long canoes, for the river has run this way for thousands of years.

"Used to be hellish good fishing here," calls a man from his olive drab metal boat. "Sure ain't what it used to be." The river changes. From far off comes the lonely cry of a towboat's horn. In the backwater a heron stands on one leg contemplating the water's surface. Far to the south, a sailboat emerges from a little cove and heads cross wind, her lee rail nearly awash, a trail of spume kicking up in her wake. The sun is halfway across the sky, burning away the mists until there is blue water, blue sky. Another beautiful day on this beautiful river, this fat lake, this Pimiteoui.

Along the Spoon . . .

> *Where are Elmer, Herman, Bert, Tom, and Charley,*
> *The weak of will, the strong of arm, the clown, the*
> *   boozer, the fighter?*
> *All, all are sleeping on the hill.*
>   —Edgar Lee Masters, "The Hill"

The Spoon River flows slowly these autumn days, carrying golden and but-
ter-yellow leaves from the old elms and cottonwoods lining its bank, winding
across silent valleys where crickets chirp, past the quiet cemeteries along the hillsides and the peaceful little towns, some of them now deserted and forgotten.

At London Mills, northern end of the Spoon River Valley Scenic Drive, the
river moves beneath a rusted bridge at the edge of town that was put up by the
King Iron Bridge Co. of Cleveland, Ohio in 1893. In an adjoining park along the
river near a copy of the Statue of Liberty are old mill stones that have long since
ceased to grind. A sodbuster lies there within earshot of John Deere and International Harvesters pulling eight-bottom plows through the rich loam of the
river bottoms.

London Mills is one starting point for the newly opened drive. The other
is at Dickson Mounds, 65 miles away. The route, marked with red and white
signs, carries the driver mainly along back roads through a land that has changed
little in the past century. It is being opened in connection with the Illinois Ses-
quicentennial year and the 145th anniversary of Fulton County.

Farther down the road from London Mills is Ellisville (Pop. 140) where the
old curtain in the opera house still advertises the services of drayage firms, people
named Giberson, Dr. Cluts and Cadwallader, the blacksmith. In the tiny post
office are posters of men wanted for various crimes and in the window a football schedule of Valley Senior High. An adjacent building, now deserted, has its
windows pasted over with Nixon signs.

Back of the town in the old cemetery overlooking the valley of the Spoon,
there is an eloquent silence amid the tumbled stones. Among those sleeping on
the hill is George W., son of Jacob and Jane Hand, who died Dec. 13, 1841, at
the age of two years, nine months and 25 days, and John Culver, who died Jan.
10, 1816 after 17 years, two months and 17 days of life.

Some of the tablets have been worn smooth by time and those who lie
there are forgotten. The wind that once fanned their cheeks sighs through the
pines. From high overhead there is the sound of a jet.

> *Do the boys and girls still go to Siever's*
> *For cider after school, in late September?*
> *Or gather hazel nuts among the thickets*
> *On Aaron Hatfield's farm when the frosts begin?*
> *For many times with the laughing girls and boys*
> *Played I along the road and over the hills*
> *When the sun was low and the air was cool,*
> *Stopping to club the walnut tree*
> *Standing leafless against a flaming west.*
> *Now, the smell of the autumn smoke,*
> *And the dropping acorns,*

And the echoes about the vales
Bring dreams of life. They hover over me.
They question me:
Where are those laughing comrades?
How many are with me, how many
In the old orchards along the way to Siever's,
And in the woods that overlook
The quiet water?
                    —Edgar Lee Masters, "Hare Drummer"

On the route winds a gravel road, wide at some points, narrowing to a
twisted, but passable track at others. It leads across old iron bridges, into
sections of Fulton County that seem to be unchanged by time and which look
the same as the river valley of a century ago. But where there once was a
thriving mill at Babylon Bend, there are now only a few houses, a clubhouse
and a sense of quiet desolation.

At Bernadotte, where thousands of soldiers trained at Camp Ellis during
World War II, there is little of that era to be seen.

The road runs through Lewistown, site of the major part of Masters' anthology and ends at Dickson Mounds.

And always there is the Spoon winding slowly along, the leaves of another autumn flowing with its gentle current, scattered like a shower of coins.
It passes through sleepy valleys and under bridges where cars seldom cross any
more. Trees in places bend almost to the water, the maples, elms and willows,
and sometimes they meet across the middle. There are still clamshells buried
in the soft mud along the banks and the water occasionally splashes with the
jumping of fish. In the fields, there is the ceaseless sound of the crickets and
the old cemeteries along the hillsides with their crooked tombstones are immensely peaceful in the chill wind of an October afternoon.

One passed in a fever,
One was burned in a mine,
One was killed in a brawl,
One died in a jail,
One fell from a bridge toiling for children and wife—
All, all are sleeping, sleeping, sleeping on the hill.

The Other End of the Spoon

Up here in Knox, Stark, and a small wedge of Peoria County, the Spoon River is not nearly so celebrated as along its lower end, which Edgar Lee Masters made forever famous. Nothing quite like Babylon Bend up here, or Sievers orchard, where the boys and girls once stopped for cider on those long past autumn afternoons. Or those cemeteries where the dead will not lie still.

Different up here, even more remote and unknown with these little towns, Elmore, Modena, Dahinda, that are seldom mentioned unless a tornado passes through, or a flood. It is the same river in a different setting. Here it comes, wandering out of the fields north of Wyoming, carving a deepening scar across the rich corn land. Then widening as another creek joins, and another, until it becomes a dark, rich artery wandering through this peaceful land.

Low now. "Lowest I've ever seen it," says one old timer. But there are high water marks from springtimes when the river sang a different song, and cornfields along its edges where the black ground is thickly sown with rocks and boulders.

It runs beneath quaint rusty bridges as it follows its twisted, winding way. One minute there it is, right beside some gravel back country road, and the next minute it is flying off across a field and almost disappearing. Way off there, a distant line of trees snaking along the far ridge. Then back again, slicing right beneath the road again, beneath another of those 1895 Clinton Bridges with their board floors and sturdy turnbuckles and angle irons, all rusted in place as if they have taken root and grown here.

This is rich country, unlike some of that along the lower Spoon. Here are wide fields of corn, tasseled out now so that they look like some vast chenille spread laid across the land. The back roads seem to have been cut through the corn, like firebreaks through a forest, for it rises on all sides, an impenetrable black-green wall. And everywhere that scratchy, rustling sound, like heavy paper, picked up by the wind, and that miraculous fetid odor of pollination and fertilization "first the grain, then the ear, then the full grain in the ear" in a process that repeats itself across the endless acres in almost infinite proportions. This truly is the proverbial land flowing, not with milk and honey, but with corn and beans to feed the world.

And flowing, too, the Spoon, slowly now around another bend, its surface flecked with foam that passes with a slow majesty, like ships in some endless flotilla. Running down a long, leafy trace where the maples and cottonwoods hang low over the water, dark and cool, filled with birdsong and muted rustlings, and the fiddlings of the first katydids. It is the fullness of summer. Wild mustard and chickory thick along the roadside and sudden bursts of purple. Queen Anne's lace nodding in a fencerow, sumac prematurely crimson, elderberry and wild grape and a startled quail darting for cover.

Now another bridge bearing the badge at its top, "Clinton Bridge 1895." It is a most admirable example of simplicity and ingenuity. Most of these bridges are all alike, shipped down and put together like so many erector sets. The main piers, of stone, so many feet apart. Next attach girder A to crossbeam B and tighten turnbuckle C. Not quite so simple as that, perhaps, but beautifully uncomplicated, and surely put together in days and weeks rather than the months and years it takes for a bridge these days of technical wizardry.

They are deeply rusted now, genuine antiques. Old planks held down with huge spikes hammered through hard oak, many bent and twisted. They have served their purpose and they are slowly being replaced. At Elmore there is a new and expensive state aid bridge nearing completion and another one at Maquon, so functional and modern that it seems not to be a bridge at all and many passing over it will not know the Spoon flows beneath.

Then Dahinda and another Clinton Bridge. Right near it is the huge Sante Fe steel bridge, built in 1910. "The Spoon is the only river in Knox County," says Doris Gale. She remembers them cutting ice from the river. Used to be marvelous skating, too. And there is a legend at Dahinda of a pot of Indian gold. Some brave is supposed to have come back once for it. And a Knox College professor arrived one day 16 years ago and dug a hole big enough for a foundation. He found nothing. If the legend is right, the gold is still at Dahinda.

Farther downstream is the Old Wolf Bridge, only covered bridge to cross the Spoon. It looks like some bucolic calender scene, needing only a horse-drawn surrey and a few cows grazing in the distance. Instead there is a John Deere tractor nosing onto the bridge, pulling a cart loaded with pigs. The bridge's undersides are scrawled with graffiti and obscenities and its little parking lot is littered with beer cans and remains of campfires and careless picnics.

On goes the Spoon, sweeping past more corn and bean fields, dropping here in a sudden rush of water that foams white and catches the sun and splinters it into glittering fragments. Then it slows to a crawl, lapping peacefully along muddy banks where raccoons have drunk, and other nocturnal animals, too, for it is the only natural watering spot in the entire area—the rest is corn and beans. On toward Maquon, once the site of an Indian village, and to London Mills, where the more famous scenic drive begins and where the Spoon has become famous.

Up here, there is beauty too, and it is coming into its own. There is a Knox County Scenic Drive along the upper Spoon, and this may all change soon. But not yet. In some areas up here a roadmap and a compass are necessities. There are the weak of will, the strong of arm, the clown, the boozer, the fighter, sleeping on their hills up here, too. Until now, they have remained discreetly silent about it all along this secret, almost unknown other end of the Spoon.

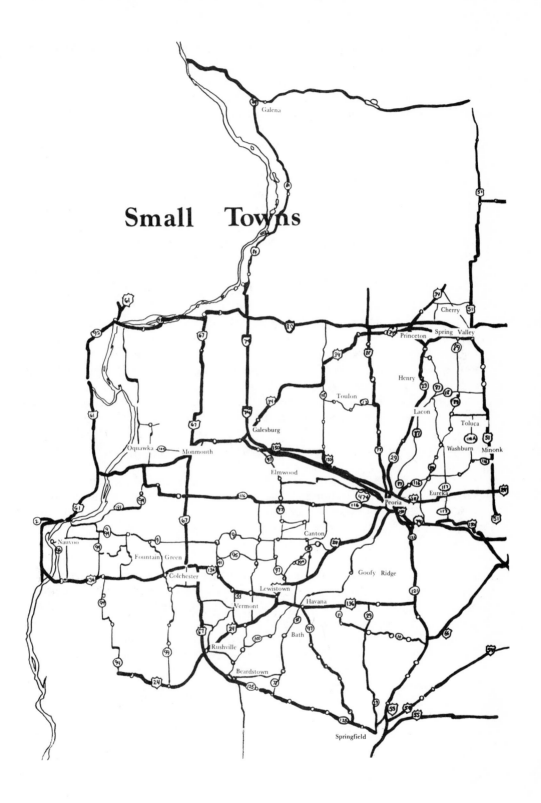

Small Towns

A Winter Day in Vermont, Illinois

A winter day in Vermont, gray and wet with a raw east wind slowly furling and unfurling the flag high above the square. Empty sidewalks under canted roofs, like the arcades of old western towns and the soft sounds of sparrows. A truck passes by. A door slams. A man in a red farm cap nods. "How do." "Hello." It is not possible to remain a stranger here for long.

There are porch swings hoisted up against the ceilings for the winter, old houses with washing machines or gas ranges outside the doors, a yard with a small cannon in it. A boat, badly needing paint, with its bow emerging from a door of a shed that is beyond salvation from paint. And those grand Victorian houses, ten or more, ante bellum mansions, really, of soft red Vermont brick, widow's walks at the top, gingerbread and foundations three feet thick, as solid as forts.

One was the home of Col. Thomas Hamer, where Lincoln was a guest on Oct. 26 and 27, 1858. Outside is a sign that says Col. Hamer painted the house black in mourning at the news of Lincoln's death. It is now white.

There are other stories of somewhat less historical significance. One is about a famous prank that began to unfold when a buggy was hoisted to the top of the water tower. They still talk, too, about Camp Ellis days when soldiers lined up three deep to feed silver coins into the slot machines.

Farther back in history was the cholera epidemic. And the way the town was named, after its founding in 1835, by a native of the Green Mountain State who offered to provide a jug of whiskey for the privilege of calling it Vermont.

And there is in C. C. Mercer's store everything from Alf Landon pins and arrowheads to old-time miner's pails, a cigar store Indian, dolls, 2-cent candy and racks of confession magazines. On the wall is an ad from Mershon's Hall, once located above the bank, for "Uncle Tom's Cabin," "The Two Orphans" and "He's a Lunatic," all highlights from the 1875-76 theatrical season.

"You know, I'm the wealthiest man in town," says Mercer. "Oh, not in money, but in everything else. I'll keep going here so long as I can make change." He and his wife are about to celebrate their 50th anniversary. He is the older brother of the late Judge Frederick O. Mercer—"probably the most famous man to come out of hereabouts." He moves, more slowly now, to a roller concert organ, turns the crank and sings along in a clear, strong voice to "In the Good Old Summertime," stirring long, dusty echoes of distant summers and faces that have gone back to the earth. Then to the Regina Music Box and "Under the Double Eagle," and there are bright visions of men in blue coming home, a war won, cracked and brittle saddlebags.

Sparrows chirped then, too, as they do now in the cemetery where the high statue of a Union veteran leans on his long rifle so long as stone lasts. The eternal flame before this GAR-WRC monument has been extinguished. Nobody seems to know why for certain.

"Too costly," say some of the townspeople. "It was supposed to cost forty dollars a year and the first month's bill was twenty."

"No, that wasn't it. It was supposed to burn until the Vietnam war was over. Well, it's over now."

"It was the energy crisis last year," says a third. "When we had all the shortages. That's the reason."

The opinions in the American Legion Club on Main Street vary almost as much as does the character of the patrons. There are men in yellow Caterpillar caps and red farm caps. A businessman. A retired Navy man. A small girl on her grandfather's lap. The man who takes care of the cemeteries says the flame died because of the cost. "You should have seen that thing in the wind. You could have cooked a meal over it."

"No, that wasn't it . . ." The debate goes on. In the restroom is a rudely scrawled cardboard sign. "Please use stool instead of wastebasket. Thank you." There are a kitchen table and four chairs, empty now beneath an overhead poker lamp embossed with clubs and diamonds. The Legion sells something like 300 lottery tickets a week. There were five winners during the week of Sept. 3.

Nine hundred people, according to the signs at the edge of town. Three grocery stores. Aubrey Neilsen has been in his for 30 years and intends to keep going. "You know, you don't last too long if you just go and sit down somewhere." The stores have spools of string in iron holders, sack racks, butcher paper rolls. Mrs. D. K. Miller says that lots of people come in from Astoria since there is only one store there. Neilsen's store and the Millers' both deliver to some older people. "Our customers are our friends," she says.

In almost every public place in town is a Kost Memorial Home calendar, dated 1919, with a Gibson type girl on the cover. There is one in the newly panelled office of Kenny Kessler, who founded the town's only industry, then Ken-Ray Brass Corp., back in 1946. He is now assistant sales manager for Fall River Foundry Co. of Fall River, Wisconsin.

"At one time we had a hundred and thirty employees here," he says. "Used to do four million a year. Our goal was to be the number one employer in the county. Never quite made it as big as International Harvester in Canton, though."

He no longer owns the brass foundry, which now has about 60 people at work. "My hobby is to keep the old town primed."

He has also been building some new houses and says that property values have doubled in the last nine months. But for the next 10 years, he says, he looks for things to go down. Until recently, his wife operated a recreation center and restaurant a few doors up from his office. It is closed, its pool tables covered, the big rooms dark and quiet. "Some people have offered to pay ten bucks a month if we'd open it," Kessler says. "And some of the wives would pay twenty just to get their husbands out of the house."

The Kesslers live in a 120-year-old home that is meticulously restored and furnished. The same man built five Victorian mansions before the Civil War and built them good.

"It's an old, interesting, dead and dried-up town," Kessler says. "A good place to live. Good schools. More history here than you'd imagine. When I was a kid I couldn't wait to get away from the place. Now when I go to the big town, I can't wait to get back."

He stands behind the bar of his pine panelled recreation room, swirling brandy around in a short, wide glass. In one corner is a player piano made in Oregon, Ill., his wife's hometown. Kessler threads a roll onto the spindle and begins pumping the pedals. Another old, old song. "The Roses of Picardy."

The school buses have come again and the high schoolers are back from their day at VIT (Vermont, Ipava, Table Grove) a few miles up the road, within sight of the few remaining chimneys of Camp Ellis. A train rumbles past off to the west on the Burlington, which still uses Vermont as a junction point. Once there was a railroad station and 12 or so passengers a day. Now there is an occasional freight, carrying coal out of the nearby Amax mines, heading north.

The streets are almost empty, save for men in a truck removing the last of the overhead Christmas decorations. They say there are more people in the cemetery than in the town. One of them is Andrew Koons, who lies securely behind the double locks of his stone mausoleum, his Civil War veteran's tablet propped up against the base, a tin soldier leaning on a non-existant rifle outside and an inscription in memory of the Union dead of Co. B, 84th Illinois Infantry. There are remnants of snow on the tall pines, whispering, whispering.

Someone orders another round at the Legion and the Michelob spurts into the glasses. "Too costly. That was the reason." Echoes. "The Roses of Picardy." "In the Good Old Summertime." The flag still waves softly against the dull, wet sky. A winter day in Vermont.

. . . except perhaps an occasional freight bearing coal or a load of granite.

And the huge, old elms vanished long ago. Once, they formed a cool, green arch high above Main Street. Beyond is endless prairie, shimmering in the warmth of early summer, houses and barns dotting its vast, unbroken sweep, which seems to run to the horizon and beyond, like an ocean.

The depot is deserted, save for the sparrows, and tar-paper siding flaps away in the long wind. The bowling alley nearby has been turned into a beauty parlor.

The door of the Elmwood *Gazette* is locked, and a sign hangs in the window: "Please leave news items or others under door. Thank you." There is a long, piercing blast as the noon whistle blows. It sets up a flurry of dogs barking. Then it is silent.

Gene Bourgoin is there amid the granite dust and gravestones of the Bourgoin Monument Co. The only remaining industry in town, it has been in the family for three generations. A sign by his desk reads, "A monument is erected not because someone died, but because someone lived."

"You know, I used to want to live in Peoria," he says. "But we really have everything here. We never even had a key for the front door until after I was married. You can walk up and down these streets after dark without worrying. It is a good life."

A good life.

He explains how huge slabs of granite from Wisconsin, Minnesota, Vermont and Africa are sawed into gravestone-sized pieces, then finished, polished, lettered.

"We've made an awful lot of things out of granite in the past," he says. "We did the granite for the Buckingham Fountain in Chicago . . . the base for the (Lorado) Taft monument in the cemetery here. There's not too much wholesale business any more. In the past, we shipped as far as Spain, Hawaii, Alaska; but we limit ourselves pretty much to the immediate area now."

A building, adjacent to the railroad tracks, is crowded with monuments in various stages of completion. One is being redone, because a dealer left a letter out of a name. The sand-blasting machine hisses, etching names and dates deep and long. On one stone is the heart-stopping "Our Little Boy," and on another is the picture of a school child, sealed and fitted onto the marble.

One monument has been brought back to be lettered in Hebrew, a job too complicated to be done with the monument in place in the cemetery. And there are others, all of them telling of pacts finished, lives ended, stories completed, all of them now condensed, abbreviated and edited down to a name and two dates.

Born. Died. Remembered. In solid, substantial granite that we imagine will outlive memory.

In the Elmwood Cemetery, a few blocks away, there are acres and acres of monuments, many of them large and imposing, many of them of red or pink marble, some dating from the time when survivors measured prestige by the size of a grave marker.

There is the inevitable Civil War soldier in stone, leaning on his long rifle; stone obelisks dating from 100 years ago. They become more dense as the summers pass, filling in the empty spaces on the rolling green lawn, one by one, more names, more dates.

A good life.

The Taft monument here is a memorial really, for his ashes were scattered here in 1938, across the grass beneath his bronze figure "Memory." The base is inscribed, "The Handicraft of Their Work is Their Prayer—Lorado Taft, April 20, 1860-October 30, 1936."

His statue of "The Pioneers" dominates the town square. The figures rise heroically, massively—the protective, indomitable man, the strong, determined woman with the baby cradled in her arms, the dog, the long rifle. The base is inscribed, "To the pioneers who bridged the streams, subdued the soil and founded a state." It is said that there were as many as 12,000 people here the day that the statue was dedicated, in May of 1928. It was perhaps the biggest crowd ever gathered here.

The other landmark is the old Congregational Church, built on the site of Don Carlos Taft's Elmwood Academy. The church is locked these days, and it appears to be abandoned, almost in danger of collapse. Its age is put at 120 years.

"Abandoned? I should say not!"

It is Roma Shively, retired school teacher and unofficial historian, speaking. "We have a preacher in every other Sunday."

She sits in her bright, sun-splashed living room with its nylon curtains and oval rug, leafing through yellowed papers, photographs, deeds, notes, minutes of long adjourned meetings. A post card has a view of the old Elmwood, when the trees overhead formed a vaulted arch, cool and lovely in the summertime, bare as stone gothic ribs in the winter.

"The biggest change here over the years has been the loss of our elms. And the next big thing was the automobile. People can go so far and so fast nowadays," she says.

"I remember when father would hitch up the horse and we'd ride up and down the street and have quite a time. I suppose that wouldn't be fun for the kids these days."

She has been teaching in Elmwood since 1938, mostly seventh and eighth grades. She graduated from Knox in 1929 and goes back to the Galesburg school now and then.

"I think I'll go for my 50th reunion, and then that will be that. There are too many people who talk about the money they've made, and I can't stand that. I just stayed here, and taught, but that's what I wanted to do," she says.

More scraps float up from the past. The post office. The paper mill. The railroad. An old ordinance assessing a fine of $5 for having a horse or an ox on the sidewalk. Stories of the town founder William J. F. Phelps and how he would raise the price of lots for people he considered undesirable, and how he would almost give land to those he believed to have particularly good character. As the twig is bent so the tree grows. He seemed to extend that philosophy to the village, too.

We walk out the front door. School children are passing on their way back to classes. One of them has thrown an empty Pepsi Cola can in her yard. Miss Shively picks it up, patiently, resignedly. "I don't know why . . ."

A good life.

It is almost the prototype of the small town, peaceful, insulated, serene and intimate to the point of people discussing one another's problems—health, marital, behavior—in public bar or private club. Peoria is just beyond the horizon, but in some ways, it is years away.

The village's character is enhanced by the feel of space. There are few 60-foot lots here. They are large enough to insure a physical privacy that is unknown in much of Peoria and its suburbs. There is elbow room here, a wide-shouldered feeling that leads one to consider the thought that small town life has its points and that the rush to the city may have been one of the greatest mistakes of our time.

There is quietness, peace. Young people and old stop in at Wilson's Recreation for coffee and talk. Pool balls click in the back room. People talk about a bargain in bowling shirts at K-Mart. Young mothers with their children and old men and women sit and drink coffee out of thick, white mugs. Hash browns are 30 cents. Cube steak is $1.25. The conversation, the companionship, the sense of community are free.

And people nod. They say hello to strangers. They smile.

A good life.

In the early afternoon, the Elmwood Tap is nearly deserted. "The Edge of Night" is on television, all anguish and torment and no one to watch. Jack Buck is announcing the Cardinal game on the radio. There are three young men with long hair pounding on the pinball machine. The bartender stands yawning behind the bar. Sometimes on rainy days, the back room is crowded. Cards snap onto the worn table tops. The old spindly chairs scrape back. "Hey, bartender, let's have another round back here . . . "

The Taft Museum, located in the Kemp family home, is seldom open. Taft never lived there; his home was torn down long ago. In one room of the museum are documents, pieces of his sculpture, pictures. A flag waves above the green lawn, and sun spills through the old windows. Out back is a barn with fly nets, collars, hames, a cutter, a sleigh, a democrat, wooden ox yokes, old farm implements, most given by Mr. and Mrs. Herman Glick.

There is an English taxicab in the driveway of Bob Lott, the banker. A long row of trees leads up to the Maple Lane Country Club, which has its own pool and golf course. The wind seems to blow endlessly, and the countryside rolls away forever, filling up now with corn and soybeans and green wheat, with white houses bobbing like ships in the haze, and green patches of woods.

On June 5, 1879, on the 25th anniversary of the old church, William Phelps recalled when the village and the surrounding countryside was a wild and unbroken waste.

"When standing on that eminence, still so inviting, our western border 300 feet above the level of Peoria lake, and looking abroad over the thousands and thousands of rich acres, stretching away as far as the eye could reach, we could nowhere find a trace or a sign of civilization, where in musing reverie we would forecast the future of this tenantless domain which a prince might envy . . ."

And still might. The elms are gone, but the prairie remains like the names cut deep in the red granite, unchanging save for the colors of its season.

It is quiet in town. The newspaper office is still closed. The library has not yet opened. The sidewalks are empty. Two men are working at the site of the new bandstand in the square. There is the soft sound of wind blowing through the trees. The temperature light outside the bank winks up by a degree. The train hardly ever stops here any more.

Here's Looking at Toluca

It is said that certain connoisseurs and gourmets, upon driving in a northeasterly direction out of Peoria, begin to detect the faint but unmistakable odor of Italian cooking at the point where Rt. 116A begins its lonely course to the north.

An exaggeration, to be sure, but there is something about that locale out there on the prairie just west of Benson that sets the nose to quivering and the salivary glands to reacting, particularly among those for whom the journey to Toluca has become a hallowed gustatory pilgrimage.

The great slag pile known as Jumbo still lies beyond the horizon, and there are miles to go before one eats. But Toluca has amassed such a reputation as a mecca for Italian food lovers that many even rate such widely heralded spots as Mama Leone's in New York or the expensive Italian Village in Chicago as decidedly inferior by comparison.

For more years than some people care to mention, gourmets and gourmands alike have made that long trip again and again. On busy weekends they wait at the bar, like immigrants, for the magic summons to the inner sanctums of Capponi's or Mona's, tempted all the while by visions of waitresses gliding by with monstrous platters of ravioli and spaghetti.

Famine. Despair. Then, at last, the sudden, blessed summons. The soft rustle of napery. Dishes clatter. The scratch of a pencil on an order pad. The wait goes on, more bearable now.

Then there is bread, savory, warm and crisp. Salad . . . and finally the ravioli, the spaghetti and a kind of bliss that can only be described by the peculiarly Latin gesture that consists of kissing the fingers and raising them upwards like blown dandelion seeds.

There are stories, easily verified, of people eating enormous quantities of food at ridiculously low prices that seem to have changed little over the years. One group of 11 recently consumed ravioli, spaghetti, chicken, wine, spumoni, coffee, repeat orders, and so on—all for $34.

It is possible at any given moment—theoretically—to seat half the town's entire population in the three Italian restaurants of Toluca. Mona's and Capponi's are known far abroad. The third is Cap's, to the right along Main Street, lesser known, but carrying on in the grand tradition.

The owner, Aldo Capponi, stands behind the bar, talking. There is a high, embossed ceiling, a heater fan that comes on with the surging sound of a wind tunnel, the pervasive, mouth-watering scents of spices, sausage, tomato sauce, pizza . . .

"People came to Toluca from all over Italy," he says. "My folks came from around the Piedmont area. They couldn't even understand people from the other side of the hill.

"There were 400 or 500 people working in the mine here at one time. It closed in 1924. That hole was more than 500 feet deep. When the mine closed, all the guys who stayed on here went to work for the railroad. There used to be more than 30 taverns here. Now, there are five."

There were mainly Irish and Italians, and there were even special places for the North Italians and others for the South Italians. The Irish had their own church, St. Anne's, and the Italians had theirs, St. Joachim's. It is gone now, but the Italians and the Irish lie side by side in the tidy cemetery just outside of town, the Palumbos and Santinis alongside the Kellys and the Dalys, with a scattering of Polish and Germans.

Nobody knows exactly how the town was named. The story goes that an Italian, upon viewing the site some years back, commented in broken English, "I just came to look-a."

It is said that today there are more Germans in Toluca than Italians. There is also a remarkable Czech, Anton Hanus, who, at 86, still operates the Toluca Garment Co. and complains that "Business is terrible."

"When I came here 32, 33 years ago, they paid the people eight cents an hour. Came in an Ohio car, a big car that held 12 people.

"What do we do here? Well, you go to a tailor to get a suit made, and he doesn't really know how to make a suit. He sends it here to me, and we make it. We do this for 175, 200 tailors all over the country. Where the hell you gonna get a tailor today?"

Hanus' firm, which now employs about 185 people, receives measurements, instruction and material from tailors throughout the country, coast to coast. Sometimes, when a suit or coat is half-finished, the Toluca firm sends it back to the tailor, who then calls the customer in for a fitting.

"He shows him he's making it," Hanus says. "But he's not really making it. We are."

The coat or suit is then sent back to Toluca, finished down to the point of sewing in the tailor's label and shipped back to the tailor. Presto—a handmade suit from Toluca. Believe it or not.

"We can make a suit in one day," Hanus says. His firm has made suits for men who weigh 500 pounds. One special was for a man who took size 86, not likely to be found on your average ready-to-wear rack. Hanus touches a new topcoat, nearly finished, beautiful, of camel's hair, or something even better, alpaca, perhaps.

"I get $40 to make it. The tailor sells it for $240." (The tailor, of course, supplies the material.)

Machines whirr, heavy, industrial Singers. Instant buttonholes, already slit, bound, hemmed. Whole bolts of shiny, expensive lining material flash across tables, as if in the warehouse of some Venetian merchant. There are acres of bobbins, spools of thread, spinning, brightly colored. Chalk marks and the crunch of scissors through the rich material.

"Anybody who's a tailor today is a darned fool," Hanus says. I do not believe him. His eyes twinkle, his skin is smooth. It is hard to believe that he is 86.

Outside is the main line of the Sante Fe; a fast train, bearing semi-trailers on flat cars, thunders past. It does not stop at Toluca.

The depot is gone. The coal mine is gone. Across the tracks are old, empty buildings, abandoned stores, surrounded by scrub trees, broken concrete, bricks. It is called old town, where Toluca began. But the mine is closed, and the town's population dwindled from around 4,000 to its present 1,300 or so. All that is left of the mine is Jumbo, the red and weathered pile of slag.

John Boresi remembers that mine. It opened in the 1890's, he says, and he started working there in 1913.

"Got 80 cents a ton for working coal. Nineteen fifteen, I started driving mules in the mine and made $2.87 a day. There were about 600 men working there. Still a lot of coal there. But strip mines today have veins 15 feet. This one had three-foot veins. The Italians and the Irish worked that mine. Germans never went down. Too smart."

When prohibition started, Boresi said that people in the town got together and brought in 28 railroad cars of grapes to make wine. And Jumbo, he says, once was 40 feet higher than it is now. The rain washed it down. Kids used to slide down its steep sides in old fenders from junked cars. They don't do that any more. The fenders are no longer either the right shape or thick enough, and the kids get their adventure from television.

Once the company houses of the Toluca Mining Co. stood here in long rows. They are gone. The coal is still there, 500 feet down, the shaft plugged, the equipment gone, the miners, most of them, scattered to the winds.

The modern, pub-like bar at Mona's is crowded at lunchtime, although the cavernous dining rooms at the rear are not normally used until evening. Nilda Bernardi opened Mona's 43 years ago and named it after the theme song of an orchestra that he had long ago. The tune, "Oh Mona," dates from the 1920s.

Bernardi took over Capponi's 11 years ago, after Leno Capponi retired. But each restaurant continues to serve its distinctive cuisine. Capponi is retired now and living in Arizona, but the names go on and on and so does the fame of Toluca, which has, for an old mining town, fared rather well.

There are three churches now, a relatively huge and modern supermarket, a park, a swimming pool, a school with a long tradition of basketball excellence, an all-volunteer library and neatly kept homes, a sense of peace and order.

There is the noon whistle again, stirring long echoes. It caroms off the furrowed sides of Jumbo and reverberates off across the prairie.

The bartender in Mona's passes along and offers samples of garlic pancakes. Where else? Capponi's is closed on this day, and John Boresi stands beside the cash register in the darkened dining room telling old stories.

"There is still a lot of coal down there," he says, and he remembers the inky darkness and the sputtering illumination of the carbide lamps. In Cap's there is the rich smell of pizza and sauce and another episode of "As the World Turns" unspooling on the television. Two men sit watching, beer glasses clutched in their hands.

The scents, savory and lingering, remain almost to the very end of Rt. 116A near Benson. It is Toluca's road. No other town on it. Toluca. Even the name stirs visions, glorious visions of platters heaped with spaghetti, that incomparable ravioli, of lasagna, warm and soft bread with hard crusts. Say it slowly. Toluca. Toluca. I came Toluca.

Goofy Ridge, Where the Living Is Easy

It is a place from which architects, city planners, and zoners would probably fall back in panic and bewilderment. It is a chaotic collection of old and new trailers, pig houses, shacks, sheds, cabins, outhouses, permastone cottages, garages and old buses that appears at first glance to have sprung from some gypsy encampment that stopped one day and took root.

It is a non-town, listed on no highway maps and possessing no governmental entity. It has four taverns, a real estate office, a coin laundry and a public telephone booth. The closest thing to real government is the volunteer fire department and the school bus that comes past twice a day. Otherwise its people have achieved and stoutly defended an individualistic democracy of near Jeffersonian proportions.

Were Goofy Ridge to have a motto, which it does not, it would likely be the same as that of our first flag, "Don't Tread On Me."

There is an almost fierce sense of the individual here, an unwillingness to meddle, and at the same time a certain casual freedom that has caused some people to refer to it as a kind of geriatric Peyton Place. People discuss one another's affairs, amatory and otherwise, with an openness that would singe the ears of the normal suburbanite. And yet it is neither hostile nor bitter, but has some sense of community, of family even.

"We're one big family here," one resident says. "Not all happy. There's too many of us for that. But still it's like one big family."

And how many members?

Nobody knows for certain. Maybe 400 or so. Most of them live here year 'round nowadays. It used to be that Goofy Ridge was occupied summers only. People came down on weekends to fish, drink beer, lie around in the shade. It was a common man's summer place—a little shack in the woods away from it all where a person could just go and be himself. People didn't have to worry about their neighbors, their appearances, what kind of car they were driving. It came to be the kind of life many people found enormously appealing—400 or so.

Goofy Ridge.

Gabby Hartnett and other big people from Chicago used to come here for something different. Drink and fish with the local folks down along the Illinois. A midwestern Dogpatch. Quaint. Good fishing. Great hunting in the fall.

Then a few people started staying on all year long. First there were retired people, many of them from Caterpillar. There were fewer expenses than most places. Low taxes. Living was cheap and pretty good. And now there are people of all ages, including the bus full of young people who are hauled every day back and forth to school through the Sand Ridge Forest to Manito.

"It's been a puzzle to a lot of people how it ever grew up," says Kenny Weyhrich. He runs a real estate business in the low-ceilinged front office attached to his house. It is located right off the hard road, not properly in Goofy Ridge, but in the newer part, which is shown on the plat maps as Miller's Haven.

The ridge itself is a spinelike rise that runs across the wooded land just before it drops toward the beach at Lake Chautauqua.

Weyhrich says most lots are 50 by 100 feet. Lots of people own more than one. Houses go anywhere from $8,500 to $35,000, he says. And the legend persists that the name of the place came from some kind of hijinks that involved

36

the famous John Darling shooting a walnut off somebody's head. And somebody else saying what a goofy place it was.

Even deeper in antiquity is the story about Slim Bouchet drinking away one day during prohibition and suddenly jumping up and shouting that this was the goofiest place he had ever seen.

Goofy Ridge.

"When I came here twenty-four years ago only a few people stayed all year long," says Elizabeth Buchanan, who runs the Goofy Ridge Tavern, also known as Buck and Liz's. It is the oldest tavern in town and used to have a dirt floor. Even now its linoleum-covered dance floor is nearly worn away by the shuffling of many feet. No band. Just a jukebox. "I don't care what anybody says, it's been a wonderful life down here. People just want to be left alone."

She still likes to talk about old Johnny Darling—"a marvelous person, always full of fun. They used to play great jokes. They got the game warden drunk one time and took all the fish they could haul. Shooting walnuts off heads. Things like that. Nobody got mad. It was all done in fun."

There are clippings from old newspapers in the drawer behind the bar. Stories about the crowds that used to gather for Ditch Day, a political and social celebration held in honor of the dredging of the Goofy Ridge ditch. Taverns weren't supposed to open on Sundays until after noon, but there was an unofficial kind of church at the Goofy Ridge Tap. Early. When they opened the doors at noon, everybody would go home. Mrs. Buchanan was a widow for a time after Buck died. She has a new husband now. A young one.

There are, according to reports, several May-December liaisons, even March-December ones. Somebody suggested that it might have something to do with the water.

"Wouldn't know about that," one resident responds, hand wrapped tightly around a glass of beer. "Never touch it."

Goofy Ridge.

The social life in late winter centers largely around the taverns, as it does much of the year. Weekend nights bring people out of their houses and trailers to huddle around the warmth of the bar. One of them is Deedee Meyers, who is the Hialeah in with her 75-pound Malemute Huskey. She came back to Goofy Ridge from Santa Cruz, Calif., and Keokuk. She likes it. The dog, roughly twice the size of a timber wolf, is only half grown. It is friendly and everyone who comes in to the Hieleah stops to pet the dog. The tavern has a pool table, tables and chairs and a U-shaped bar. It burned in June, reopened in September.

The Lamplighter has just reopened. Closed temporarily for some license infraction. John Denver is singing "Back Home Again" on the jukebox. There is the click of pool balls, the rolling hum of conversation. Goldie Dickerson is in her kitchen around the corner from the barroom and will fix a rib eye steak dinner for $4. A good one. Diners are sometimes in danger of being rapped on the head with the back end of a pool cue and learn quickly to lean away from the pool players circling the table and chalking their cues.

Again there is that almost familial camaraderie, and the outsider feels instinctively that he is going to be rejected out of hand or else find an arm thrown across his shoulder in friendship. It is the latter. A small boy, two and a half years old, racks balls for his father and it makes both of them laugh. The front door swings open. A young couple. The man stops to talk and the girl moves eagerly along the bar to somebody else.

Goofy Ridge.

Quiet now. No one out in the yards yet. Dusk settles slowly through the woods. Lights come on in the old prewar trailers. Stoves glow. The door bangs on an outhouse. One has polka dots on the outside and the sign, "Sapphire Beanery." Another appears to be made of brick. One has a screened-in porch. There are new moons carved into the doors. Street of sand with tree roots causing unfamiliar bumps. Not a car moving now. Old oaks with the last of autumn's leaves still rustling dryly, waiting for the spring wind and the swelling buds to send them flying. Ice breaking up alond the river. Soon the long lines of geese going north again. Fishing. Warm days. And the easy, easy livin'.

Goofy Ridge.

Perhaps not so goofy at that.

Welcome to Washburn

Driving up along the smooth new blacktop surface of Rt. 89 brings the slow realization of the benefits of non progress. No huge factories belching smoke here, no subdivisions crawling across the landscape, no plastic roofed fast food franchises. Not yet. This is still Grade A, uninterrupted, all-American countryside, just like grandpa used to make.

Hardly any trucks along this peaceful and lovely stretch of road, either. Very little traffic, in fact. Only billboards are those small ones, advertising seed corn or the Lutheran Hour on WMAQ. It has changed little here over the years, at least on the surface, and it has quite clearly been for the best.

This country rolls slightly, stretching out far to the west into thick wooded valleys that are green and cool and flow down toward the river. Out to the east is the prairie, a vast and fertile patchwork, mostly dark now with the colors of earth, neatly hemmed and stitched with fences. Old wire here, and time weathered posts, deeply ridged by the wind and the ice and bleached by the sun. Islands out there, too, homes and barns and summer green trees and the sound and feel of the long wind. Then a turn in the road, the water tower above the trees and the sign, "Welcome to Washburn."

Twelve hundred people live here, the sign proclaims. Not many, maybe, in the great global scale of things where births and deaths in a single week may run into the millions. But its own place, this, unique and different from all the rest, just as faces are, or fingerprints.

Welcome to Washburn.

It is true that there may be hundreds of places like Jack's Restaurant where the farmers sit on the stools and push their hats back and drink their coffee hot and black from the heavy mugs. Flapjacks on the grill this morning, sausages sizzling, somebody ordering a "mess of eggs" and the men calling back and forth, "Feeder cattle looking pretty good this year, huh?" or "Hi, you old son of a gun." But nowhere else exactly the same. This is Washburn. This is a golden May morning.

Just up the street is Elsie Strauch, washing the windows at Walt's Superway until they gleam in the morning sunlight. She and her husband have been in business here for 42 years and they have been good years. Open at 6 a.m. Life and the town pass by through those clean windows. "Two big things here in the past few years," they say. "Miss Illinois and the bank robbery."

Many of us remember those, too. The robbery was almost three years ago now. A September Friday afternoon. Two men came into the bank and herded the employees into the vault. They left with just over $25,000, the accounts said, and six hours later they were captured.

And while the robbery was going on, Miss Colleen Metternich, Miss Illinois of 1973 and a teacher at Lowpoint Washburn High School, was in Atlantic City for the Miss America finals.

The bank is quiet now and Colleen Metternich has gone on, but the school where she taught is busy as ever, maybe more so. It has an ag department with five different courses—agriculture mechanics, power and machinery, crop production, animal science and introduction to agriculture, plus classes in electricity, welding, soils and fertilizer and an ag economics class. Plus the academic curriculum. Plus music.

Two hundred and forty students now, says Jack Simpson, new principal, who looks as if he used to play tackle for Ohio State. But many of them absent the day before judging by the stream of kids pouring into the office to get their admission slips signed.

"Where were you Friday, Rich?"

"I didn't hear the first bell."

The excuses go on.

"Can't you get up in the morning?" Simpson asks.

"I did. I took a shower though."

"Well, get up ten minutes earlier."

Another was out chasing cows which had gotten through the fence. One was ordering flowers for a school affair when the first bell rang. Another simply shrugs and doesn't care.

Simpson says lots of kids want a car and then a job to support that car and that's all they care about. Nothing changes. The last bell has rung and silence falls across the hallways.

The post office looks like a historic building, a depot, perhaps, where famous men once detrained or politicians spoke. It isn't. Used to be a contractor's office. But the post office remains the social center of town. People stop, pick up their mail from those quaint glass-front boxes with the combination locks, and talk. Along with the usual "Wanted" notices, there are items of more pressing concern on the bulletin board: "Pork Queen Contest—contests must be 18 to 21. Contack Mrs. Don Heck by June 10. Sponserded by Wood Ford Co. Pork Producers" and "Free sand box fill. Sponserd by LW Jaycees."

Nelson Iunker is here and so is Elmer Zoss. Iunker has been in the trucking business here for 43 years. Zoss has Box No. 1 at the post office. Had it ever since he moved here in 1955 and before that it was his son's. Yes, they remember that bank robbery. September 7, 1974. Put eight people in the vault. Another bank robbery long time ago, too, so long ago the robber got away on horseback, but nobody remembers the details. And they say they built the first car in this town, at Duryea Bros., down on Main Street. Had five blacksmith shops at one time. Now there are none. J. Frank Duryea was, however, a native of Washburn.

Across the way, in the Supreme Dairy cheese store, John Damerell displays his Quasquicentennial Shaving Permit. Big days here Aug. 12 to 15, when the town celebrates its 125 years. Store proprietor Bonnie Jenkins says no cheese is made here any more. Nobody has dairy herds now. The cheese comes drom the Supreme Dairy in Ogelsby and she passes out samples. Longhorn. Colby. Brick. Cheddar.

Friendly, these people. A man in a pickup says he's not sure just when they built the unique log cabin American Legion post headquarters. Sometime in the 30s. He'll find out and let us know. He does. 1938. And they raffled off a bull in 1946 and used the $1,200 proceeds to refurbish the place. Somebody has gone to get a key to show off the inside. Inside Tom Mikos' tavern, only one right in town, four men are playing Euchre beneath a Tiffany lampshade from Old Style. They are drinking Pabst. They snap their cards onto the formica table top in the same way men everywhere do. They look almost the same as the men in the wine gardens of Vienna, or those in the little bars in Paris. Mikos has come here from Wheaton. A bright place with neat, checkered tablecloths. Mikos says he plans to redo the front.

40

The park at the south edge of town is empty and peaceful on an early weekday afternoon. The grass is mowed, the tables painted and there is a sense of order. Nelson Iunker's truck pulls in with a load of gravel. One keeps running into the same people here. Twelve hundred in all. Enough to choose from.

And to the south of town is the Snag Creek Golf Course. Busy already, its flags snapping in the breeze, its fairways clipped. Men stand in their golf caps and windbreakers, shading their eyes as they stare out across the green, eyes forever on the ball. In one direction is the town with its water tower and its 1200 souls and its "Welcome to Washburn" sign. In the other is the prairie again and the soft wind blowing and the birds singing across those old fields. A card snicks onto the table beneath the Old Style Beer lamp. The cash register in Walt's Superway rings once again. A man in Oshkosh B'Gosh overalls extracts a *Successful Farming* magazine from his box at the post office. A redwing blackbird salutes the new season from atop a gnarled fencepost and out there somewhere a lark practices its trills. Summer is icumen in again in this changeless land. Indeed it is.

Princeton, a Page from the Past

An early summer morning along South Main St., early enough so that time seems, for the moment, to have slipped backwards.

Take away these parking meters, the neon and plastic from the store fronts, the mercury vapor lights and the tubular aluminum furniture from the porches of the big houses nearby and it is something else.

Carriages clattering across the bricks. Horses' hooves. The old inter-urban clanging in on its way to Spring Valley. The men emerging from all these enormous houses, nodding sagely to one another, checking their gold watches and going off to their businesses or farms or wherever very rich and prosperous men go once they leave their mansions.

They are incredible, these houses. One is reminiscent of the Custis-Lee mansion on the hill above Arlington National Cemetery in Virginia; another has soaring mansard roofs like something out of Charles Addams' cartoons. Many of the homes are of mellowed native brick with ornate Victorian trim that looks, from a distance, like white lace. They are columned and porticoed and turreted with widows' walks, and there are huge shutters and high old windows from which eyes have gazed at the passing scene for 100 years and more.

Students of architecture revel in this unprecedented collection of American classic homes, and there are the sightseers, driving through slowly, like those tourists in Beverly Hills, saying to one another, "Look at that one," or, "How about this one over here!"

They are a rare treasure, these houses, most of them surprisingly well preserved. Some have fallen, and others have been sided with aluminum or similarly modernized, but dozens of them have been saved or are being repainted and restored with an eye toward authenticity. Throughout the town, ladders and scaffolding arise in profusion, and one calculates that the amount of paint being sold here must be keeping someone in clover.

But Princeton is not lost in dreams of its past. The city's motto, "Where Tradition Meets Progress," may sound as if it were the winning entry in a high-school contest, but it is startlingly accurate.

The early-morning ghosts linger but briefly. They are soon chased away by a growing clamor of traffic along Main St., and the shoppers, the businessmen, the kids on bikes all bring an unusual sense of vitality.

Downtown has not been diminished by shopping centers or malls, and its charm remains in its age and state of preservation. There is apparently only a single empty store, that one gutted by fire.

The old hotels have gone into and beyond genteel disrepair. One has been changed into apartments, and in the lobby of the other is the bus depot and a television-repair shop. The sturdy oak tables in the dining room are still set, but no one eats here any more. A color television beams out its daytime fare; there are no viewers. The sign on the front door says "Pull Hard."

Coming up along Main St. From the south, up from Tiskilwa and past the silent farmhouses and the deep green yards, to the soaring Soldiers and Sailors Monument and beyond, is a trip through history. The town grew this way, starting with those first settlers from the Hampshire Colony Congregational Church of Northampton, Mass., in 1831, and John and Cyrus Bryant, brothers of William Cullen Bryant. Cyrus's house still stands at 1100 S. Main. Princeton expanded north, up toward the railroad tracks, which came in 1854, and out farther, to Interstate 80, of more recent vintage, which has sprouted with motels and franchise-food shops that look exactly like those in a thousand other cities.

It is the old business district that remains unique, that brings people to Princeton. There is the old American House Hotel with its faded lettering—"European" and "Home Cooking"—and an iron-grill balcony facing the monument in the square, small shops along the street level and apartments now up above.

Across the street is one of the last of the old-time grocery stores, Nelson's Grocery and Meats, which looks, behind its heavy Colonial Bread screen door, like something that Walt Disney Productions might have spent months and millions to create.

Nelson has been in business since 1938. He still charges groceries, keeping the duplicate tickets in an old McCaskey biller, and the store delivers. Nelson is particularly proud of his delivery boys; many of them are now distinguished citizens. One is a state's attorney, another is a West Point graduate; others are engineers, professors. He keeps their photographs and displays them proudly. They are his boys. And it is not, despite the wooden screen door slamming, the sound of the old adding machine, the old cases and shelves, a scene from Disney's "Pollyanna."

Farther north is Country Casuals, the kind of small boutique that one might easily find in a far more sophisticated setting. Its basement, home of the Strawberry Patch Dining Room, has an almost Parisian ambience. There are bentwood chairs and a bistro-like setting. Light filters down from a grate window, and there is an intriguing view of the street. There are imported greeting cards, a Franklin stove, a roll-top desk, racks of tasteful clothes, an unexpected air of discreet elegance.

The basement across the street at Hoffman's Jewelry is somewhat less stylish but an attraction nonetheless. J. A. Murphy operates it as Patterns of the Past, and there is a bewildering collection of discontinued china and crystal patterns, stacked in unbelievable profusion.

There are orange crates full of dishes, shelves full of dishes, aisles full of dishes; one is afraid to move for fear of causing some enormous crash. Customers edge through gingerly, examining the elegant—Limoges, Haviland—and the curious, such as a commemorative plate of the Great West Baden Spring Hotel of West Baden, Ind., "The Carlsbad of America." Murphy says that he has had customers from as far as South Africa and Anchorage, Alaska, on the same day.

And there are the drug stores with their savory, cosmetic smells, dress shops and shoe stores, department store, a cigar store where a man stands looking through the girlie magazines. There is a theater, the new colonial style Prouty Civic Building, real-estate offices, barber shops and antique shops through which women in their summer dresses browse silently and critically.

The newer part of the business district sits near the railroad, and there are still the high embossed tin ceilings and long narrow rooms. Roland Eckdahl, who has been Princeton mayor since 1960, is behind the counter of his clothing store, which he says is doing three times as much business per square foot as the national average.

He says that perhaps the best thing about his city is the way it looks, even though it has lost most of its elms.

"This used to be known as the city of elms," he said. "But the disease came, and we lost 8,000 of them." Many of the elms were planted in 1875 and

43

had grown until they formed cool green gothic arches high above the streets.

Ruben Noble's hardware store, just up from the mayor's store, is said to be the oldest business in town, dating to 1854. Beneath its high ceiling are long racks and bins of endless varieties of hardware, 16-penny nails, coal scuttles, kerosene lanterns and machetes. The highest racks are accessible from tall ladders on tracks, like those in old libraries. Rope is stored in huge reels in the basement and is fed up through slots in the floor that have worn perceptibly over six-score years and then some.

And, just beyond, are the tracks and the railroad station, a solid brick paperweight of a place that looks like one of those accessories to a Lionel train set of the late 1930s, even to its ornate outside lights, like those once sold in toy stores for $1.98 (plus bulb).

Inside is Phyllis Pozzi, one of the few women station agents in the business. Hers is a large oak ticket office that still has its telegraph key and the old desk piled high with receipts, weigh bills, bills of lading. This is an Amtrak station now. The Illinois Zephyr passes twice a day, and the station handles about 70 passengers a week, most of them going to Quincy.

Out past the seed stores and lumber yards, Princeton becomes more nondescript. A sign on Mr. Quick, a hamburger drive-in, extends congratulations to Linda and Ed, for what, heaven only knows, and the city trails off, almost, to a junction where trucks whining past on Interstate 80 create a jarring, modern sound, like that of an overly amplified guitar. A little farther along is the old red covered bridge across Bureau Creek—the structure is 115 years old now and still solid as a rock.

And there is still City-County Park, a cool oasis of oaks and shade, so scrupulously maintained that the Massachusetts settlers would be pleased. Joe Pratt, park superintendent, is there with his dog, Sandy. He does everything from cleaning the latrines to talking with the people who stop by. Sixty-eight acres, he says. Put in during the days of the Work Projects Administration. One Sunday, Pratt says, the park was visited by 1,400 to 1,500 people from 17 states and Canada.

And the people of Princeton like to point out other things about the place—the swimming pool, the churches, the new subdivision, the high school that looks like a set for "Our Miss Brooks," the Bureau County Fair, and so on.

But what fascinates the visitor is the look of the city, so solid, deep-rooted and seemingly permanent that, were the final trumpet to blow right now, there is little doubt that this would be one of the last places to crumble.

There are, to be sure, glaring exceptions to all this heritage and splendor, such as the New Deal courthouse, so evocative of the WPA that it lacks only the statue of a man leaning on a shovel. And the historic jail is being torn down and replaced by a new, more efficient building.

This is no Greenfield Village or Williamsburg; whatever restoration has been done has been largely voluntary, which makes Princeton all the more admirable. And the results are visible throughout the community, whether one drives along Peru Rd., or South Main St., or along any of a dozen other streets.

One of them leads to the house of the abolitionist preacher Owen Lovejoy. It was once a station on the underground railroad and is now restored as a historic site and tourist attraction. Out back is a little red schoolhouse, brought in off the prairie and rebuilt as a monument to the one-room education of early Illinois. In one of its windows is a Fedders air conditioner, a somewhat unexpected example of tradition meeting progress.

There remains somehow that futile and hopeless wish to have been here when the elms were at their peak, when people walked in silent wonder beneath them on late summer days, like pilgrims at Chartres, and when the New Englanders still lived in their tall castles far back on the green, green grass.

Every town has its ghosts, its silent past. But on a quiet August morning, before the doors open and cars come, before the parking meters and aluminum light poles are perceived, yesterday is alive and well and remarkably preserved in Princeton.

Lewistown

Life goes slowly here, geared almost to the great ebb and flow of the seasons and the even greater coming and going of life and death.

There have been boom times and slack ones. Busy Saturday nights when the coping around the old courthouse was so full there was no place to sit. Times when the troops from Camp Ellis poured into town. It was like Las Vegas, they said. Buses coming and going. Soldiers three and four deep at the bars. Slot machines. Then the quiet times again. Peaceful. Soft and slow autumns. Sap rising in the springtime. Something leisurely, too, that people who are always in a hurry find immensely appealing, like those signs one sees in the windows. "Gone to bank. Be back soon." "Gone to meeting. Be back Wednesday."

This is like many of the towns along the Spoon River which once rejected Edgar Lee Masters for being a tattler and a troublemaker. Imagine him dredging up all those stories about the dead. They saw in the characters of *Spoon River Anthology* an uncle, maybe, or someone whose piety was unquestioned in life. But all has been forgiven now and the fact that Edgar Lee once lived here is one of the town's attractions. His boyhood home is preserved and so is that of his father, where he frequently stopped later in life. And Oak Hill Cemetery is generally regarded as "the Hill," first made infamous and then famous by the Anthology.

The old graves here go back a hundred years and more and there is at this time of year a sense of deep peace. The wind in the newly leafed trees takes on a new sound. It is not the dry and scratchy rustle of winter, but a warmer, full-throated, urgent plea. And the ground is soft, springy. Bird songs and stirrings. Lichen on the headstones.

Some of the more prominent graves are surrounded by wrought iron fencing, partly fallen now, the gates with rusted hinges. There are stones with masonic symbols, or with a hand pointing skyward and the legend, "We meet above." Above one grave where a young girl lies sleeping into another springtime is the motto, "This lovely bud, so young so fair, Called hence by early doom."

But Masters's hill and Masters's people range all along the valley of the Spoon, the merchants, the bankers, the brawlers, in quiet little cemeteries where the crickets sound on warm afternoons and the tall grass bends in the wind. And Petersburg, where Masters now sleeps on his own hill, has been his heart's home rather than Lewistown. But Lewistown remains the historic seat of a county so relatively empty that population explosion alarmists quickly look elsewhere. Less than 50 people per square mile.

"I've got nine hundred and seventy-five square miles to patrol here," says Sheriff Meredith Ellsworth, first Fulton county sheriff in 100 years to get elected again. He says his old jail was actually built in 1863, not in 1850 as the historical brochure proclaims. But it has seen horse thieves and lynch mobs, and none of its prisoners has ever been given the death penalty.

There are, on this day, half a dozen prisoners there, oldtimers most of them, and Sheriff Ellsworth is on the telephone. On the other end is the distraught mother of a young man busted on a dope charge, an affliction these days that has lapped beyond the cities into once-untouched rural areas.

The courthouse nearby has recently been redone, remodeled and enlarged last year at a cost of over a million. It is not the type of building to inspire architectural rapture, being rather simple and block-like, but with a pleasant plaza out front. At one side is some kind of Gatling gun and at the other a 37milli-meter piece of French artillery from World War I. The plaza is dedicated to the veterans of the Revolutionary War who lived in Fulton County. And many of World War II notables, MacArthur, Eisenhower, Patton, Halsey, Nimitz and Marshall.

These were the big years for Lewistown, during World War II, when there were as many as 70,000 soldiers at nearby Camp Ellis. People remember buses going to camp every five minutes and troops lined up for blocks. Two movie theaters then. They opened at 11 in the morning and were packed until closing time. Boom times, they were. But then it all went away almost as quickly as it had come. The camp shut down. Everybody left. And Lewistown settled back into what it had been before.

Talk to people about it now and they might not remember. "Lot of people here in those days are dead now." All that happened over 30 years ago. Third of a century. And the memories are partly gone, out on the hill now, beneath the spring turf of Oak Hill. Lots of people die in 30 years time. Lots of new people born, moving in.

The Spoon River Hotel looks almost the same as always. Built in 1850, they say, and many dignitaries from the Civil War stayed in these rooms. When they were building Camp Ellis, the workmen sometimes piled nine to a room and slept in shifts. The hotel is still full, mostly with workers from Central Illinois Light Company's Duck Creek project. But much of it is being converted to apartments, according to Harold Glaser, who runs the place now. "Eventually, we'll make an apartment house out of it and rent out the lobby," he says.

But there are still some hotel rooms left, rented usually on a weekly basis—$28 a week without and $31.50 with bath, or $7.50 and $8.50 a night. Sixteen rooms and 12 apartments now. Glaser has been here a while. He says things are going well around the square and that most businesses have changed hands.

One of the best of the buildings on the square is the so called Beadles Block, a 100-year old jewel of a place that promises all sorts of architectural and historic surprises, but it has been panelled inside and most of its secrets are boarded up, accessible only through a furniture store. Once there was an opera house on the second floor, later it was a roller rink. It remains a strikingly ornate and brooding building with its tin roof arcade and lovely sculptured windows.

The historic Rasmussen Blacksmith Shop and Museum opens later in May and there is a sign in the window, "Closed for the year, see you next spring." Across the way is Bob Zempell, member of the fourth generation of his family to be running that huge drafty old store filled with crockery, hardware and dusty memories. He says he used to be lucky to get out of the place by 10 at night when he started working. Now business is not so good. "Used to have two movies in town. Now there are none." Lewistown is not getting the best of things right now, he says, with things like Chicago sludge on one hand and a facility for delinquents on the other.

"It's my home town," says Mayor Alwilda Gaskill, a gracious and articulate woman who retired after 28 years of teaching in 1971 and is busy as ever. "When the mayor resigned, the citizens party asked me to run and I did. I really think the women got out and voted." Her office in city hall is small and cramped. It seems almost as if there should be a piece of chalk on her desk, and an apple. "I've always liked knowing everybody in town. It's just a home town."

With a past. Lincoln spoke here between the pillars of the old courthouse on August 17, 1858. Dusty, tired travelers climbed down here from the stage coaches that passed between Springfield and the Galena lead mines a hundred and fifty years ago. Now it is billed as capital of Spoon River country, boyhood home of Edgar Lee Masters. And his hill. Spring's soft wind sweeps in from the prairie out to the west, plays across the surface of the Spoon and whispers through the trees and weathered gravestones of Oak Hill. More than 50 people per square mile here. Each one a story that has now been edited down so tightly that there are only names and dates left. And the certainty that when the long sleep on this hill is over, "we meet above," all of them. The merchant, the banker, the brawler, "this lovely bud."

In the meantime, life goes slowly here. There is time to think about things.

Grass May Be Greener Beneath Eureka's Snow

There is perhaps too much familiarity here, not the kind that breeds contempt, but rather the kind that numbs the vision and makes what is everyday seem somehow less appealing. Here are these old familiar roads in and out of town, crisscrossing right at the center; the courthouse raising its graceful, open spire above the treetops, and the grand old college, its buildings looking like some set from an antebellum movie, all so well known, so familiar that the grass has simply got to be greener elsewhere.

Or does it?

When the political editor of the Los Angeles *Times* followed Ronald Reagan back here ten years ago to dedicate the library, he became so fascinated by Eureka that he wondered in print why it was not listed as one of the choice places in the world to live. Paris, he said, was at the top, with Rome and London second and third and Los Angeles 15th . . . "and Eureka, Ill., didn't even get a mention," he said. But it was "a little bit of what's left of America as it was when I was a boy." Could be.

No smog. No crime. No pickets. No litter. And there are some kind of long ties here, deep and certain, and things do not seem to change much. There is the new shopping center to the east of town, not draining away business from downtown so much as complementing it, nor do the rambling houses that have grown up around the wooded shores of Lake Eureka really alter the character of the town. There are still areas where nothing much ever changes. The old is saved. Painted. Fixed up. The feeling is one of stability.

Burrus Dickinson, publisher of the *Woodford County News* for about as long as anybody can remember, seems to be the kind of man meant to lean back in a chair, fix his hands behind his head and talk. Used to be the president of Eureka College. Fifteen years, as a matter of fact. Taught journalism, too, at the University of Illinois. Some of his students still around these parts. He is 72. Looking as good as new.

"Place was originally settled by members of the Christian Church," he says, "way back in the 1830s. Before that there was no town at all, only log cabins a mile or so apart. This was part of a big walnut grove that ran all the way from the Mackinaw River to north of Cruger. That was its first name. Walnut Grove. Had to change it, though. There was another Walnut Grove down somewhere near Bushnell."

Dickinson's family has been here since 1834. He bought his paper in 1937 and was president of Eureka College from 1939 to 1954. "We were down to 54 students during the war," he says. Yes, the college still has its ties with the Christian Church, but there are more Catholics now than anything. "Where do they go to church? Over in Washington, if at all."

People still walk the streets safely here, day or night. Dickinson says that after they have done it once or twice, the students from Chicago think nothing of getting off the bus and walking out to the college. Back home they would never dare.

When Carl Greenburg of the Los Angeles *Times* was here with Reagan, he wrote, "I saw a people who appear to be living in contentment, who probably don't have to lock their doors at night, who mind their own business instead of yours . . . The last holdup in town was about 10 years ago and that was by some bird from another city . . ."

At one time it was pumpkins that made Eureka famous. This was the undisputed pumpkin capital of the world. Street signs were made in the shape of pumpkins, and every other fall at harvest time Eureka blossomed with bands and floats and beauty pageants in celebration of the great pumpkin. But in 1960 Libby McNeill and Libby, which had owned the Eureka cannery since 1929, moved its headquarters to Morton, shut down here, and Eureka became the ex-pumpkin capital of the world. Not much to go on. The last festival was held in 1961. The street signs disappeared after pumpkins disappeared and the pumpkin is gone these days, treasured only in souvenir Pumpkin Festival programs, particularly the centennial issue of 1959, and in yellowing newspaper clippings.

But who needs pumpkins? Eureka has its other distinctions. It is one of the area's relatively few dry towns, with a tavern on the east and one on the west, but none in town, a situation so carefully preserved that a recent annexation went right around a liquor store.

Eureka has its own college, so old and venerable that its administration building was built with a front at either end since nobody knew at the time which way the town would grow. And the college adds its own flavor to the town with its cultural activities, its athletics, its Reagan Center, its pool. Eureka has its own movie theater, community owned, but closed now because of a structural problem with one wall. It has its own distinctive judge, Sam Harrod III, a pariah among his peers for bringing common sense to the administration of justice by having offenders get haircuts or pick up beer cans along the highways, but a hero to the people. Eureka has its own hospital, which has grown from a streetcorner establishment into an efficient medical plant without losing its sense of mission; it has its own park, golf course, two homes for the aged, its sense of peace, of stability.

Right by Rt. 117, which bisects the town north to south, is the gem-like First Christian Church, looking from the outside much like Jubilee College at Kickapoo once did, and on the inside like some beautifully preserved English abby with its dark beams and Tudor trappings. Across the way, the Woodford County courthouse, a tall drafty old building which looks from a distance like some elaborate clock tower. Some of its original flavor is still intact, although the third floor courtroom badly combines suspended ceilings and fluorescent lighting with high old doors and marble floors. Young men here on this winter day in PAC hats and FFA jackets. Traffic offenses mostly.

And over across Rt. 24 is one of the town's oldest buildings in which an antique shop is now maintained by Robert Herschel, retired Peoria industrialist. There is the ticking of many clocks here, an awareness of seconds, minutes, hours, passing one by one, and Herschel himself, beaming like some extremely civilized English shopkeeper, telling how he has lived here for 40 years, how he bought the old building mainly to preserve it. Originally a millinery shop, he says, built by a certain Mrs. Bradbury who had a house here when the town was organized. Moved to its present location about 1900 and it has been somewhat crooked ever since, leaning noticeably to the east. It used to be a dentist's office, and the patients would look through the drastically out-of-plumb windows at the courthouse across the way and comment, "Well I see the courthouse is still crooked."

And there is, of course, Ronald "Dutch" Reagan of the class of 1932, who

50

remains in memory like some fabled legend, although still in the flesh. He is unquestionably the most famous person ever to come out of here. But the greatest? The happiest?

Who knows. He or she may still be here, living a peaceful, quiet, unspectacular life. Maybe one of the men in the senior citizens bowling league who gather on Wednesdays at 1:30 at the Star Lite Lanes, roll respectable enough games and call themselves, laughingly, the Holy Rollers, the Over the Hill Gang, the Has-Beens. Maybe somebody along the street who stops to explain the sign in the barbershop window, "Will be back around April 5, 1977." Gone to California and the road maps are still spread out inside the shop, showing the way across Wyoming.

Back here nothing but winter. The old walnut grove, or what is left of it, rises off the prairie like a black etching on white paper, hard-edged and sharp and knife cold now. "Say something nice about our town," Robert Herschel calls out as we leave his shop. All right. The grass is green down there beneath that snow. Maybe as green as anywhere.

Spring Valley

Hard to believe these days that this once was considered one of the toughest towns in the whole country. Sixty-nine taverns, there were, plus five bumboats along the river, places noted for wild drinking, wild fighting, wild women. There was a famous madam named Red Slippers who used to take her girls down Main street every Saturday night in a surrey with a fringe on top, and it was said, "She knew the value of good advertising." From here she went to the Klondike and became lost in legend.

This, too, was one of the centers of the anarchist movement, but it seems to have been peculiarly tame here and funloving. The Prosperity Club, built by the anarchists, had the longest bar in the state. Any thirsty citizen, and there must have been plenty of them, could buy six schooners of beer for a quarter to help wash down the coal dust. The movement's newspaper, *L'Aurora*, had a circulation of 3,000 and it was rumored the assassination of President McKinley was plotted in Spring Valley.

There were 32 national groups represented here in 1905, including one Chinaman. The big groups were the Italians, the Poles, the Germans, Irish, Lithuanians. Often they arrived in town wearing their native costumes, still ticketed and tagged from their point of entry. The English, the Welsh, the Scotch came first. And then the miners from middle and southern Europe. It was a boom town and must have looked at the turn of the century like one of those brawling frontier towns where the sheriff would be somebody along the lines of John Wayne.

The Spring Valley Coal Co. advertised for miners in 1885, offering "steady employment and good chances for a home." Much of the country was suffering from an industrial depression at the time and advertisement like this one brought a near stampede.

"They came expecting their choice of jobs and high wages," noted the Bureau County *Daily News Tribune*. "Instead they found the mines, the mills and the smelters. They dug coal and got a dollar a day."

John Mitchell, who was to become famous as a respected pioneer union leader, came the following year. He was 16 and already a member of the Knights of Labor. He became known as the father of the eight-hour day and was a longtime president of the UMW. But those were times of strife and lockouts. In April, 1888, four years after the opening of Spring Valley's first mine, the 700 men in shafts three and four were told to take their tools and report back when notified. The following April, the rest of the miners were sent home.

It was the infamous lockout of 1889, which brought destitution to the town. The Bureau County paper reporter wrote, "Women with a babe in one arm and a bucket in the other have walked from house to house all over the country adjacent to Spring Valley begging for a little food. Falling wages must stop somewhere for working men must eat as must also their families."

While it lasted, it was like some tumultuous epic, something out of *How Green Was My Valley*, with the mine owners and the superintendents locked in a long and bitter struggle with the miners and the union organizers. "They treated us with silent contempt as if we were brute beasts. That is what irritated our men most. They ignored us entirely. It could not be worse in the old country."

The peak came around 1910, when the Spring Valley Coal Co. operated five mines, three in town, one in Dalzell and one in Seatonville, employing over 2,500 miners. Then came the slow shift to southern coal and the last mine was dismantled fifty years ago. A few old miners are left with their memories. And those red slag piles, crumbling pyramids of an age when the mines brought waves of immigrants into this valley, men who spend their days working on their knees, lying on their sides, hacking out coal for 10 hours a day in small black tunnels three or three and a half feet high.

No more of that, now. And only a remnant of those 69 taverns. The building that housed the longest bar is a youth club. And Spring Valley, once known to the Indians as the Valley of the Springs, wears a peaceful, prosperous look. Main Street has its stores and shops and looks vaguely like an Edward Hopper painting. Many of the signs bear the name of the merchant family, Cassiday. And many of the stores and shops are covered with stucco, or pebbled ash. In one is Dave Fassino, now owner of Vallero's Bakery, which sends hearty European type bread (no preservatives added) with hard, crumbly crusts throughout this area of the state.

"It's what you don't put in that makes the difference," he says. "American bread has dough conditioners to keep it soft. Most bakery bread comes out of the oven two hours after the dough is started. Mine is still rising."

He is the fourth generation baker in his family. His father skipped the profession because of an allergy to dough. Fassino does all his own baking, and he makes anywhere between 350 and 1,000 loaves a day, long French loaves, a shorter and fatter Italian Vienna style and hard rolls. While he continues the old traditions in his profession, he is not totally bound. He is married to a McLinden from Peoria and it is one more step in the melting of the old ethnic ties.

For when they came to Spring Valley, each national group built its own church. There is the Irish church: Immaculate Conception; the Italian church: St. Anthony's; the Polish Church: St. Peter and Paul; and the Luthuanian church: St. Ann's.

People still go to "the Polish church" or "the Irish church" or "the Italian church." The latter has a brand new building and there are people who remember the old one, with its benches out front for the men who dropped off their women and children and remained to socialize—outside. For them, religion was synonymous with women. Their old church is now owned by the Baptists and the new St. Anthony's has no benches out front.

But it is St. Peter and Paul that brings tears of nostalgia to old line Catholics who are horrified by sterile, modern churches. It is dripping with statues, blazing with near rococo splendor. There are on its altars at least a dozen statues plus a soaring mural of Polish and Italian saints proceeding across the heavens: St. Stanislaus Kostka, St. Tarsisius, St. Maria Goretti.

"There will be no changes so long as I am here," says Msgr. Joseph Kapala. He comes to greet us wearing suspenders and carrying a white rosary. He has celebrated the golden jubilee of his ordination in March of this year. He was born in Wilmington, Delaware, and went back to the old country with his parents shortly thereafter, where he became eventually the youngest monsignor in all of Slovakia. He returned to the United States in 1946. On the wall of his rectory is a special commendation from Pope Paul VI on the occasion of his jubilee.

"Read it," he says. "Go on. Read it." Fifty years a priest. "Yes, the town is mostly Catholic. We used to sing Christmas carols here in Polish. There are still a few people who come to confession in Polish." He leaves us a small holy card showing priestly hands breaking the sacred host. "In memory of the Fiftieth Anniversary of Ordination to the Priesthood of Rev. Msgr. Joseph Kapala. Ordained in Rome March 12, 1927. Golden Jubilee Celebration Spring Valley, Illinois, March 12, 1977. Please pray for me." A man of humility, simplicity. "You know what somebody told me. You are not old. You are just closer to heaven." Amen.

Mamie Reinsch, who runs her own tavern now that her husband is dead, looks as Irish as anybody in town, but is Italian. Her maiden name was Picco. "It doesn't matter what people are," she says. "They're all just good or bad." She stands behind an antique bar, bought by her and her husband in Chicago nearly half a century ago. A canary runs through its trills in its cage by the window and a small dog reclines comfortably on a pillowed chair. There is something solid, entrenched here, the same feeling one finds in those family-run bistros in Paris, some sweet shop in Vienna.

But this is Spring Valley, and just next door is Pete Alfano, one of the pioneer pizza makers in the entire area. He is from Palermo and speaks more Italian than English. He has been making pizza here since 1958, when hardly anybody else was doing it. We can carry glasses of beer from Reinsch's tavern to Alfano's, but carefully. The police might not like it. But it's all right, says Mamie's son. "I used to be chief of police." Alfano's pizza is excellent, made and baked on the spot, from the dough on up, and to order. "Now everybody makes it," Pete Alfano says. He shakes his head sadly.

No signs out on this street of the turmoil of the past. Mrs. Cyril Sweeney, who is Welsh, Italian and French, says that during one of the anarchists' parades, one of the citizens grabbed the red flag, stomped on it and marched down the street carrying an American flag.

"During the Pullman strike, they say Emma Goldman was here preaching from a soap box. She is supposed to have baptized a baby in beer, too."

We are sitting in her kitchen and she is sifting through the historical collection of her late husband. "I started to read it," she says, "and I got hooked." She talks about the famous Red Slippers, about the editor, Pat Mahoney, who got off a riverboat one day on his way to the Klondike, and never made it, for he spent the rest of his life here. And there was Reinke's Opera House, where the Foys played, the traveling vaudeville, all the old newspapers.

"When McKinley was killed they chased the editor of the anarchist paper out of town and anarchy died here that fast. There is not one son, not one grandson left to carry on anarchy here. They were swallowed up in the melting pot of Spring Valley."

From the south, the best approach to the Valley of the Springs is up old Rt. 29, which winds its leisurely way through cool forests of cottonwoods and oaks. Past the new St. Anthony's at one end, and the St. Margaret's Hospital, to St. Bede at the other. The east-west boundaries are the river and the cemeteries that line the ridges overlooking the town, all silent as Edgar Lee Masters' hill, and as eloquent, too. Seven churches in town now, the four Catholic, the Congregational, the Greek Orthodox, the Baptist and a synagogue.

The old Spring Valley Mine company houses are still here, covered with stucco now, many of them, and expanded, but looking as if they will last as long as the slag piles. Enough industry to keep things going and for a "help wanted," in fact, at the Stewart Warner plant on the edge of town. A 1912 Carnegie Library in a sea of green grass, churches, serenity. And down a cool, shaded street, running and laughing, members of a gym class returning to Hall Township High.

"Steady employment and good chances for a home," read the advertisement of 90 years ago. It has all come true now. Ticketed and tagged they once stood, wearing babushkas, carrying their clothing in cardboard fastened with rope. For their grandchildren and great-grandchildren, the melting pot that is Spring Valley may be as close as anyone can come to realizing the essence of the American dream.

Bath

Drive south of Havana along Rt. 78 and Bath may flash past the windows almost without a thought. A church, a gas station, a little square with huge sycamores, a couple of taverns and then the countryside again, sandy lowlands fringed with cottonwoods and willows. Only 400 people and not much going on, it would seem.

But look again and Bath takes shape as one of those unique little towns where history has left a deep mark. There are long echoes here on a summer's day, memories as easily stirred as the soft white cottonwood seeds that float down like the tentative snow of November.

Lincoln slept here, surveyed the town, in fact, and spoke here. For it was here in 1858 that he delivered his famous "A house divided against itself cannot stand" speech, a score and two years after he had come through with his chain and transit. People saved pieces of wood from the oak grove where he spoke. The last of the so-called Lincoln oaks died and was cut down in the late 1930s and carvers made souvenirs which have become family treasures.

History comes and goes and there are no great monuments to recall Lincoln: a house, a room, a marker. But there is something else here too, a strange fondness that seems to express itself in simple, unaffected verse, full of sentiment and the memory of bygone days. Inside the cover of the 125th anniversary book of the village, an event celebrated in 1961, is a copy of Lincoln's original survey, and a poem that reads, in part,

To those who know our town so well,
Whose pride in it is plain to all,
By old time stories they've loved to tell,
By familiar tales they so fondly recall.
To the hours of research of facts herein,
(We honestly hope they've been a great joy!)
To all who may have kith or kin.
In our fair, friendly village, Bath, Illinois.

One of the legends has it that Bath received its name after Lincoln gazed over the east channel toward Grand Island after a day's hard work at mapping the town and commented, "That'd be a good place to take a bath." It is perhaps not likely, since the time of year—November—was not particularly conducive to river bathing. Slightly more credible is the story of an Englishman who felt some nostalgia while passing by and remarked on the similarities between here and Bath, England, although they must have been then as now wildly imaginary. It is, nevertheless, the generally accepted opinion, and Miss Mae Sisson, late of here, even represented the village at a pageant in Bath, England, in 1909. Thus are legends cemented.

Bath (Illinois) seems to have fostered an almost fanatical devotion from those who have lived here. There is something of the typical mid-American small town, with echoes of Huckleberry Finn in that slow and peaceful river, and summer memories of childhood along those quiet streets, of days that seemed to stretch on forever then, but now seem as short and tenuous as the life of the Mayfly.

For the 50th reunion of the Old Schoolhouse, celebrated in 1955, Harry Ohl of Chicago wrote another poem that reads, in part,

I want to go back to the years that have passed,

Where time made a play with me in its cast,
To a schoolhouse of brick that the present can't see,
And tho' it is gone, it's a fond memory . . .

The old school house stood on the site of what used to be the courthouse before the county seat was moved to Havana in 1851. The building was condemned in 1940 and replaced in 1943 by a concrete WPA style building which does not seem calculated to inspire poets.

One that might, however, is Bath's old red brick mansion known either as "The Big Brick House," "The 1850 House" or "The Tara of Sangamon Valley." It was built sometime in the 1840s or in 1850 by Maj. Benjamin H. Gatton, founder of Bath and a man of considerable wealth and influence. He had so many servants that the high cupola at the top was reportedly built so he could watch over them as they worked in the fields.

There are nine major rooms, high ceilings elaborately decorated at the cornices, and a coffin grand piano in the living room that Lincoln was supposed to have played, although Lincoln's pianistic abilities are somewhat suspect. The house was modernized to some extent by its former owners, even to shag carpeting and a swimming pool out back, but it is in admirable condition otherwise. Present owners are Mr. and Mrs. Wayne Shields, who plan on enjoying its room, its grace, its sense of history.

The riverboats and showboats came here and Bath had the reputation of a tough river town. These days an old barge, a fish house once perhaps, now a floating tavern, rests broken along the shore. There is a Stag beer sign on top, and it looks, almost, as if it settled there and fell to ruin after some enormous all-night brawl. Somebody is supposed to have been killed on the boat once, or drowned, nobody knows for sure. But the showboats came too, happier times, happier memories, the "Cotton Blossom," "Frenches New Sensation," "The Majestic," "The Golden Rod,." And there is a poem about those days, too, by C. D. Hulburt:

Ah a steamboat whistle,
So early in the morn,
Tis show boat day and hip hurray,
And the summer day is warm . . .

All gone now, and lots more, too. But Bath slumbers into its 140th year with considerably more life than might be apparent at that first, fleeting glance. For there is a kind of momentum to the tradition and things go on and on. Every Memorial Day since the Civil War, young people of Bath have marched down to the riverside and placed little boats bearing flowers in the current and sung "Illinois" in memory of the dead of many wars.

The Bath K. J. U. Women's Club (Kum Join Us) sponsors a Lincoln lore tour in June with stops at the places where Lincoln stayed, the feed house, the Oak Street ferry which leads over to Grand Island—owned by Chicago hunters and reportedly for sale for half a million dollars. And there is on July 16 and 17 another Bath homecoming with free fish and such crowds that it is hardly possible to get into town.

Olster Parrott, who was born in the same room where Lincoln was entertained in the Ruggles House, has been in business with his wife, Elsie, for over 45 years here and knows almost everything there is to know about the town. He remembers when they sold hamburgers three for a quarter. He remembers old baseball games in the summertime, the fights that sometimes followed,

Lyle and Nyle Finch, sportsmen and truckers who grew up here, the late Sen. Scott Lucas, the great fishing days in the summertime, the duck hunting in the fall, the old cemetery at the edge of town with the wind in the high pines, and more.

And that strange affection again for so small a town. Cliff Hulburt again, with his poem, "Dear Old Bath":

If you every stop at Bath,
And meet their lovely people
You won't see big edifice,
Topped by sky-high steeple
But the people you will meet
Will chant as one big choir
Their love for you and just true blue
Suffices for the spire.

If I must choose another home
And opine with my voice
I'd shun New York and Paris,
BATH would be my choice.

Henry. Pop. 2600. Best Town by a Dam Site

The sign at the south edge of town still proclaims this to be the best town in Illinois by a dam site, although the dam is hardly more than a relic and is of little consequence these days.

Folks say that a minister tried to get rid of the motto one time. He failed. The signboard remains at one end of town, and, at the other, are the walls of the dam, which look like the remains of some crusader watchtower.

In between is the kind of town that people like to have their kids grow up in—clean, quiet, safe, stable.

It is Monday morning, and, in the cool breeze, clean wash floats from dozens of clothes lines. Children on bicycles cruise along the shaded streets, where old white houses seem to be resting on their wide lawns, looking just as they have for 50, maybe 100 years.

At noon, members of the Rotary Club gather in the banquet room of the Hotel Henry. A bell sounds, and they break into lusty song: "My country tis of thee . . ." From the riverfront comes the hiss of grain spilling into a barge, and, from far off, comes the sound of a train whistle echoing along the river valley.

There is a powerful sense of the past here, and yet there is nothing faded or yellow about it. It is no incredible time machine reeling backwards to the rotogravure era of scratchy woollen bathing suits, people hurriedly changing clothes behind the drawn shades of old square cars before hurrying into the limpid waters of Lake Senachwine.

The beaten-down mud underfoot looks no different there today. I remember that. Cowering, one time, beneath an old cottage along with the daddy longlegs as the hail beat down, and my father watched helplessly as the leatherette roof of the car was shredded.

There are long memories here, a sense of yesterday that seems almost to have been photographed with a Brownie box camera. But there is a liveliness too, a sense of vibrancy, not the feeling of a crumbling river town dozing into another August.

Hardly.

"The unique thing here is the number of young businessmen," says George Ziegler. On this day, he is sitting in a panelled cubicle at the Henry *News-Republican* and chewing on a cigar stub. The phones are ringing, the tape punchers going full tilt. He is in the process of putting out two editions of his four papers so that he can take a week's vacation.

"Anybody in his 40s is practically an old man. That's what really makes this town," he says.

Jim Koehler, partner in the Watercott Department Store, says that it is a Goodrich plant that has helped keep the young people here.

"It wasn't possible before that. There was nothing for them to do. Before Goodrich came in 1958, it was a sleepy little town, lots of retired, although business has always been good. The population was 1,800 then. Now, it's 2,600. That may not seem like much, until you figure it out percentagewise.

Koehler, who is 33 and looks younger, seems to be faintly astonished at his good fortune in living in Henry. He was a traveling salesman once for a furniture company but he left that job. "I had a friend visit here last week from Kansas City, and he's ready to move here right now," Koehler says. "He can't get over the fact that I walk to work. He drives, and it takes him 40 minutes."

The store is 97 years old. It was founded by his great-grandfather, who did, one year, $1 million worth of business.

"And that was when suits were selling for $4," says Koehler. The store does well today but has never managed to equal that figure. On the top of the old building is a huge, high-ceilinged room that was once a theater, later a roller-skating rink. It is now the furniture showroom.

"It's a nice, peaceful town," says Bill Brennan, whose parents used to operate a funeral parlor here. "I've got everything I want right here. You can buy your clothes, get your car and have it fixed here. I lived for a while in Montana. Loved it. But I came back. There's no money out there."

Dr. Walter Bayne arrives for the Rotary meeting and says that he doesn't give a darn for the big city. Likes it where he is. His view carries considerable weight, since he has traveled in more than 100 countries. He always comes back to Henry. He was born in Chicago but has lived here most of his life. He has been "sort of" retired since a year ago June, after practicing dentistry for 54 years.

It is hard to find community detractors among members of the Rotary and the Chamber of Commerce. Other residents, however, think that Henry is dead: they comment on the number of empty stores.

Among the things that Henry does not have are parking meters and bicycle locks. Hundreds of bikes are jammed into the racks outside the municipal swimming pool every afternoon, or left along the sidewalks wherever their riders happen to stop, without ever being locked.

There is not much crime here. Not many bicycle thieves. Where would anybody go with a stolen bike? Some people even leave keys in their cars and don't lock their doors.

"One of the worst things that happened to us was when somebody siphoned some gas out of one of our trucks," says Jim Koehler. The police are there, however, alert and cruising, to make sure that it stays that way.

The only readily discernible problem seems to spring from bicycles and accidents. The editor's son is recovering from a broken leg. In the hotel bar, a young girl is sipping a noncola drink, and the female bartender signs the cast on her arm, caused, she admits, by a bicycle accident.

Farther down the bar, two men talk about the old days of duck hunting. "Filled the rumble seat of that Whippet with ducks in three hours. Hell, you couldn't do that nowadays if you hunted all season."

The big duck clubs still abound. They are private now, and the people come down from Chicago when the skies turn gray and the wind cold. Among the Chicago visitors, they say, is Oscar Mayer, the hot-dog king.

Along the riverfront, cottonwoods flap in the summer breeze with a sound like that of children clapping. Two barefoot girls are wading through the waves lapping against the shore near the ornate old waterworks. Up near the old dam are three boys rooting through beer cans left from boating parties.

"They're for my beer can collection," says Bill Jamison. In the basket of his bike are cans from Coors, Olympia, Kingsbury. His prize is a Schlitz tallboy. His friends, Al and John Karls, are helping. They say that their mother won't let them have a collection of their own. Who can blame her?

The back bar of the Blue Ribbon Inn is covered with stuffed fish, turtles, shells, a frog, mostly from the Illinois River. They are from the old days. They are brown now from years of cigarette smoke.

The old days have a way of lingering appealingly. Some of the flavor has gotten away, however; the interior of the old ice cream store on Edwards Street was moved lock, stock and barrel to Scottsdale, Arizona.

There is a renewed attempt on the part of at least four enterprises to re-capture some of the elegance of the past, to return to the old Victorian style of architecture, instead of succumbing to plastic, glass and neon. They are Watercott's, the Jigger and Jug, the Merdian Drug Store and the post office.

In the old library, there is a bird's eye view of the town in 1878. It shows, among other things, a paper mill, Granit Mill, a foundry, an elevator, a lumber yard, Bower's Mill and the dam in glorious operation.

There is an illustrated advertisement for the "2nd Annual Peoria Henry Colony Homecoming Excursion" on the steamboat Verne Swain on Saturday, Aug. 14, 1915. Round-trip fare from Peoria to Henry was 50 cents for adults, 25 cents for children. There were a band concert at Henry, speakers and a 25-cent supper served by the St. John's Guild. "No gambling or other objec-tionable features aboard our steamers," the ad concluded.

Henry supposedly is named for Gen. James D. Henry, who led the Illi-nois Volunteers to victory over hostile Sac and Fox Indians in 1832. At one time, lots sold for $1 and anybody with $1.25 to spare could pick up a whole acre. Five years later, the same lots cost $300 to $500.

In 1850, the town's population was 401, and, by 1854, it hit 1,306. A historian noted that the location was particularly favorable because of an un-derlay of gravel. Henry's streets would be dry and dusty, while those of the prairie towns were still hub-deep in mud.

The steamboats faded, the dam closed and the railroads ebbed until there was—and is—only one passenger train a day. Today, about 10 passengers board the Rock Island each week at the mini-station, according to Inez Thompson, de-pot master. If there were any more, they would have to wait under the trees.

She says that the railroad is doing $4 million business at Henry, mainly with Goodrich, but also with Grace Chemical and the Riverside Press. The latter is owned by Richard Finfgeld, who prints 20 or more papers and publi-cations.

"A good town," he says. "It's diversified. Good, active business com-munity. It's got the river, schools, scenery. And it's the hub for a consider-able area."

There are still signs in the windows from recent ceremonies honoring Capt. John Philip Cromwell, who was born Sept. 11, 1901, in Henry, and went down with the submarine Sculpin near Truk in November 1943. The crew was captured by the Japanese, but he went down with his ship, saying, "Go ahead, I know too much to go with you." The memorial consists of brass plaques and a torpedo at one edge of the square.

In the window of Dr. Robert Seaman's office are copies of Walt Whitman poems—"I Hear America Singing"and "O Captain, My Captain." Flags fly regularly in dozens of yards throughout town.

To the north are two widely different resort areas. There is Walnut Grove, with its 1920-style cottages that seem to have changed not a bit in half a century. Farther on, to the west, is Lake Thunderbird, with its hundreds of acres of woods that look as they might have when the Indians were still here.

The land is dotted now with chalets and A-frames.

Goodrich and Grace rise from the corn and bean fields along the river, shimmering in the afternoon heat. In the cemetery is a statue of a golden retriever with the inscription, "Freddie, March 29, 1869." The county fair has ended and all that remains are half a dozen cars on the infield, left, it appears, from a demolition derby.

It is afternoon. Monday. Tall trees. Cool and shaded streets. A sense of permanence, as if Henry will be here tomorrow, too. The Rotary meeting is over, and the men have gone back to their offices and stores. Most of the washing has been taken down. The swimming pool is nearly filled with young bodies, none of them clad in scratchy wool. A boy rockets down the slide and knifes into the water. There are almost as many bicycles on the streets as cars.

The jukebox in the hotel tavern comes alive with "Back Home in Indiana" and "Paper Doll." People on the street smile and say hello. A breeze rustles through the high, old trees along Edwards Street and sets the cottonwoods in motion near the river. A houseboat inches into the marina. There will be more beer cans. Coors. Olympia. Kingsbury. It is a good town to be a boy in. A girl, too. And to hear them talk, an adult. Best by a dam site.

Fountain Green, Junkyard Town

Should some geological team elect to dig hereabouts in a few hundred years—or a few thousand, depending on the way things go—it might well conclude that this represents the final resting place of the American dream. For even now much of this once lovely town has become a kind of reliquary, an enormous cemetery filled with wrecked and junked cars.

There is something uncomfortably prophetic about this little town of some 90 souls, for it is a microcosm of urban blight, the ultimate pollution. Here is the old grocery store with its windows gone, its meat case empty, and it is now used to store used transmissions. What was once a Phillips 66 gas station is buried beneath a lapping tide of tires and wheels. Some of the streets are sprinkled with spark plugs, flattened hub caps, bolts and bits of ignition wire. There are whole fields of broken and twisted cars bisected by narrow, rutted lanes like those of some medieval slum.

Kermit Bouseman, who operates the Bouseman Auto Supply, is understandably reluctant to talk much about this. He is not unfriendly, only gun-shy around news people. "I just don't need it," he says, describing how a photographer not long ago used a low-angle and telescopic lens to make it appear as if the yard of the United Presbyterian Church nearby was also filled with old car parts.

Not so. Bouseman's empire has its limits here, and there are islands of rare serenity in this small and extremely old town. One is the church itself, a strikingly plain and simple white building that speaks of a faith deep and rich as the old prairie loam. It is solid and homey, pews curving gently around its small altar, the cool light of morning streaming in benediction through its frosted windows. There is a long dining room table with Queen Anne chairs in a small room off to the side, and a plaque that reads: "Attendance today 69. Offering today $28.80. Attendance last Sunday 56. Offering last Sunday $25.89."

Nearby Dan Shell is working in his yard. The frost has killed his tomatoes and he has stacked the withered vines in a high mound. He is not elated about the town's reputation as a junkyard, but there are compensations. "I'd rather live here and be safe than in some of these towns you can't even walk around in," he says. "If it weren't for all these cars, what would this town be?"

Shell used to work for Bouseman. And so did 30 or 40 other people, mostly at the job of dismantling and stripping the cars. He says the business was started by Bouseman's father back around 1930. And somehow it just grew and grew until there are now something like 17 acres in town covered with cars and 23 out in the country.

"Oh, this used to be a pretty little place until it became a junk town," says Ida Jackson. She is sitting in the yellow autumn sun on the front porch of her grandfather's magnificent Civil War home. And she talks about the town, the past with the sure knowledge of one who has lived here all her life, who has seen a lot, and who has written about much of it for a number of area newspapers.

The brick for the house was made on the grounds, she says, fired in a kiln right here that was run 24 hours a day. The house was started in 1862 and once enough bricks were made, the crew of men laid up its 17-inch thick walls. But then most of them were called away to serve in the Union Army and work didn't resume until the war ended and they came back to Fountain Green. Most of them, anyway. One craftsman spent a whole year here doing all the woodwork, the ornate walnut bannister, the elaborate doorframes, the molding. There are 17 rooms and the mansion is in need of a little paint these days, for it has been weathered and checked by a hundred and more winters.

But such elegance. We sit on the front porch and talk in the sun, and for just a moment the years seem to fall away and out there past the tall grass of the front yard it seems as if the young men might be coming back any time now, feet shuffling in the dust, singing their old songs, souvenirs packed away in their rucksacks and kit bags.

But no, it is 1976 and there is nothing much left of Fountain Green to come back to. Once there was a blacksmith shop, a general store, a grocery store, a post office. The school closed last spring, even though it is the newest one in the La Harpe district. Time goes on and Miss Jackson still writes about the town for the *Hancock Quill*, among others . . . "The McConnell reunion was held in the Fountain Green Park Sunday with over 100 in attendance . . . Melvin Latherow is presently a patient in the Carthage Hospital" . . . and occasional feature stories, including one about her own venerable home.

Now most people in town take the cars as a matter of course, she says. She is grateful that the lot across the street, once owned by Bouseman, has remained blessedly free from junk.

There is only one other business in town, Marj and Ed's coffee shop, a combined grocery store and cafe where men sit a noontimes at dining room type tables. We ask for hamburgers, but Marjorie Meyers says she doesn't fix them. "Don't like the way they smell." Her accent is unmistakably English. A war bride, it turns out, from Portsmouth and here for 30 years. She has been back home just twice in that time. But this is home now, in nearby Joetta, and she likes it.

And there are two other local attractions they talk about. One is alive, Sherm Willock, cowboy artist and self-styled folksinger who is working for some farmer or other on this particular day, and the old Lincoln Cemetery east of town with its graves of Lincoln's distant relatives. We drive part way down a field, then walk along a fence and climb across barbed wire to find the old burial ground. Cows have grazed here and the tablets are broken and lie among the weeds.

There are several Lincolns buried here, James, who died in 1837, Robert whose tablet bears the misspelled inscription "Resquiescat in Pace" and an Abraham Lincoln who died Jan. 22, 1852. His tombstone is broken and his grave overgrown, a striking contrast to that of his relative in Springfield, who sleeps in his elaborate and much-visited cool tomb. This one is quiet and almost unknown, out on the prairie, under the open sky, amid the broken stones.

And the town is somehow like the cemetery, quiet now beneath its incredible accumulation of cars and parts. These seem to have flowed across lots and streets and alleys like lava from some eruptive volcano. The gas pump at the 66 station still reads 32.4 cents for regular. The sign creaks in the wind. There is a 1967 calendar inside. Surprisingly, the dusty telephone still issues a dial tone, an eerie sound, like something from "On the Beach."

And to the west, in those jumbled acres of hulks there are long silences and long echoes. Some of these cars died of sedate old age, refusing to start one cold morning, or breaking an axle or a tie rod and deemed too old to repair. And others went violently, with that awful crumpling of metal, shattered glass, screams, sirens and the excited voices that attend public death. Some have been there so long trees have taken root and grown up through open hoods. There are DeSotos and Studebakers, rusted cars from abroad come these many miles to die, there are fast models which never made that last curve. And there are, in the whispering of the wind, those sounds, those memories:

"A real creampuff, this little baby. Twenty thousand miles of easy driving and not a scratch on her."

"Headon Crash On Rt. 9 Kills 2"

"And just listen to those doors. Solid, huh? And how about that loop pile carpeting all the way through?"

Dead dreams now, gone to earth. Rust to rust. One car still has half a dozen beer bottles on the floor behind the grotesquely twisted hood, beneath its windshield so obviously shattered by a head. Stripped and empty now, the elegantly upholstered seats frayed by wind and rain. In one van, the sunlight pouring through, the broken windows explode into a mosaic, like some exquisite piece of leaded glass. Elsewhere the cars are piled up like geological strata in which epochs of automotive progress might be traced, from long stick shifts on the floor, to column-mounted levers, automatic drive and, again, to gear shift levers on the floor.

But it remains the lifeblood of the town. Slowly, slowly, all these cars are stripped until only the carcasses remain, the generators gone, the water pumps, transmissions, wheels and hubcaps. The great American new car dream ends here and becomes, in the harsh glare of daylight, an epic nightmare.

But other echoes remain. In another old cemetery, along the blacktop to La Harpe, are more old stones and people who lived and died long before the cars came and sleep with their own memories. On one stone is the inscription:

Weep not for me
 my companion dear,
Shed not for me
 the briney tear,
As I am now freed
 from pain,
Your loss is my
 eternal gain.

And there are, in town, those tidy and neat houses with their trimmed yards which stand in proud and stunning contrast to the tide of metal. And the little church with the dried flowers in its window and the hymn book opened on this October morning to no. 351, "March On, O Soul, With Strength!"

Havana: the Memories Linger On . . .

The fishing is only an echo of the great days, the steamboat whistles and cries of the drovers have all died away and the sounds of the slot machines—cherries clicking into the windows and the silvery gush of coins—are only memories now, but Havana still has the flavor of a rugged town out of the Twenties, maybe earlier.

Something of the frontier seems to have stopped here and taken root at the edge of the Illinois River, not the artifice of those South-western restorations where actors stage gunfights outside the Redeye Saloon, but the real item: honest, tough, individual and uncompromisingly nonconformist.

Havana is a town where a man can paint his house purple and leave a rusted car in his back yard if he damn well pleases, where the next man can collect art and travel to Europe and where nearly everybody shares an interest in at least two things—fish and ducks.

Ah, but the fishing is almost gone, if not the ducks. The old men talk about it, and their eyes light up, and the stories come tumbling out. "They once took a carload of fish out of here every day for 30 days straight. That was back about 1915 or so, and there was 20 to 25,000 pounds in each car.

"We had Thompson Lake to fish in then. And Spring Lake. Now they're all levied into farms, and the fish have got no place but the river. The traffic takes care of them there.

"We used to see boats once in a while, the Bald Eagle, Golden Eagle, the Commanche and so on, but now we get up to 15 boats a day, and it tears hell out of the river."

This is Bill Riley talking, 79 years old now, sitting in the back room of Foster's Fish Market, where a few pitiful bucketsful of buffalo and catfish are gasping and twitching.

"I helped make the last haul at Thompson Lake. The dredge boat was waiting for us to get out, and when I got out, he closed the levy. Took 40,000 pounds of fish. We worked two nights and three days to get 'em out of the seine."

People say that this used to be the biggest fresh-water fishing area in the whole world, this area along the river between Liverpool and Havana.

Not now.

"They've made this river into a racetrack for towboats," says Chuck Anderson, who now operates the fish market. "But we don't have any real fishing any more. They've shut off the backwaters. The current's too fast. Fish can't lay eggs there. No, you can't make a living off the river any more."

Just north of Foster's, the workboat "Roy K" nudges a barge up to the Illinois Grain dock, and from high in the white tower comes a golden rush of grain. At one end are the farm trucks from Topeka and Bath, pulling up one by one to unload the riches from Illinois fields, and at the other are the barges, miles of river, the ocean, and tables somewhere waiting for bread.

And, to the north of town are the enormous orderly mounds of coal, mixed and stacked like some Mayan pyramid, waiting to be barged upriver and converted into electricity—lots of it.

There are other things that go out of Havana in huge quantities, among them green beans and turkey eggs. The one comes from irrigated farms that utilize double-cropping, a mechanized picking operation and heavily loaded semi-trailers thundering to the Green Giant canneries in Wisconsin. The other is a product of the Bonnett Turkey Farms, which exports poults throughout the United States and eggs as far away as Germany, France and Italy.

Irrigation here is cheap because this is so-called "hidden river" country. Desert plants and deciduous trees exist side-by-side, and it is said that you can drill 100 feet down and pump 2,000 gallons per minute from an 18-inch well forever. Fields already are lined with those huge, walking pipelines that can create rain at the punch of a button. They have made the sandy, desert-like ground bloom with the wealth of beans and potatoes.

The riches are seldom evident. Those who have them and those who don't coexist in a peaceful and ambient elbow-to-elbow rapport. One of the grandest old houses in town—a gem right out of the great days of Natchez, with an interior like a Parisian salon and a garden from "The Great Gatsby"— sits next to an implement yard with its changing inventory of tractors and combines.

And the old Victorian houses that rise along the rim of the hill alternate their casual elegance with houses that are far more modest, to say the least, and the effect is a quickening and heightening of character. It is a mixture that seems almost Southern in its tolerance and forebearance, and the feeling is quite unlike that of the numbingly plastic order of so many new towns and subdivisions.

Main Street is still brick, wide enough for diagonal parking and lined with two-story brick buildings that go back to another century. There are ornate cornices, narrow staircases and old second floors with dark hallways and overhead fans.

Bud Cullinane, a local landholder, sits in one of them, near his grandfather's roll-top desk. Old Irish, from settlers who came over impoverished from the potato famine, found land, and, ultimately, wealth. On his desk is a copy of Strunk's *The Elements of Style* and Stephen Birmingham's *Real Lace.*

Cullinane lives in the house built by a Maj. Fullerton of Natchez; Lincoln once stayed in it. And Cullinane has a hunting lodge in the country where pianist Arthur Rubinstein was once a guest and was served his favorite wine— Mouton-Rothschild.

Cullinane is equally at home in Paris, which he loves, or in Havana, which he also loves. "An exceptional town," he says, and he waves at people as he passes. He has friends in high places and in low and talks with ease about Baccarat crystal or a sagging farm gate.

An exceptional town.

In the window of the Harvest Time Fellowship International Tabernacle is a sign:

Coming Soon
  Jesus

Nearby, in the window of the Lawford Theater, is another sign: "No shoes, no shirt, no ticket." And, in a clothing-store window, is the announcement, "Non-slip streaking shoes $5.99."

Plum Street is wide and quiet. Old houses, iron fencing, sparrows chirping in the late morning, and women hanging out their washing. In some places in the sidewalks are rusted iron rings.

And in Laurel Hill Cemetery, U.S. Senator Scott Lucas lies at rest beneath a simple marker that reads: "The Honorable Scott W. Lucas, Sr., Feb. 19, 1892-Feb. 22, 1968." There is an American Legion emblem and a faded American flag waving in the wind.

Matanza Beach, south of town, has a peaceful, deserted look in the spring, like some unused set from "Bonnie and Clyde" that lacks only a 1933 Ford V-8 and people who look like Estelle Parsons.

Once it was a slum, similar somewhat now to Quiver Beach, north of Havana. But Matanza has gone through the gambling era to become a colorful settlement that has a quaint and somewhat dated character. Clusters of tiny cabins named "Pac-um-in," "The Cove," "Elaine and Rich," "Sans Souci," and "Sunova Beach."

For a whole era before Adlai Stevenson became governor, Havana was virtually synonymous with gambling. Some people referred to it as Little Reno, and it was known as a resort for Chicago hoods, who virtually subsidized the town. Slot machines whirring. Roulette wheels. Blackjack. Craps.

People do not talk about it much, except to say that it wasn't too bad. Or they remember the days when Camp Ellis, an Army camp, was only a few miles away, over in Fulton County, and there were slot machines in drugstores, and people couldn't even get near a bar for the crowds. Some people even say that it was pretty good then. Others say children stood on boxes so they could reach up to play the machines.

Mayor Clarence Chester leans back in his chair in city hall, a former bank. "The old days are gone. They brought a lot of money to our town. We don't change fast. Just a little at a time. We make some advancement each year."

He has been mayor almost as long as anyone can remember—25 years—and is now in his seventh term.

"Our sales tax is gaining each year. We're above several towns our size, and that's a good indication." He leans forward and shakes hands. "Come back again. Any time."

Along the street, the merchants display their goods, lawn mowers, potting materials, roses, rakes. A Union soldier stands atop his pedestal in the Mason County courthouse yard, and the markers tell of Lincoln's passing.

Near the riverfront park is a small block of cabins, full during the Camp Ellis days, but now almost all empty. The high spring water laps up almost to the grass line. Now and then a car stops and somebody gets out to watch the water go past or to look at the "Roy K" shoving a freshly loaded grain barge away from the docks, a different, newer kind of wealth.

There are remnants of the old. The Towne House is still there, a quiet restaurant where the sound of ships sliding across the table, cards being shuffled, wheels spinning have long vanished. It was opened 25 years ago, and its great days—when the crowds surged in, the croupiers raked in crisp bills and the long black cars pulled up in front—are gone. Money does not flow any more in Havana in a silvery rush of nickles or thrashing fish, but more slowly, more surely. Now it is the color of gold for grain, black for coal, green for beans . . .

Times change, but not the echoes, not the memories. Never the memories. The fishing may be gone, but there will be another season, another fall after the high geese have passed, and the ducks come winging in on frosty mornings. The people from Chicago will come again, not in long black cars this time or in felt hats, but in hunting gear, their guns broken open, shotgun shells in their pockets. The echoes remain. And the memories.

Toulon: They're Still the Good Old Days

Late summer now. Almost autumn. The corn at the edge of town is changing, and there is a different sound in the wind, dry and rustly as old newspapers. New smells, too, sharper, of tanin and sumac. The deep green is fading from the soybean fields, as if they have been bleached by the heat and sun of the long season and are now paling and yellow. Low clouds roll in out of the west, like fog off the sea. The sun disappears. "Think it'll rain?" somebody in town asks. "Naw, it's forgotten how."

Sheriff Kenneth Dison drops into a chair in his panelled office in the old courthouse and sets his summer trooper's hat aside. "Last murder we had here was about 14 years ago, when a guy cut a lady's throat in a shoe store. He got 199 years for that. No, sir, now we've got dope problems and stuff like that, people breaking into farms and houses. Used to have bootleggers and chicken thieves. But we never had a bank robbed." He knocks on the arm of his oak chair.

The courthouse where he sits rises over the town square in simple, classic splendor, neo-Greek and looking somehow southern with its tower, its portico, its white columns and the bench on its porch. Out front is a marker signifying that Abraham Lincoln spoke here on Oct. 6, 1858, when the building was only two years old.

The exterior is little changed, but within are carpeted floors, paneling, flourescent ceilings. The corridor leading to the airy courtroom is lined with pictures of former county judges, most of them frowning majestically. "Some of them look like hanging judges to me," says the sheriff.

His jail, right behind the courthouse, is the only one in the county. The jail is empty now, occupied on weekends only when people serve part-time terms for misdemeanors, vandalism and so on. In one of the cells is a copy of *In the Heat of the Day*, a copy of *Frontier Times* and a wrapped Hershey bar. There are also jigsaw puzzles and a stack of *National Geographics*.

The steel walls are marked with years of graffiti. A prisoner who served time for molesting a girl had written, "Big-mouth female," and another had neatly engraved the message, "Paid in full. My room. Keep out."

"I knew most of them," the sheriff says. "Take this one"—he points to a name—"I've had all his kids here, too. One time, we had five boys in for marijuana. It was Thanksgiving. I opened up the jail doors and invited them into the house to eat with the family. They couldn't believe it. I still hear from those kids. You know, that's pretty good."

The clouds have lifted now, and the sun spills along Main Street. Brightly painted steel benches. Clusters of petunias and geraniums. There are plans for a beautification project to further enhance the character of the buildings and to add even more flowers and green.

High embossed tin cellings. Fans droning through the heat of an early afternoon. A grain truck rumbling through town. A tractor pulling a wagon down Main Street. Two men underneath a wooden manure spreader to work on the chain drive: "There, I think maybe that's got it . . ."

Ben Parker is standing in front of the Historical Society home and chipping away at the grass in the sidewalk with a slender hoe. He has a red FS (Farm Services) hat on and chews the stump of a cigar. "Ought to come out Sunday," he says. "We're having our big doings then . . . ice cream social,

73

cake, a speaker—your Mr. Dancey, as a matter of fact."

Parker is a catalyst for the Historical Society, which has a collection that puts those of most bigger counties to shame. "They'd like to get their hands on this down in Springfield, but, no sir, it belongs right here."

The house, formerly the McKeighan Home, seems to contain virtually everything of conceivable historical value from the whole of Stark County— swords, rifles, musical instruments, furniture, clothing, a homemade harp, a high-wheeled . . . "C'mon, you've got to see the rest," Parker says. He is like a boy in a toy store. He serves up vast amounts of information about this piece or that. "Here, listen to this." He cranks up an Edison phonograph and carefully lays the needle on the cylinder. There is the scratchy sound of a long forgotten band.

Other items: a clock dating from 1752 that still works, a copy of the Ku Klux Klan Bulletin printed in Toulon in 1869, decorations, paintings, mementos, books. "Guys in Springfield sure would like to get their hands on this stuff."

Growing near the porch is the second largest American chestnut in the state. "Planted right after the Civil War," says Parker. Nearby is an American hickory from the same date. There is a building full of old farm equipment— "450 items in all"—and the incredibly preserved office of Dr. Thomas Hall, a pioneer physician who built the office of walnut in 1847. His greatgranddaughter is on the porch with a broom. Mrs. Mary Hall Grieve. "He was a proud old Englishman," she says, "and I'm proud to be his granddaughter."

The office remains virtually complete. Hundreds of jars for medicines, boxes for herbs and leaves often gathered in the nearby countryside, the doctor's saddlebags, records. "That's the chair where Lincoln had his tooth pulled," says Mrs. Grieve. It is said that he had a toothache while in town for his speech and had it taken care of, then and there, by Dr. Hall.

There are, on a shelf, the remains of an amputated arm and a leg, pieces of bone. Nobody knows for sure how the building managed to survive through years of apparent neglect, when it stood empty and surrounded by weeds, but it has. Sound as a dollar. Parker reverently unfolds the pages of a huge record book of Civil War veterans treated by the doctor. "Those state boys sure would like to get their hands on this."

High old pines in the cemetery on the east edge of town, a small forest of them, really, clean and savory and cool. They must have been there for years, 100 or more, and, in the wind, they make a sound that is all whispers and sighs, muted and serene as some lingering pedal point. An uncrowded little cemetery where the old stone tablets and the markers over the Civil War veterans in Dr. Hall's book stand side by side with new granite and freshly engraved dates. There is room for everybody there . . .

Life goes on. The radio in Slugs Zelin's tavern blasts out popular music, and all the men at the bar have on farm hats, IH (International Harvester), FS or Pfister. A sign on the wall advertises imported beers—Konigsbacher from Germany, Ringnes from Oslo, Sacres from Lisbon and Ceres Lager Stout from Denmark. A man comes in with a woman in a long green skirt slit up past the knee.

Carl Lehman is unloading 50-pound sacks of calf feed at his store with its high tin ceiling. 1907. He stops for a moment and mops the sweat off his forehead. "No manufacturing here nowadays. Kraft's plant is used mainly for storing and aging. Mostly farming now. But we don't have any empty buildings in town."

They once manufactured buggies and wagons in the building. Now it is hardware, farm supplies, feeds. There is another feed outfit in town. Competition? "Not really. If their equipment breaks down, they can borrow ours. And we've borrowed some of theirs. That's the way it works here." There is a fan humming in his glass-lined office. Two massive roll-top desks. "Lots of people have wanted to buy these desks. No sale."

There is a sign in Ed Rice's barber shop. "Vote for Somebody, but Get a Haircut." He barbers part-time only in his little shop, where he also sells fishing gear and shotgun shells. "They tell me 50 per cent of the barbers in Illinois are going out of business." He is cutting Bill Franklin's hair, which is young and long. Franklin has not had a haircut for five, six weeks.

Down the street, in Jimal's, a restaurant and cocktail lounge, there are furnishings that came from the Rendezvous Room of the Hotel Pere Marquette. There is also the ornate steel grill from the bar that used to be just off the Main Street lobby of the Pere. Jimal's is crowded at noon, and with good reason: the food is good and reasonably priced, and the place is comfortable.

Outside is Mary Ryan, probation officer and county health nurse, shaking her head sadly over the case of a 15-year-old girl and a man from Kewanee. She cannot do as much as she would like. Not enough time. Not enough help. And the problems go on. Statutory rape. Venereal diseases. Countless trips to the Zeller Zone Center in Peoria.

Seven thousand, four hundred people in the county, more or less. Two hundred eighty-nine miles for Sheriff Dison to cover with his deputy. 1920-era roads that wind along the section lines like buggy trails and link the small towns—Wyoming, Bradford, LaFayette, West Jersey.

A county named by Col. Henderson for Gen. John Stark, supposedly the man who said at Bunker Hill, "Hold your fire, boys, 'til you see the whites of their eyes." And Toulon, the county seat, named by Col. Henderson after Toulon, Tennessee, and not Toulon, France. A rich land with wooden rills, the Spoon River winding right through the middle. And the wind . . .

The radio crackles in Sheriff Dison's office. The familiar police talk: "Ten-four, ten-twenty . . ." The manure spreader is fixed and gone, and there is the sound of a heavy hammer against angle iron, loud and ringing. Two men stand in the street talking. One has several ears of sweet corn clutched in his arms. The time and temperature sign on the bank blinks off another hour. The clouds are coming in, low and fast again. There could be some rain. Too late, though, to do any good this year around here. Late summer now. Almost autumn again.

Canton—the 30s Stay

Driving into Canton late on a summer evening brings the feel of going backwards in time into the 30s, when kids played kick-the-can on quiet streets or roller-skated in the lingering dusks, when the soft summer nights folded themselves around little towns leaving long echoes of familiar sounds. Car tires whining on brick streets. Bugs swarming around street lights. Distant voices crying, "You're it" or "olly olly ox in free." Porch swings creaking. The slam of a car door. Mothers calling their children across darkened yards. Radios all tuned to Fibber McGee and Molly or the Joe Louis fight. The whir of electric fans, the far-off wail of a train rushing through the night to some far-off place.

It is still there somehow in the night streets at Canton. At the south end of the square, young people lounge on the hoods of their cars or on motorcycles. One will occasionally race off, shredding the silence of the night, but it returns, flowing back from all sides until there are only the crickets, soft murmurs, a screen door slamming. A lonely attendant sweeps the driveway of a service station. At the International Harvester plant, a guard pours a cup of coffee from a thermos and leans back in his swivel chair. The steam rises from the cup and high above is another tower of steam rising from a stack atop the building.

It is all still there, startlingly familiar, a pace and an atmosphere that seem hardly to have changed since I was a boy and my family used to drive to Canton in a green Oakland with wire wheels for Sunday Picnics in Big Creek Park. There are the same roads, the same hot summer smell, the same look, and a feel so powerfully unchanged that it can almost be touched and tasted.

On summer afternoons, the changes that have come are more obvious, most notably the cars, the clothes and the manners. But something indefinably nostalgic remains. The red-tipped water tower still rises just beyond the square, looking like an old-fashioned skyrocket about to be launched. And below are the old buildings, many of a style and age to raise images of fiery July 4 speeches, parading bands and boys in knickers.

Spoon River College is located in an antique gray building once a cigar factory, Two doors away, past a Schlitz sign above a tavern entry, is the Salvation Army, where women sort over old clothing and peer out through the dusty windows. Up above are apartments, with women sitting behind screen doors with the crying babies and the interminable soap operas. It is no longer "Just Plain Bill" or "Stella Dallas" but "The Secret Storm" and "As the World Turns" with real people on the screen, and in color, too. But such changes are less than meet the eye.

In the Fulton County Democratic Headquarters, two old men bend over a pool table. The Sports Center has T-shirts in the window that read, "Canton High School Deutsche Klub—Nation's Largest." In the Hotel Canton, an overhead fan turns sluggishly. The man at the desk says there are 31 rooms in all. The next few months will be bad, he says. Summer is the slowest time. Most of the residents are permanent.

A cab dispatcher radio blares out a sudden summons. The hotel has tin ceilings, television in the lounge and a coffee shop that has been long abandoned and locked.

The stairs are lighted by 15-watt bulbs. Its long carpeted halls creak with the echoes of over 60 years of footsteps. Old hotels have long memories and whisper things. Nothing is forgotten.

Along the square is one of the last of the old-time grocery stores, Tony's Fruit Store. It is run by 73-year-old Tony Pusatere. The store has been there since 1901 and he has run it since 1930. Inside is a dark and savory clutter, with high shelves stacked with a bewildering array of food. "There used to be forty, fifty stores like this in town," Pusatere says. "Now I'm the only one left. The rest is big markets. People will be sorry one day."

A man passes by and kids him about being the sex symbol of the square and Tony laughs. A boy comes in for candy, staring and pointing through the glass counter. "I'll take one of those and one of those . . . " It seems strange that he is not wearing knickers.

The Canton City Building is an airy old structure filled with light and magnificent oak. Despite its aluminum framed front doors, it has a durable, changeless look, like some solid brass paper weight. Across the street is the William Parlin home. Parlin founded the P. & O. Plow Works, now International Harvester. Parlin bought the house in 1864 from Judge William Kellog, a personal friend of Abraham Lincoln. It is now the Murphy Memorial Home.

At the Association of Commerce, manager Terry Crank says, "International is our bread and butter." It employs roughly 2,000 people. The mines give work to another 600. There is little else in the way of industry aside from coal and farm machinery.

In the Canton News Stand across the street, a lady carries out a copy of *Personal Astrology*. Among the new arrivals in the paperback section are *Deep Throat* and *Inside Linda Lovelace*. Men sit in chairs on the sidewalk outside the Churchill Hotel. And in his drugstore just off the square is Edward Lewis Jr., who probably knows as much about Canton as any man dead or alive. His 1967 book *Reflections of Canton, in a Pharmacist's Show Globe* is something of a definitive history of the town. Besides he has the kind of memory that begs to be picked.

"It's one of the two cities in this area named after the celestial cities of China. Canton was at one time the largest center in the Midwest in the cigar business. Any time you see a three-story building you can just about be sure it was a cigar factory at one time. A lot of them were just one or two man operations. They made twenty million cigars a year here at the peak. Then it was all gone. Once there were eighteen to twenty factories and even a special factory where they manufactured cigar boxes. A couple of them remained into the forties, but the machine-made cigars put an end to it all."

Lewis's drug store has a turn of the century look. It was built around 1885 and the fixtures come from 1913. There are white and black checkerboard floors, heavy wood and glass cases rubbed to a shine by the years, and even an old cigar lighter, built in and made for the gaslight era, but inoperable now.

One of the garages downtown has a Studebaker sign hanging over its door and there is a Lark 4-door wagon in the street. Many business places have signs in the windows that say, "Yes, we're open" or "Sorry, we're closed." There are intriguing empty buildings, one a former auto agency with old pieces of cars and oak office furniture, all covered with deep layers of dust.

And off to the west of town is a lonely, windswept area that is reminiscent of the Badlands or the moon's surface. Across the desolation is the distant roar of huge shovels and the area is surrounded by signs that say "No

Fishing! No Hunting! No Swimming! No Trespassing! Consolidated Coal Co." In one stretch is a rusted and abandoned shovel, looking like the remains of some extinct creature, a mechanized dinosaur. And beyond is an empty north-south road, looking so much out of the past that it seems to cry out the peaceful blipping of a Model A or a long green Oakland with wire wheels and two spare tires in its front fenders.

It is when night falls that the feeling of having retreated in time becomes strongest. Dusk lingers and then fades. There are crickets, then fireflies. The backyards are empty and no one plays Kick the Can any more. A boy goes past on a bicycle, a 10-speed model that clicks as he coasts. From a television set comes an eerie glow and the sound of laughter. It is not Edgar Bergan and Charley McCarthy, or Al Jolson and Eddie Cantor, but something newer. Car tires whine across the brick and the lights wash across curtained windows. A motorcycle tears into the night and then it is silent again. It is a deep and peaceful silence that has worn so well and lasted so long that it is hard to realize that it is 1973 and not 1937 all over again. But it is. It is.

Oquawka

At the end of main street here, which happens to be called Third, is a standard octagonal red stop sign where the street, the town and the state of Illinois all come to an abrupt end. Just beyond is the Mississippi River, tumbling and icy these days as the surface of some enormous frozen Daquiri. There is no record of anyone being arrested for running this stop sign, although it might not be unlikely on one of those grand summer weekends when the boaters are here in force, when the fishermen are embroidering their stories over beer, when the young people are cruising up and down and when the town's seven taverns are running hell bent for leather.

Seven taverns in a town said to contain 1,401 souls calls forth the simple, arithmetically bald truth that there is one tavern for every 200.14 inhabitants, which may or may not set some kind of record. Fans of other statistical and historical jetsam might like to know that Oquawka is supposed to be the Indian name for Yellow Bank, that Lincoln slept here one time, that the state's second oldest courthouse is here, that the county contains 381 square miles and that the town has its own elephant burial site.

A story goes with that, of course, and almost anybody in sight will tell it without asking. Seems the Clark and Walters Circus was stopped here back in the summer of 1972. Hot, muggy day with a storm coming. Circus had an elephant named Norma Jean. Afternoon. Norma Jean was tethered to the lone tree in the field where the swimming pool is located now. Well, sir, lightning struck that very tree, travelled along the chain affixed to Norma Jean's leg and killed the beast right on the spot. Knocked her keeper 30 feet, too, although he survived. The tragedy was lamentable enough for a small circus. More pressing was the problem of what to do with the late elephant. Well there was, thank heaven, a backhoe working nearby and a large grave was dug for the unfortunate Norma Jean, who was suitably interred. The story was carried nationwide by the Associated Press and Paul Harvey and people who had never before heard of Oquawka did. And there is to this day a marker at the spot:

> *Norma Jean*
> *Elephant*
> *1942*
> *Died July 17, 1972*

Wade Meloan, who has the only drug store in Henderson County, displays on his wall a carefully inscribed award he received for mowing the grave of Norma Jean. There are clippings of the elephant story, other mementos about Oquawka and pictures, one an autographed photo of Cesar Romero, with whom Meloan served during World War II at Alameda. Another of his shipmates there was actor Gig Young.

Meloan says he seldom dispenses drugs anymore. He is 66 and says the business is dying. People hereabouts go over to Monmouth or down to Burlington when they need a prescription filled. Meloan is philosophical about such things. Only Coke and other soft drinks pass along that counter now. No more sodas, sundaes or thick chocolate shakes. On the wall back of the counter is a copy of Murphy's Law:

> *Nothing is as easy as it looks.*
> *Everything takes longer than you expect;*

79

And if anything can go wrong it will;
At the worst possible moment.

But Oquawka is booming, its residents insist, a claim that may be belied
somewhat by the somnolence of winter, although hardly by the prices of real
estate. A 50 by 100 riverfront lot, if available, can go for $10,000 or more.
And with any kind of rude hut or cabin, it is simply out of sight.

Many of the cabins are both rude and crude, reminiscent in places of the
habitats of Goofy Ridge, in other places of the cottages of Quiver Beach or
Matanzas Beach near Havana, or in the best parts, the kind of discreet and
pleasant residential sections not unlike those of scores of old towns strung out
along the river's banks. It is a strange mixture of the old and the new, rock
hard and permanent on one hand and on the other as temporary and shifting
as the sands on which the trailers and vacation cabins rest.

This is a tough old river town with memories of the days when the water
was so shallow only the sternwheelers could navigate here, of shifting sands
bars, of leadsmen calling out "mark twain" and deckhands and drovers drinking and fighting.

Trouble still rears its ugly head and there is talk of a recent knifing in
one of the town's places. It is rare enough to excite comment. Bernice Ten-
nant says her place, Bernice's, is peaceful. Any trouble and she calls the sheriff, two blocks away. Wall to wall with people on New Year's Eve, she says.
Didn't all leave until 7:20 in the morning. "Not one cuss word. Not one
fight," she says proudly. The house rules are printed on the mirror behind
the back bar:

The bartender is always right.
When the bartender is wrong,
See rule 1.

Near the door, a tall, lean man arises from a stool, waves farewell to Bernice, and leaves. He is one of the regulars, seven days a week. Sometimes he
comes before opening and waits, and he has had on this day 15 shots of
Seagram's in three hours. He gets a special price.

Next door is the senior citizens center where 40 to 50 people gather each
noon for a good meal. They pay whatever they want, or can, usually 75 cents,
and the menu on this day includes liver and onions, mashed potatoes, green
beans, slaw and apple sauce. Afterwards there are games of cards, crafts, time
to talk.

Fairly quiet these days at Delabar State Park just north of town along
the river. Ranger Doss Hinshaw says the place is really jammed in summertime. "People come from as far as Chicago. It's all river-oriented recreation."
Fishing. Duck hunting. Boating. People swim off the sandy islands. There
is space for 58 trailers at the park, but it often holds many more beneath its
cool, second growth stand of oak. Only squirrels moving there now.

The park has a launching area of its own. There is also a city boat dock
and a marina. Covered bridge south of town, too, and the big old house
where Lincoln is supposed to have slept. The opera house over the hardware
store has long been empty and quiet. And once there was a button factory
with something like 80 employees. Also a dance hall and people remember
crowds of 5,000. A Japanese company has taken over the Wayne Bros. elevator and it is being expanded. Otherwise there is no industry any more. A

resort town with its picturesque street that runs into the river, the covered bridge, the churches, the old cemetery.

"Quiet here now," says Gene Schertz, a former Peorian who runs Ruth's place. "A weekend town only in the winter. But wait until summer."

Then, they say, the streets are alive with people. They come into the stores and taverns in their swim suits. The harbor is awash and all the spaces at Delabar are taken. There are mayflies that come on some strange night and then disappear, parties on the sand beaches, the smell of charcoal fires and steak drippings. The hoot of towboats in the distance and that long white light stabbing out of the darkness.

Not now. All ice and cold and a sense of desolation. Life goes on, slowly. The senior citizens have cleared away their plates and the cards come out. There is another card game at the Blue Goose, first tavern off the water's edge, where the cold seeps under the door. The wind rattles through the brown oak leaves at Delabar. Afternoon lovers are parked near the covered bridge. And the harbor is frozen solid, like a bowl of ice cubes. The little shops advertising

African Worms
        and
Smoked Fish

are closed and it seems as if the town at this time of year has just about heeded that sign at the water's edge.

Stop

A Touch of New England in Midwestern Monmouth

It would be possible here on some fine September day to be touched with a sense of disorientation in which one might easily mistake this west Central Illinois community for a very old New England town. It is not only the name of the place, its massive trees, the houses on some of the grander streets far back on their green, green lawns, or the college, which looks like an eastern prep school, but a feeling of propriety and tradition, of deep roots and long memories.

There is the modern colonial here, to be sure, predictably brick and white-trimmed with accents of Williamsburg blue, but there is the real Victorian article, too. Fine old buildings with their high-arched windows, sculpted cornices and elaborate bric-a-brac, many of them recently redecorated.

There is the red stone courthouse from 1894 with its broad staircases and its fortress tower and the soldier out front on his pedestal, standing above the veterans' names from Warren County who fought at Fort Donaldson, Vicksburg, Lookout Mountain, Nashville and Mobile. Something neatly trimmed about the place, tidy almost as the entries in the old brass hinged books of chattels and mortgages from long ago . . . "Know ye by these presents . . ."

Downtown is hardly dying, despite the fire two years ago that wiped out a whole block. But it is changing. There is said to be a city plan to make Main Street into a shopping mall with no cars, but the merchants are against it. Right now, traffic pours through in an almost endless stream, looping around the curious traffic circle in a way that makes walking hazardous, to say the least. It will change, they say, once the bypass to the west is opened. And most people agree that downtown needs wider sidewalks.

But nothing drastic. Jeweler Milton Stout says that it is the personal touch in towns like this that keeps customers coming back. "I know people who came back from Galesburg and complained that they can't get waited on in the malls. But we're different. And we're a farming town. That's the big thing here."

The other changes are almost predictable, same as almost everywhere. When Russ Strong went into the barber business in 1950 there were 23 other barbers at work in Monmouth. Now there are only six working full time. Strong moved into a tiny antique building two years ago, after the fire, and plans to move again soon. The building, he says, is way over a hundred years old. It was a harness shop once, later a shoe shop. It is like a relic, shrunken with age, looking oddly out of place among the normal-sized buildings surrounding it. Strong charges $4 for long hair, $3 for regular cuts. "If they don't wash it, or I can't comb it, I charge four."

Monmouth College wears its 1853 founding date like a proud banner. That was long before the Civil War after all, before Lincoln and Douglas even began debating, in fact, and there is a sense on all these green and lovely campus acres with their massive old trees of permanence, of stability. A little rust seeping into the trees now and on this particular day the fall term has not yet started. A few joggers beneath the trees. And there is the school chaplain, Rev. Paul McClanahan, here since 1964, of old Scotch-Irish stock, eyes gleaming beneath his soft, snow white hair. His greatgrandfather was one of the charter signers of the college. He is looking forward to the term. He is a bicyclist. He looks, in fact, something like Robert Donat as Mr. Chips.

Back downstairs Victor Moffet, now in his 80s, still runs the *Review Atlas*, a daily 10-cent paper with a run of about 6,000 issues. It is an old fashioned operation, with hot type and the quaint clicking of the typesetting machines.

Moffet is dressed like a printer, wedging sticks of type into a form as if deadline is minutes away. The paper rolls off an 1894 Straightline press, which may or may not be an antique. But somebody at the paper once saw its duplicate in a historic newspaper exhibit. Jud Jones is still sports editor at 74. He retired 21 years ago as a high school coach in southern Illinois. He came home to Monmouth and Moffet talked him into the job even though he was not a writer. "Hell, you can learn, can't you?" Jones was told. And he has. The pressroom at one time was the site of the longest bar in the world.

And there are the big houses, along Euclid and 8th, the cemetery on one side, the college on the other. One of the more curious has a long cave beneath it that has been turned into "Hobbitt Heaven" by its owner, Nan Gerding, and another, where the president of the college lives, is all belle epoque grandeur, so splendid and gracious that it seems there should be tours, for a charge.

The sun this late summer day still has that butter yellow look and feel. Not long now before the gold comes, brushing the big old trees and sifting onto these vast green lawns like seasonal coins. A town for all seasons, yes, with its golf courses and beef festival, nearby Lake Warren and the Mississippi River and Delabar State Park. But maybe best in autumn when the cool mornings come and the colors in the treetops flame against the clean skies and distant fields. The time when that strange sense of de ja vu comes so strongly, so urgently, of having seen all this before, perhaps even somewhere else.

But this is not somewhere else. This is west Central Illinois. This is Monmouth. This is the good life after all and it is not some other time, some other place.

People keep coming back to these small towns along this vital river, amid these fertile green prairies. More than ever now, they say. Part of a national trend. People beginning to get out of the big cities with their smog, traffic, crime and chaos. Back to towns where people know other people, where they are individuals with names rather than numbers, where they can walk the quiet, shaded streets and feel a part of something.

"These are no longer rural communities," says Dale Parsons, who runs his own men's store and is president of the Lacon Businessmen's Association. "They are urban. People can do whatever they want, go where they want. This is a mobile society."

But not too mobile. Not the restless surge of the city strips, all plastic and franchise. People walk these streets and nod to one another. "How's it goin'?" they say, or "Think it'll rain?" There is a softer pace to life, an easier flow. On rainy summer days the town fills up with pickup trucks. Farmers swarm around the counters of the huge Jolliff Implement Co., located now in what used to be the old woolen mill. It is John Deere all the way, from massive tractors with ear-rattling power on down to lawn mowers and bicycles. Outside are fields of used "Johnny Poppers" whose distinctive eruptions are still heard from many a corn and bean field. And in the dusty back rooms is an incredible collection of old cars, trucks, tractors, wagons, farm gear. An antique Buick with a square cavernous interior which makes one reflect that leg-room and passenger comfort began to decline with stream-lining. A Rumely Oilpull Tractor. A Model T pickup truck with a wooden bed. A 1936 Ford. Old wagons and buggies and cultivators and rakes beyond number. Owner Bob Jolliff grins. "I buy old tractors. Everybody's got a bad habit, I guess."

Not far off, a truck from Varna pulls into the Illinois Grain Co. elevator, one of two in town, and looses a golden waterfall of corn. Seven to 10 million bushels of grain go through this one elevator alone, all siphoned in from a 40-mile radius, loaded into barges that hold between 45,000 and 60,000 bushels, and sent south. To New Orleans where huge vacuum hoses suck the grain from barge into the holds of ocean going vessels. And outward bound, to the world.

This was once known as Strawn's landing in 1829, after John Strawn, first settler in the area. In 1831 it was renamed Columbia, presumably after "Columbia the Gem of the Ocean" which was so movingly sung by the circuit riding ministers that it became greatly admired. But there was another Columbia in Illinois and Lacon finally became the name that stuck. It is based on a volume of philosophy by an obscure and forgotten Englishman which bore some relationship to Laconia, one of the regions of ancient Greece, and which gave us the word laconic, for curt or Spartan.

Once there was a rare pontoon bridge here, a perilous and creaky affair that was made more stable by a design of Capt. David Swain. It was said in its later years to be one of two in the world, the other being somewhere on the Nile. And the town was famous for almost 100 years for its woolen mill, a rarity outside of New England or the South.

Lots of the fine old houses remain, some with their ornate Gothic bric-a-brac and high rectangular windows. But some of them were destroyed in the tornado that roared through town in March of 1942. Rasho Krowlek, known widely as Poncho, remembers it being two blocks wide, going catty-corner right through town starting at the cemetery. Five dead and lots of houses wrecked. One can almost follow its path to this day by the age of the houses along certain streets.

Everybody worked at the woolen mill for a while in those days, Krowlek says, "at least until they got a better job." He says he made 50 cents an hour there in 1942, then went to work for a carpenter for 75 cents an hour, and later hired on at the shipyard in Seneca where they were making LSTs, getting $1.20 an hour as a painter. And driving 65 miles one way. And coming back to Lacon the other 65 miles.

Lots of others came back, too, and will remain. The Barnses and Lagranges beneath that impressive obolisk in the big cemetery at the south of town, back from Redlands and Hollywood, Calif., back from Columbus, Neb. Back to Lacon along this vital river. Titus Lovelace is back home, too. Killed on the Camden and Amboy railroad near Burlington, N.J., on Aug. 29, 1835 at 40 years, three months and 14 days—in a time when even a man's days on earth were considered worth numbering. A thousand and more stories here, one beneath every stone. Now they are all edited down to the barest journalistic terms. Who? Where? When? One reads simply. "Arcene Pichereau. A Native of France. 1822-1913." and on another antique tablet sunk far into the ground by the weight of years is a willow tree and a cross and the legend "Pray for the Soul of Andrew J. Grady, who Died Aug. 10, 1853. Also Andrew J. Jr . . ." and the rest is already gone beneath the green summer grass.

No obvious signs saying so, but Lincoln was a frequent visitor here. On one October evening in 1854 he dropped in on the Wightman family as they were eating dinner. Mrs. Wightman hurried off for another plate, but Lincoln said not to bother, that he'd just eat from the bread plate, and he did. Afterwards, Lincoln took three-year old Laura Wightman on his lap and rocked away on a rocking chair, which proceeded to break, dumping the man and the baby girl onto the floor. The rocker was mended and used for many years on the porch of the family home. So the story goes.

The courthouse dates from these same years. It was completed in November 1853, a simple and stately building that has suffered from modernization over the years. There are dropped ceilings, flourescent lights and droning air conditioners. But a few things remain, the ornate iron railings, the high-backed wooden jury chairs, like those from some farm kitchen still alive with the rich odors of chicken gravy and buttered corn and hot bread in the oven.

Lots of other old things gone, too. Immaculate Conception is one of the early churches of the diocese, but it has a vaguely modern interior to go with its age and its grand windows. The old convent of the Sisters of St. Francis has given way to a low and rambling building which is a far cry from your traditional ecclesiastical style, but there remains the feeling that things have not changed here at all that much. The steamboats are long gone from the river and now the towboats churn downriver with their enormous cargoes of grain or coal. The pontoon bridge has disappeared and the standard Illinois River model pours traffic down into town smoothly and efficiently. On the third floor of Cookie's Village Tap nearby old shreds of lace curtains hang silently in empty windows, for this was once a hotel, and now the action is downstairs in the busy bar and dining room where someone may yet be found to talk about the tornado. And farther out, to the east, like one of the last great chateaux of the aristocracy, is the Ira Norris Thompson home, occupied only occasionally now by the great-great-grandson of the Strawn who founded Lacon, but still full of rich smells and glorious memories. The house was built in 1900 and the Thompsons live these days quietly in Winnetka most of the time, but Thompson talks about the house with affection, for his heritage remains here, as does that of many another.

Yes, it is a mobile society and these people are urban, with a difference. For there is a softer pace here, an easier flow, smooth and steady as the river in August. And that small town friendliness. When people say, "Think it'll rain?" or "How's it goin'?" they still smile.

Beardstown

"You get on that river and you just love it . . ."

Mention Beardstown and the mind will sketch a series of quick and lasting impressions: a sleepy river town that still has the melodious notes of the packet boat whistles ringing in its ears; the river forever rolling past, bank-full and treacherous in the spring, more lazy come July; memories of stage coaches clattering off to the east, to Springfield, and a tall circuit-riding lawyer, boots thick with prairie dust, riding into town to defend Duff Armstrong; a boy sitting along the levee watching the water and waiting for a catfish to strike the hook at the other end of his bamboo pole.

Somehow the images still fit, and Beardstown wears them willingly. But if anyone looks beyond the men sunning themselves on the steel chairs outside the Hotel Park or the grass sprouting through the cracks of brick streets, he will discover a quiet boom and a healthy pride that are making life in the small, old-time river town uncommonly rich.

Around the perimeter, away from the old square a block off the riverfront, is a bruising activity in which wood carriers that look like busy elephants stack hardwood logs with steel claws, in which thousands of hogs stream through the expanding Oscar Mayer plant, and gleaming tanks pour from Trinity Industries, like so many bright, steel eggs.

As a Wednesday committee meeting at the Chamber of Commerce broke up, an uncommon number of young men emerged from the board room. Among them was President Joe DeSollar, who at the age of 24 is assistant cashier and trust officer at the First National Bank.

"I never thought I'd come back to Beardstown after college," he said, "But after job interviews in big cities, I couldn't see working in some big office building and fighting traffic. The old home town started to look pretty good."

Merle Griffith, who publishes the local *Illinoisan-Star*, said it seemed to him people were starting to come back home. "Younger people are taking part in the community life here. It's a hopeful trend. In our Chamber of Commerce alone, eight out of nine directors are somewhat around thirty."

The roots run back far. The signs at the edge of town indicate 6,100 people live in Beardstown, which was laid out in 1827 by Thomas Beard. The town's old Lincoln courtroom is the only one still in regular use, and its fame rests on the fact that Lincoln came for the sake of a mother's distress to defend her son, Duff Armstrong.

Armstrong was charged with having killed a man at a camp meeting in Virgin's Grove. Lincoln won the young man's freedom after a witness swore he had seen Armstrong deliver the fatal blow by the light of the moon. Lincoln sent out for an almanac and proved that the moon had not risen at the time the crime was committed and it became known as the Almanac Trial.

Opposite the upstairs courtroom is a quiet museum filled with models of old riverboats, arrowhead collections, racks of Civil War rifles and other artifacts. At the old cemetery south of town the soldiers from 1865 lie in neat rows in an area surrounded by iron arches. There is a statue of an infantryman leaning on his rifle, a rusty flagpole and a sundial that works.

Across the lane is the gravestone of Ezra J. Ebaugh, who died Nov. 10,

1884 at the age of 66. It is carved in the form of a chair and beside it is a rusted buggy seat. The inscription reads, "Thou Shalt Be Missed Because Thy Seat Will Be Empty."

In the 100-year old Arrow Restaurant along the riverfront, where 25 tons of catfish are served a year, Abe Lynn tends bar and has the time to talk. "Somebody figured at one time we had a hundred and twenty-five people who lived here and made their living on the riverboats. Lots of them were captains."

He rushes off and pulls on the Michelob tap and carries the beer down the bar. "No flood problems here. They put up that seawall in the twenties and raised it seven feet after the big flood of 1943. Even then, the water didn't come in. They piled sandbags and boards up on top."

The building has hand-hewn 10 by 12 oak beams, some measuring over 40 feet long, but its age is camouflaged by a modern front, neon signs and a beer sign, and its inside is chrome and naugahyde.

Nearby, at the Park Hotel, men sit in the sun waiting for something to happen. Signs at the corners of the square indicate that pedestrians have the right of way and cars stop to let people pass. Near the big Critic Feeds plant, sparrows peck at spots where piles of corn have been spilled. A man pushes a wheel barrow down the street. And if one waits long enough, Frank Jamison Jr., known as "Happy," may come along on his one-speed Hawthorne bicycle, an event somewhat out of the ordinary only because he will be 79 on Sept. 3.

Wearing Big Mac overalls and a lumberjack shirt, he settles into an overstuffed chair in his home at 818 Second St. opens a voluminous scrapbook and begins talking about the old days on the river. One can almost hear the faint hiss of steampower as he goes on, feel the decks trembling, and see the long corrugated wake rolling out astern.

"Now wait a minute," he says. "First I've got to tell you about my first boy and then we'll get to that." Four of his own boys and a brother were captains on a river boat, plus two grandsons. Another grandson is an engineer and three of his brothers were pilots. He talks about old boats and old days and the sharp memory keeps dredging up names and places—the barge Pearl, Treadway Lake, Mascoutin Bay, the Meridosia Bridge, Little Beardstown, Throckmorton's Button Factory, the David Swain, the Clendenin Slough, Little Field Spreads, and on and on.

"Had lots of pecan trees along the river in the old days, before they cut that Chicago Canal, hundreds of 'em. Water killed all that stuff off. I've fished and hunted all my life. Had a hundred ducks laying on that kitchen floor one time. You get on that river and you just love it."

On the walls are pictures of dogs, Renoir prints, family pictures, a picture of Christ. "Now wait a minute, first I got to tell you about . . ." He puts on steel rim spectacles, runs his hand through his snow-white hair and leafs farther into his scrapbook. He remembers the big days of clam-digging and button-making, when just about everybody in town was busy sewing buttons on little cards. He said he's never owned a car. Just bicycles. He worked for 12 years for the railroad and 35 for the Central Illinois Public Service Co. And when he looks up from his scrapbook, his eyes seem to be gazing far out across the water, which is kicking up a swell with a few whitecaps here and there. "You get on that river and you just love it."

Outside the cottonwood seeds blow in the wind like a soft flurry of snow. The men outside the Park Hotel are gone. A towboat looses a deep, piercing blast on its whistle and there is the heavy sound of diesel power. The town looks almost asleep, but isn't.

They say nearly every kid in town is a Little Leaguer. Hogs squeal in the pens over at Oscar Mayer and a mower stutters to life in the old cemetery, cutting out the sound of the wind high in the trees. At the Chamber of Commerce, they pass out the kind of statistical information that Chamber of Commerce people invariably assemble about their town—"50 hospital beds, 45 hotel rooms, three parks, 1 library, 7 doctors, 1 golf course, 1 marina, 1 swimming pool . . ." and they display a section of Griffith's paper showing the way industries are bustling and growing—Illinois Glove, Burlington and Northwestern, Kent Feeds, Alton Box Board, Beardstown Hardwood, and the rest.

They say the young are coming back to the good small-town life and the old are still there, either with their memories or their headstones. And they all seem to have something to say that is worth listening to.

"Thou shalt be missed because thy seat will be empty."

"I never thought I'd come back to Beardstown. But the old home town started to look pretty good."

"You get on that river and you just love it."

Minonk

Leaf smoke rises in the early November afternoon like some indelible perfume, some hazy dream of lingering Indian summer. The streets are almost deserted. And quiet, save for the occasional scratch of rake tines along hard ground. Then that sudden boiling pillar of smoke which diffuses into an aroma so nostalgic and soul satisfying that one wonders it is not bottled and sold in towns which prohibit bonfires.

An elderly man shuffles along the street, feet scuffling through the maple leaves. A porch swing creaks in the soft wind. In a field adjacent to the high school there are excited cries and the sound of pounding feet in a girls' game of flag football. Stores along Main Street exult in the school's unblemished record and urge the Minonk-Dana-Rutland Mohawks on to even greater feats.

Just outside of town, Route 51 flows north and south like some spinal column carrying its incessant, pounding traffic up and down the state. And yet Minonk remains an almost untainted example of the great and wondrous American small town.

There is something still distinctive and unique about towns such as these. They retain their character and personality, and a sense of history, too. They have not been molded into the plastic, franchise sameness that has stripped so many places of their individuality. Not yet.

It is true that from Route 51, Minonk looks like almost any other town out here on the prairie. Black soil stretching away as far as the eye can see, incredibly rich and fertile. The church steeple rising above the trees and the red and gray slag piles from the great days of mining. It could be Roanoke, Toluca, one of a half dozen other towns that wear similar faces, at least from a distance.

Its Main Street is bisected by railroad tracks, as are those of El Paso and Colchester. There are brick streets and old buildings with their Victorian trappings. But it has its own identity, its own sounds, its own memories.

Here are proud old homes with wraparound porches still echoing the conversations of hot, still evenings and long rainy afternoons. Nothing has bettered these porches, although the new homes have patios, sundecks, balconies. Here they are numerous and inviting, a part of the older houses and the greater and the lesser. Polish and German miners once sat on these porches. So did the managers, the merchants, the bankers. They saw the same sunsets glowing along the western rim of the prairie, the same dusks, purple and gray, stealing in from the east, heard the same crickets and cicadas throbbing in summer nights and smelled the same leaf smoke in the autumn afternoons.

The mines are closed now. These days most of the people work at Caterpillar and drive back and forth every day, making the best of the good life at work and at home. It is, they say, a bedroom community.

Frieda Kettwich, who runs K's Kitchen, says there are six churches and six taverns in town. Mostly Germans, Irish, Poles. Still the two railroads, the Sante Fe and the Illinois Central. The movie theater. Three garages, Ford, Chevy and Buick. Lots of new subdivisions. Her place has evolved into a combined restaurant, delicatessen and catering service and features the kind of things that do not come out of cans.

"The tailor is gone now," she says. "That's a cellulose insulation plant now. But we have a dairy, a bakery that employs about thirty or forty people, and the insulation plant."

On the walls of the post office, where Bill Hart has presided for a dozen years, are old propellers, a string of 50 caliber ammunition, photographs. And a story goes with everything. The big propeller came off a plane that crashed near town shortly after World War I. It was an Aeroking, Hart says, something like a Jenny, and it was flown by Tom Livingston. Livingston not only survived the crash, but still lives in town. Hart was with the 9th Air Force in World War II, flying a B-26 in France. He arrived during the Battle of the Bulge and flew out of Cambrai, bombing bridges and railroad yards. He flew very little after the war. "I still like it, though," he says. "Every chance I get I go up with somebody around here."

Just down the street is Jim Daker, who has just moved in to what used to be Spanky's Hideaway, now known as Gentleman Jim's. He has come from Aurora and on his first day admits he knows very little about the tavern business.

The town has gradually changed. Bob Denson of the Minonk *News-Dispatch* ("More than 10,000 Readers") says the mines have gone, of course, along with the brickyard and tileyard. "Now we have people moving in from Chicago. They want to get away from the big city. And we have old people, a lot of retired."

His paper is 104 years old and keeps its readers with a heavy dose of homey news, not only about the football team, the obituaries, the anniversaries, but with pieces about a children's Halloween party, wedding showers, and those inimitable personals in which visits and dinners and tours are recounted with such care as to make the simple life seem decidedly gracious. And the small column by "Alice" with its pungent philosophy. "It's hard work being so glamorous. The older I get, the harder I work, the longer it takes, the shorter it lasts and the less it means."

The oldest of the town's cemeteries stands near the foot of the slag pile. Old stones from the 1860s with the Civil War soldiers and the young children lying side by side beneath their weathered tablets. Nearby, too, is the swimming pool, and the tennis courts, empty save for the scuffling leaves.

The small bits and pieces that make up life and another day go on. A white-haired lady bicyclist pedals slowly past the theater on a balloon-tired model. "Smokey and the Bandit" is on the marquee, with "The Bad News Bears Go to Japan" coming next. On a deserted porch across from St. Patrick's church, an empty swing sways in the wind, creaking softly.

The PE classes at the high school have ended and it is quiet. The high and low last Tuesday, reports the newspaper, were 61 and 36. December corn is $2.18. There is an item about children visiting their grandparents and others about visitors from Iowa, a family moving into a new rural home.

They say Minonk is an Indian name meaning "good place." They believe it.

Colchester

"Multum in Parvo" (much in little) is the motto and corporate seal here, adopted when Colchester was incorporated 121 years ago. And it seems at first glance to be oddly inappropriate, as if it should be the other way around—little in much.

It is late morning. The rails that bisect the town are empty, stretching off toward the flat horizons like a silvery chalkline. On either side of the great swath of railroad right-of-way cars are parked nose up against the curbings, the way horses and buggies used to stand.

The sidewalks are empty and the rows of deep red brick buildings seem to be deserted. Momentarily.

Somewhere within the new high school at the edge of town a signal has sounded. Doors swing wide and young people pour into the streets and flow down the sidewalks. Farther out, a tractor plows across an enormous expanse of field, looking as insignificant as some trawler on its prairie ocean. The school year winds down. Summer flows across this broad, wide-sky land. Slower than usual this year, but it does not wait long.

Multum in parvo. It is, on second glance, perhaps a fairly accurate description of the town as it is today. Time has marched on and pretty much passed this old English mining town and it seems, to the casual passerby, to be if not a ghost town, then the next best thing. The mines are all shut down, the brick-yards are quiet—one turned into a gift shop—and there is a somnolent air to these streets, although the same can be said of most small towns and several bigger ones at that.

But Colchester is not precisely down nor out. The visible signs of decline are not so much a malaise as a sign of evolution and it may be a good one.

All the growth and progress hereabouts have happened to the east, at Macomb. And with that growing realization that progress is not necessarily good, that big is not always beautiful, has come a new appreciation of the values small towns have to offer.

Many of the great problems innundating the modern world—slums, traffic, congestion, violence, racial tension, crime, smog—are all happening elsewhere. Here time runs more slowly and there is silence in which to ponder the deeper truths.

Multum in parvo. Colchester is almost a shell of what it once was. There were 45 coal mines here in 1886 producing 86,021 tons of high-grade coal. It was said at one time that a man knowing his way around down there could go underground near Tennessee, just to the west, and, by following the old mining tunnels, come up between Colchester and Macomb, about four miles away.

At one time, too, the Miners' Picnics were huge, jostling affairs, drawing as many as 15,000 people, it is said, for a day of races, bands playing, games, contests and tables heaped with chicken, ham and potato salad. There would be a speaker, too, and sometimes a balloon ascension. The town had two cricket teams, so deep-rooted was its Englishness.

Colchester was a booming center of manufacturing. Bricks, cigars, windmills, brooms and harnesses poured from its shops and factories. The Englishmen came here for coal and they stayed beneath these broad skies, finding better lives than the mines back in England offered. Many of them now lie in the cemetery north of town, people named Foster and Taylor, Jarvis, Hall, Parnall, and Usher.

Multum in Parvo.

Almost noon now. D. A. O'Hara invites us inside the Colchester *Chronicle*, ink-scented and filled with a bewildering array of equipment that runs almost from Gutenberg to IBM. He is from this area, born at Macomb. He lived in Manhattan and was a layout editor for McGraw Hill for five years around the time of World War II. He came back home after serving in Italy with the Air Force, and he and his wife started a weekly at Bardolph. He has been at Colchester since 1951.

"It is not a good life moneywise," he says. But there are compensations. "I lead a pretty austere life. I read a lot. We've got a good library here in town and would you believe our savings and loan has assets of $32 million and the bank has over $3 million. This was a farmer's market town clear into the 1920s. Now I can't quite put my hand on it. Back in the railroad days you could go to Chicago, spend the day and still get back the same day."

He says there is one major company still in town, Yetter, which manufactures farm equipment. Here for over 50 years.

There is a Johnson outboard dealer, which also sells boats and trailers. There are Methodist, Baptist and Christian churches and one of the old ones has been turned into an antique shop.

Multum in Parvo. The Colchester *Chronicle* carries little news of arms sales and terrorist attacks and government announcements on the state of the economy. Stories, rather, about the library board and the circulation of books, which is sharply up, a model airplane show, a retirement, a funeral service, den meetings and the home extension schedule, people entering the hospital, others convalescing. This is the stuff of life, this is the sleave of care.

O'Hara says he plans to put out a four-sheet daily. He seems to have the capacity for it, the imagination. He is lean, poetic and makes one think of Leslie Howard, Lord Byron or Shelley.

The noon hour ends. In the restaurant across from the empty Princess Theatre, the late lunchers are finishing their sandwiches, sitting at long picnic tables. A pinball machine erupts in a flurry of bells and flashing lights. The pool table is unused. The early afternoon sun spills through the front windows.

Next door, Ralph Beck leans on the counter of his sundries store. He has been here all his life. Sells everything from Volco Rocks to bread, magazines, tobacco, film, candy . . . you name it. There is a violin on the counter. He plays hoe-down violin and a little bit of country. Still slow time of year, he says, but Lake Argyle does him lots of good once the season gets on.

Odd thing is that Colchester has been bone-dry for almost as long as anybody can remember. Everybody used to drink in the old days, even the early preachers, but sometime during Prohibition, a local bootlegger got shot and the town voted to go dry. There have been several referendums, the last one four years ago. The drys won by a three-two margin. Nobody knows quite how a vote would go today, but there is a package store and tavern just down the road at Tennessee and no one seems to feel particularly deprived.

There used to be a curious place six miles to the west called Vishnu, originally a picnic spot but later famous for its mineral waters. Its owner

93

claimed the waters to be so beneficial that they would "cure or benefit all kinds of debility, neuralgia, rheumatism, palpitation of the heart, dyspepsia, all kinds of kidney troubles, and worms. The water beats all other medicines for female troubles and in fact we are sure that we have found the great Balm of Gilead for suffering humanity." Back in 1890, Vishnu had a 25-room hotel and more than 20 buildings. It has long since fallen into ruin.

These days, Colchester's treasure, perhaps that of the entire area, is Lake Argyle State Park, with its fishing lake and its rolling hills of virgin timber and hiking trails. It is equally attractive to wildlife, the contemplation of nature and glorious beer parties by the undergraduates from Western Illinois University.

It is said that half a million people a year pass through Colchester on their way to the park.

Not all is dead, even though the town has never recovered from a series of crippling fires early in the century. But quiet now. Tracks are empty. A few people walk up and down the sidewalk. A good place to live, close enough to Macomb for almost anything, and yet retaining its own individuality, its own rich history.

And those good old days were never all that good. In her history of Colchester, June Moon quoted an old saying, "Colchester could boast of more weddings, fewer divorces, more pretty girls, fewer loafers, a bigger trade, more dollars worth of railroad business, a bigger saloon keeper, a bigger lodge and better and more whiskey than any town in the county."

It also was said that one afternoon in 1888 there were 177 teams tied to various hitch racks in Colchester and it was not a celebration of any kind, just people who came to town to do their trading. But miners died here by the score. And there was the wild day in 1889 when the town was so full of excitement that "there was a cutting affray, a family row, a horse down and a dog fight, all within half an hour . . ."

Multum in Parvo, indeed. It may be the best of the good old days are right here and right now.

There's No Rush in Rushville

Rushville—mid-morning and already hot. The cornfields begin to melt into a watery haze far across the prairie, and the thermometer on the bank blinks into the 80s.

It will reach 90 before this day is past, and the men sitting on the green slat benches in the square will slide backwards toward the shade as the sun burns its way across the sky above and the lawn at their feet.

This is circus day. At the fairgrounds at the edge of town, the big top is going up, and members of the Sells and Grey Three-Ring Circus are going about their chores; the scene is reminiscent of the prelude to "Carnival."

An elephant gouges away at the turf, throwing cool black dirt up on its back. "Hey, get away from that elephant," a man shouts at the youngsters who stant there, solemn and wide-eyed. Yes, they have seen elephants before, at the St. Louis Zoo, but never so close.

The circus is here for one day only. Matinee and evening performances. Then it will pick up and go on again, like some Flying Dutchman forever making the rounds of the small towns and cities. It is the first circus here for as long as almost anyone can remember.

Donald Juett, retired farmer and "retired just about everything," leans on a thick square yardstick that he uses as a cane and watches the proceedings. "Used to be some pretty decent circuses here in the old days," he says. "Barnum and Bailey were here, but never Ringling Brothers." He says that he goes around every day now and "stirs up the neighborhood." He says that he will be 77—if he makes it to fall.

Hoofbeats thudding against the hot white surface, breath coming in quick, rhythmic snorts, a lone trotter pulls a sulky and rider around the long, white oval of the fairgrounds track. Circus people go about their chores, washing and hanging out clothes in the slow, wet wind.

The same wind stirs the flag high above the old bandstand in the town square, a source of considerable pride in Rushville. Justifiably so. Besides the green benches, there are, along the sidewalks, neat borders of flowers, and, around the bandstand, landscaping that is modern without being intrusive. It all imparts a sense of order and care that is formal, yet liveable.

Cars park in multiple rows around the square—diagonally against the curbings and in the middle of the wide street. There seem to be flower boxes everywhere. And, in most cases, the Victorian store fronts with their high cornices and other ornamentation have been preserved.

The courthouse has been newly tuckpointed, the old red paint stripped away. From the outside, the building looks much as it must have in the late 1880s, clean and solid—a duplicate, supposedly, of the courthouse at Monroe, Mich. The cornerstone is inscribed, "Laid by the Masonic Fraternity, June 24, A.D. 1885." The second-floor courtroom is a curious and unsettling combination of stunning historic preservation and faceless modern.

There is a huge, leather-upholstered witness chair that looks like some Burgundian throne; nearby, there is a plastic-topped table. The judge's bench is of classic oak design, embroidered with elaborate carving and piecework with a surface rubbed and checkered by almost a century of use.

For the jury there are, by contrast, mass-produced barrel chairs upholstered with vinyl. Overhead are suspended acoustical panels and flourescent tubes; the embossed tin ceiling is hidden away in the upper darkness. Dark oak floors are spattered with paint, partly covered with chartreuse carpeting.

Up in the clock tower, the bell still bongs out the hours, marked once by a man pulling a rope. The wheeled bell that came from the McShane Bell Foundry in Baltimore in 1883 has been converted now and is rapped, on schedule, by a mechanical mallet. County Clerk James Rebman says that there are times when somebody has to go shut it off, because it rings and rings.

Not today. Twelve solid, clangorous notes that echo dully in the heat. The sound begins the moment that the noon whistle has ceased its wailing. Remarkable.

The circus tents are all up now. A truck filled with animals maneuvers across the grass, a baboon peering intently from a cage.

At Mary's Diner, nearly full, service is quick, and the conversation that arises amid the clatter carries fragments of history. An elderly man is introduced as the baby of the family. "She married a third time, you know, and she had two more boys. She wasn't no spring chicken even then . . . ." "Well, it's been good to see you, too . . . ." "Don't know about this weather. Looks like it's going to be a long, hot summer . . . ."

A police car goes past, slow. Driving is E. E. VanDeventer, a policeman here for 25 years and retired now. At 73, he is, he says, laughing, "the oldest cop in the country." He works only when needed nowadays. Used to live in Peoria, he says, but doesn't think he'd like it these days. E. N. Woodruff was Peoria's mayor back then. "I s'pose he's dead now," Van Deventer reflects.

VanDeventer stops and talks with the men sitting on the green benches in the square. "Everybody sets out here, from the millionaire to the man on welfare," says one of the men. He is neither.

One of the men, wearing a P. A. G. hat, says that he doesn't know what the initials stand for; the seed man gave it to him. Another wears a yellow Caterpillar hat; there are people in town who make the round trip to work at Cat near Peoria twice a day, a trip of 72 miles or better—one way.

VanDeventer's police cruiser circles the square and heads out past Scripps Park with its swimming pool, golf course, picnic area, tennis courts, lake. The park is at the site of the old Scripps home, a gift of the heirs of James Mogg Scripps in 1923. The youngest of the Scripps, Ed, started the chain of newspapers that eventually grew into the Scripps-Howard empire. A sister, Ellen, left a trust in a Cleveland bank that matches, dollar for dollar, town funds earmarked for the park.

Paul Smith is in the park this noontime with his daughter, Paula. He has been out of work for five months and has no idea when he will be called back to the Dana Foundry in Havana. This month. Next month. Later. Meanwhile, there is the park.

One park such as this for a town of 3,300 would be remarkable, but, just south of town, there is the new Schuy-Rush, owned by the city, where a huge lake is being developed.

There is the small-town sense of peace and stability in Rushville, but there is a feeling of vitality, too. There is the Culbertson Memorial Hospital, the Schuyler County Jail Museum, several churches, an airport. The major industry remains Barlow Bros., whose Korn Top Wieners flow from the plant at the south edge of town in somewhat diminished, but still staggering, numbers. The reason for the slowdown, according to Bill Bartlow, is the high price of hogs.

There are few empty store windows in town, hardly any signs of the urban decay affecting small towns and large cities alike. One of the shops, that of barber Jerry Tyson, is named simply "League." Tyson, who has been here 20 years, works by appointment only and offers a free mustache trim with hair styling; cost, $5. The shop is paneled, its walls bearing pennants from area schools: Bradley University, Illinois Wesleyan University, Western Illinois University, Southern Illinois University; and the medallions of professional baseball teams: Chicago Cubs, St. Louis Cardinals. Business is good, he says: there is no dead time here.

The men in the square lament that Friday and Saturday nights are not what they used to be, when crowds of people surged along the streets and filled the grassy square, and when there was band music and a sense of the festive life. "Lots of that gone, now," says one of the men. "Lots of those people gone, too, planted out in the cemetery. Maybe some of us will be, too, next year you come by. Be a whole new bunch here."

Maybe.

The sun pushes on to the west, and the shade from the trees dapples the grass. The flag uncurls slowly in the hot breeze. Ninety degrees now. Two girls in short skirts climb into an old Oldsmobile and drive away, noisily. The McShane Bell in the courthouse tower clangs again, once, twice.

Almost time for the circus matinee. Barefoot boys with dollar bills crumpled in their jeans pockets begin to head toward the fairgrounds, down the wide street, past the houses with the deep lawns, on sidewalks set far back from the curbs.

Step right up. Time to start the music. Time to start the show. Time to start the summer that has, in Rushville, the gentle and easy flow of cool water through a meadow creek, a cloud drifting across a hot sky, the talk of old men beneath the trees in the square, or that of the women on the benches along the sidewalk or in the cafe.

Tomorrow, the circus will be gone. For the young, summer will stretch away endlessly, like the great shimmering prairie. Fall, for the older ones, comes far too soon.

Grant's Galena: An Illinois Town That Time Forgot

Galena is known as the town time forgot. While most places its size—
4,000 people, give or take a few—have evolved into faceless neon and plastic
franchise towns, no different from the last place back down the road, Galena
has been so remarkably unchanged it is almost as if it had been buried for a
hundred years beneath the same kind of volcanic ash that has preserved Pom-
peii and Herculaneum.

Nothing quite so destructive or dramatic accounts for the fact that Galena
today looks appreciably the same as it did at the close of the Civil War when
Gen. Ulysses S. Grant came home here to the wildest festivities imaginable. By
some happy accident of history, of economics, of fate, the world passed Galena
by. And what had been an amazingly prosperous and civilized boom town, the
biggest in Illinois outside of Chicago in the 1840s and a source of most of the
nation's lead, virtually dropped out of sight.

"Poverty saved Galena for posterity," says Carl Johnson, an artist whose
gallery on Main Street is filled with his paintings of the town. While merchants
in other places were pasting up glass block and aluminum fronts on their stores,
he says, the businessmen of Galena had no money and were compelled to leave
their vintage brick intact. Their town is now almost a national treasure, no re-
constituted Disneyland of a place or plastic restoration, but the real thing, an
antebellum architectural treasure trove and one of those rare and genuine trips
into the American past.

Galena is tucked away in a rugged, almost mountainous area in the extreme northwest corner of Illinois in one of those curiously unglaciated areas
of the Midwest. There are, in this part of the country, spectacular hills and
long, sweeping views, like those of Burgundy.

Galena lies curled along a hill reminiscent of a Greek theater, the main
street at ground level, and higher up, the patrician houses that still reflect
wealth and prestige. There are homes in a rich variety of styles—Federal,
Queen Anne, Second Empire, Italian Villa, Gothic Revival, Greek Revival—
and enough porches and New Orleans grillwork to make it readily apparent
how much of a spinal cord the Mississippi River has been for the transmission
of culture and ideas.

The town's business was lead, and these scenic wooded hills yielded their
treasures so abundantly that Galena—the name means lead sulphide—became
the wealthiest town in Illinois by 1845. There were 15,000 people here and
the town marketed 87 percent of the country's lead. More than 54 million
pounds were shipped out that year alone. Steamboats lined the banks of the
Galena River, which was 340 feet wide and deeper than the nearby Mississippi.
The town grew rich and fat.

But by the time Ulysses S. Grant arrived in 1860 to work in his father's
leather store, Galena was already beginning to fade. The gold rush of 1849 had
drained off many of the miners, and the railroad, which came through in 1854,
signaled the end of Galena as a river town. The lead market collapsed, the river
silted up, the smart money went elsewhere and for 100 years Galena fell into
the kind of slumber that might have been imagined by Washington Irving.

There were still great days to come. Grant came out of Galena to lead the
North to victory, one of nine Civil War generals from Galena. One of them was
a General Parker, a Seneca Indian, whose presence at Appomattox took Robert

98

E. Lee somewhat by surprise.

Grant came home to Galena briefly after the war, in August 1865, to accept a spacious house from the grateful citizens. He was greeted by, among others, 36 young women dressed in white waving American flags and throwing bouquets. Grant left for Washington the following month, where he continued his duties as commanding general of the Army, and returned to Galena rarely thereafter. There were two terms as President, a two-year trip around the world ending in 1879, and in the fall of 1880, Grant moved to New York. He never again lived in his large square house on Bouthillier Street in Galena.

These days, Galena is coming back into its own, for Americans are developing a new appreciation of their heritage, particularly since so little of it is left. And the old guard that has labored to keep Galena alive and in one piece is being joined by young, enthusiastic recruits, many from the Chicago area.

Among them are Charles and Linda Primrose from Lake Forest, a Chicago suburb. Their Victorian mansion on High Street is being faithfully restored as a guesthouse where visitors may occupy high-ceilinged, brass-bedded rooms for $16 to $24 a night for two. Most of the rooms have sinks, but the bath is down the hall. The rooms do not have television, radios, or telephones, but rather a sense of quiet, of isolation, of going back to something solid and good. "We have a lot of artistic people as guests," says Mrs. Primrose. "They don't mind sharing the plumbing."

The house, which sits on two and a half acres, was owned by Augustus Estey, a lead-mine owner. Grant once attended a party at the Esteys'. There are six guest rooms open all winter, and the Primroses are adding more.

Erik Jensen, who, with his wife, Marilyn, operates the 1858 Stillman Manor as a guesthouse and restaurant, sees Galena as the Newport of the Midwest. "We have dusty old New Salem, and Springfield is a walking tour," he says. "Nothing is left as untainted or as untouched as Galena. We're getting people out here who want to feel as if they belong to this planet."

The Jensens, too, are transplanted Chicagoans, and they find a curious, almost Southern attitude prevailing in Galena, that of an old riverboat town where things will get done tomorrow if they do not get done today.

The Stillman Manor has eight rooms, all faithfully furnished in century-old style, some with gas fireplaces. The rooms rent from $27 to $31. The basement restaurant offers a menu with such fare as peanut soup, New York strip steak, hash browns and salad for $8.95 and a wine list from which one can select an excellent bottle for $6.

But the heart and soul of Galena lie along Main Street, with its bewildering variety of impressions. At one end is the antique DeSoto Hotel, where Lincoln slept, reminiscent of the hostelry in the Broadway play "Hot-l Baltimore," but still thriving. And at the other end is Raleigh's, a restaurant with singing and classical music, where reservations for weekends are required in advance.

The hotel, with 70 rooms that rent from $13 to $18, is frequently full on weekends during the ski season. One of its major attractions is its dining room, the Great Galena Tea Company, furnished with oak farmhouse tables and kitchen chairs, none of which match. It has overhead paddle fans, wide flooring, antique exposed brick and huge macrame hangings. It is a popular spot for Sunday brunch, where for $2.95 you can order good eggs Benedict to go with the help-yourself buffet and the home-made pastries, fruit and juice.

There are, along Main Street, flavors reminiscent of SoHo, Greenwich Village and Montmartre, coexisting side by side with a happy blend of pure Midwest Americana.

The delicatessen called General Grant's Traveling Rations is undeniably Bohemian. Rock music blares from an expensive tape deck, overhead fans whirl beneath the embossed tin ceiling and on some evenings there are poetry readings. A lunch for two, consisting of pumpernickel buns, a variety of cheeses and sardines, costs $2.90.

Farther along is a real estate office, advertising in its window an 1830 seven-room brick house, completely restored, with patio and two fireplaces, for $50,500, a cottage with exposed log walls for $29,500 and undeveloped land from $750 to $800 an acre.

"No, the town hasn't changed, the people have," says Joseph Moes, a pharmacist here for 50 years. "All new people here. All my friends are dead. It's not the town it used to be."

To Carl Johnson, an artist who came from Chicago eight years ago, it is like a rural town, but more cosmopolitan. "People are beginning to pick up a sense of history," he says. "We've got to save the last vestiges."

He is one of the few artists along Main Street. Another is Thomas Runde, an environmental artist who uses beer tabs as his seal, reclaims old buildings and does original work for Marshall Field in Chicago. He is committed, passionately, to the utilization of our new natural resource—waste.

Galena accomodates all this, readily, and yet it owes its continued health largely to women who have kept the town afloat all these years, propagating its history and promoting the annual fall tour of homes. One of these is Gladys Ehrler, who launched the tour of Galena's more extravagant homes back in 1950 and now owns the original house occupied by Capt. U.S. Grant, who rented it for $10 a month. The Grants lived in it longer than in the official Grant House, now maintained by the State of Illinois.

She says that when the tours of Galena's homes started, half the buildings on Main Street were empty. That is no longer true. Galena is filling up again. There are two dozen antique shops, and enough customers to fill them all.

Tourists surge along the streets, window shopping and pausing for a view of the old houses perched high on the hillsides and of the churches with their slender New England spires. Where the 36 girls in white once greeted General Grant, there are young people in jeans. And in the late winter, the streets are full of cars with skis strapped on top. The ski hills at nearby Chestnut Mountain have brought a wintertime boom and a look somewhat reminiscent of a village in the Alpes Maritimes.

The town is often full on summer weekends—even the old DeSoto Hotel and the 100-year-old Ryan mansion, just north of town, where there are 24 rooms, 10 fireplaces of Italian marble and etched glass doors. One of its lavish, comfortable corner rooms with two double beds and private bath goes for $18.

There are more than a hundred mansions and cottages remaining in Galena from the days of the steamboats and lead mines, and many have been restored and furnished with regional antiques.

Thank heaven for that. Thank poverty, too.

Nauvoo, the Town the Mormons Left

Nauvoo, the old Mormon holy city in Illinois, might well be characterized as a ghost town, almost, but it is far from dead. Somewhere beneath the layered years since the Mormons left in the greatest wagon train of all time, there is life, memory, promise. A section of rail fence stitching its way westward across an empty field seems not so much a sign of something done as something continuing, and Nauvoo is not so much a tombstone to a dead past as a monument to a living present.

From here in February of 1846 Brigham Young led his people across the frozen Mississippi, westward. It was the greatest colonizing journey in United States history, and all the skills and industry and hard work that had made Nauvoo great were to make Salt Lake City even greater. The flight from Nauvoo followed persecution of the Mormons, during which the prophet Joseph Smith and his brother were arrested and murdered in jail by a mob.

At the time of the exodus, Nauvoo had 11,000 people. It ranked with Chicago in size, but it was so advanced that most towns its size were crude and primitive by comparison. While Nauvoo (the name means "Beautiful Place" in Hebrew) had 300 brick homes among its 2,200 residences, plus 20 schools, a university, five potteries, four bakeries and three newspapers, Abraham Lincoln was growing up in New Salem, barely 100 miles to the east, in a frontier log cabin community where he read by the light of wood chips thrown on an open fire.

And although Nauvoo almost died and most of the Mormons went onward, it has been reborn to become a tourist attraction that combines the sacred, the scenic, the historic and perhaps even the mystic into something peculiarly haunting.

The present population is 1,100 and there are only a few Mormons in town, including the mayor. Catholics are the majority group and the 10 o'clock mass on Sunday in old St. Peter and Paul's usually draws more people than all the other churches combined.

And yet the present state of Mormon restoration is so advanced that 163,000 visitors came last year to see the new visitors' center and the restored houses. The steamboat Delta Queen has scheduled tours of the center and its new sculpture garden, designated as a monument to women.

The visitor count is, by some measures, a drop in the bucket. Two good professional football games would outdraw Nauvoo easily in a year. But the town is so far off the interstate highway system, being roughly in the mid-point of a quadrangle formed by Chicago, St. Louis, Kansas City, and Des Moines, that no one comes here by accident or whim, but only through firm intention.

What visitors see is nothing so elaborate as Virginia's Colonial Williamsburg, nothing so well preserved as General Grant's Galena in Illinois. It is, rather, a powerfully impressionistic view of what life was like here in the middle of the 19th century. To date, almost a score of houses and other buildings have been restored and refurnished with taste and authenticity.

They are staffed by Mormon volunteers, older couples mostly, whose ministry includes 18 months service at Nauvoo—at their own expense. They work six days a week and provide an immense store of information. It ranges from details on the hooked rugs and wide-board pine flooring to the linsey-woolsey bedspreads, the antique furniture, and the so-called "sparking lamps" which were filled with oil and lighted when the young gentleman caller arrived. When the lamp went out, he was expected to go home, although more enterprising suitors sometimes brought their own oil.

There are some surprising revelations. The restored home of Brigham Young, which looks somewhat like one of the old Dutch houses of New York, is full of pine doors and panels ingeniously painted to look like white oak. There is the home and workshop of Jonathan Browning, gunsmith and mechanic, whose son, John Moses Browning, developed the Browning firearms dynasty. The elder Browning, while in Nauvoo, invented a repeating rifle and revolving multi-shot cylinders for handguns and rifles. And Heber Kimball's lavish home not only has an 1808 piano similar to one used by Beethoven, but a museum quality collection of fine English furniture.

It was Kimball's grandson, Dr. Leroy Kimball, who bought this old house in 1945, intending to restore it for his own use. The interest in the Mormon history that it represented was so intense, however, that Dr. Kimball was inspired to begin the whole idea of restoring Nauvoo. To Mormons it has become a mecca, and to others an example of cooperative effort, ingenuity and enduring faith.

Today the area occupied by the original settlement covers a broad plain with the Mississippi River as one of its boundaries and the modern town along the hill as the other. The lowlands are bisected by streets laid off neatly as a checkerboard. Many of them are abandoned. The old town was divided into huge blocks consisting of four one-acre plots, each big enough for a house, a barn and a garden. Most of the restored homes and buildings are clustered in a four-square-block area just to the east of the Nauvoo State Park.

Among them are the Windsor P. Lyon house and store, the house of Orson Hyde, who was the first missionary to Palestine sent out by the Church of Jesus Christ of Latter-day Saints, the site of the house of William Clayton, famous for composing "Come, Come, Ye Saints," and the Wilford Woodruff house, whose owner became the fourth president of the Mormon Church.

There is also the reconstructed Seventies Hall, built as a training center for missionaries in 1843, its first floor as spare and clean as a Congregational Church, and its second a museum with displays that include pieces of dishes, old glass, spoons and fruitjars excavated from the old town. Also open to visitors are the Webb Wagon and Blacksmith Shop, the bakery and the Times and Seasons Printing Office.

But the best treasures are often in the restored homes, some of them furnished down to the china and silver on the table and clothes hanging in the wardrobes. There is pewterware on the mantel, the musket and powderhorn above the fireplace and a fascinating array of old woodstoves and a wide disparity of furniture styles. They range from the formal and elegant classical pieces in the Heber Kimball home to the casual early American of Joseph Smith's homestead kitchen, which looks almost like some recreation out of *Better Homes and Gardens*.

The Mormons built this city in seven years, almost from nothing. The area had been a swamp, filled with mosquitoes, feverishly hot in summer and cold and damp in winter. It was drained, surveyed, built up and then abandoned in such a relatively short space of time that its rise and fall might have gone unnoticed, except that it was so spectacular.

Most of these Mormons were Easterners, or first-generation English-

Americans, more accustomed to civilized cities than raw wilderness. They simply transplanted their culture, their industries and their religion, which were all in glaring contrast to those of their neighboring communities.

The Mormons met intolerance, and hostility wherever they went. From Palmyra, New York, where according to doctrine, the angel Moroni had directed Joseph Smith to a hill where he found a set of golden tablets, the church moved to Kirtland, Ohio, in 1831, and into Missouri in 1839. There, too, the Mormons were victims of mob violence and bloodshed, and the majority of the congregation fled across the river into Illinois, where Joseph Smith first saw the site of his Nauvoo in 1839.

Even as the city's durable brick homes were rising, work went forth on the huge limestone temple, set on a commanding position on a hill east of the Mississippi River flats. It was intended as a beacon, a landmark, visible to every traveler for miles up and down the river and far out onto the prairie. It was a community effort, requiring a tenth of every wage-earner's income. Nauvoo's women supplied the workers with food, socks and mittens. They sewed garments for the temple ceremonies that were never to be held. This was, for its day and place, a truly massive building, 128 feet long, 88 feet wide, with its tower and gilded figure of the angel Moroni rising 158½ feet. It was an odd combination of styles, dictated, it is said, by the visions of Joseph Smith. It was not finished until April, 1846, two years after Joseph Smith's death and three months after most of the Mormons had left Nauvoo.

The temple was never used. It was dedicated on May 1, 1846. And the following day it was stripped of everything that could be moved. Those who had remained behind to finish the temple loaded the wagons and headed west, toward Salt Lake City.

For two years the temple towered over an almost deserted Nauvoo, watched over by a few custodians. Some say it was the most magnificent building in the entire Midwest. On the night of October 8, 1848, it was set afire by an arsonist. By the next morning only the walls remained. And the following spring a group of Frenchmen known as Icarians moved into Nauvoo. Their leader, Etienne Cabet, was fascinated by the ruins of the temple and hoped to rebuilt it for his colony's uses. The Icarians were at work on the temple when a violent storm struck the city in 1850 and destroyed most of the walls. Eventually the stones from the Temple were used to build a school, a dining hall and several apartment houses.

The Icarians who followed the Mormons into Nauvoo were a strange group, artisans, professional men, gentlemen. Among them were painters, musicians, lithographers, clockmakers, weavers. One of them was the bee expert Dadant, and the company that bears his name still manufactors beekeeping equipment and supplies churches with beeswax candles from Hamilton, 10 miles south of Nauvoo. Another was Alfred Piquenard, who designed Illinois' soaring capitol building at Springfield, with its curiously Parisian mansard roofs.

But like many idealistic societies, among them the Shakers, this one did not last long. Cabet was turned out by his followers and later returned to France, and most of the Icarians moved onwards, some into St. Louis. Nauvoo became a sleepy, forgotten town. For a time it was best known for its winery, now the only commercial winery in Illinois, and for its Nauvoo Blue Cheese. Every year on the weekend before Labor Day, Nauvoo holds a symbolic Wedding of the Wine and the Cheese pageant. It used to be a quaint, small town celebration, but it has grown to become a gaudy and raucous carnival.

The new town is unspectacular. Illinois Route 96 bends in from the east, passes through a business district whose only distinguishing marks are the Nauvoo Hotel, which dates from 1841, and the modern St. Mary's Priory. Then the road curves south and heads rather quickly out of town, as if eager to reach the scenic 10-mile stretch along the river down to Hamilton. It would be possible to drive through here without being aware of the rather astonishing events that took place, although a few strategically placed signs do their best to attract the attention. The Temple Square is atop the hill, along State Route 96, surrounded by a blaze of flowers and shrubbery in the summertime. There are tablets at one end and a bronze reproduction of the original temple.

It is, however, that strange and magnificent temple that best depicts the curious interweavings of cultures and religions of Nauvoo. The Icarians used the stones for their community building, which later became the Catholic school. It was eventually sold back to the Mormons.

These same stones seem to typify the peace and harmony that at last have settled over Nauvoo. It is full of long shadows and even longer memories. But not deserted. The Visitors' Center and the restored buildings remain open, as does the sculpture garden, said to be the world's largest dedicated to women. At one end are Joseph Smith and his wife Emma. He is handing her a five-dollar gold piece for the relief of the poor. There are 12 life-size figures in all.

In attendance in the homes and stores that have been restored are the polite, well dressed, helpful Mormon couples. Among them are the elder, Maurice Miller, and his wife, Yvonne, from Provo, Utah, who left eight children and 27 grandchildren back home and are outspoken in their devotion to their family and their church.

"The Mormons came to Nauvoo to find a place where they could live close to the Lord and the family," Elder Miller says. He shakes his head. "They could have fought. They had the largest militia in the state of Illinois. They didn't have to leave."

But leave they did, like all those who have been persecuted and misunderstood throughout history. But no more. It is over. And now there is a feeling of serene acceptance here. The past has been distilled, clarified and preserved with such care and reverence that Nauvoo remains as a living memorial to a highly advanced frontier civilization, and to a firm and immovable faith as well.

Cherry Mine: 481 Went Down; 259 Never Came Back

In the spring wind there are only whispers now, soft and green and punctuated from time to time by the cry of a distant blackbird, the sound of a car whining past. All the anguished sobs have quieted, all that hollow feel of massive loss has died away. The pain is gone, but it is not forgotten. Never. For the long prairie wind that flows across the twin red tips of the old St. Paul mine is the same wind that plays through the pines and cedars of all these little cemeteries, each of them with its section of tombstones marked with those same words, chiseled there forever: "Lost his life in the Cherry Mine."

They lie in the cemetery at Spring Valley, five miles to the south. James Leadacke, 42, and his two sons, Frank, 20, and Joseph, 14, beneath a tombstone that still holds their faded, cracked photographs.

And those chilling words. "Lost his life in the Cherry Mine."

They echo up and down this coal-rich valley. Sometimes the miners are identified as Polish, German, Italian, or French, as if these tombstones desperately, pathetically are meant to fix some permanent identity to those who sleep beneath them. One, Joseph Makos, was only 13 when he died in the mine. Another was 85. On one stone is written: "Gest. 13 Nov. 1909 in der Cherry Gruben Katastrofe."

Died Nov. 13, 1909 in the Cherry Mine Disaster.

They say it was a cold day that Saturday with a hard, icy rain falling in the pre-dawn darkness as the 481 men assembled at the tipple of the St. Paul mine for another day's work. And another day's pay. $1.56. Payday would be Monday. But only for some of them.

When the miners came up for lunch at 11:30, the weather had cleared a little. Still cold and windy. There had been an electric power failure in the mine a month earlier. No new wires had been installed. Instead kerosene lanterns lighted the chambers and corridors of the two levels being mined. Nobody thought too much about it. This was one of the safest and most modern mines in the United States.

Until about 1:30, when six bales of hay were sent into the mine for the mules that worked far below. On the second level, two cagers pushed the car full of hay toward the air shaft. The bales were piled high and the rafters were low. One of the bales hit a kerosene lamp and burning kerosene spilled onto the hay.

They say anybody passing by could have put out the small fire with a shovelful of dirt. Nobody bothered. About half the men working the mine that day quit about then. Their shift was up and they caught the cage to the surface and went home, their fingernails black, the coal dust in their ears, around their eyes. Down below, somebody pushed the car with the burning hay to the third level shaft opening and the hay fire was put out. But the pine rafters had ignited. Still, nobody paid much attention. The miners still on duty continued to work for the next 45 minutes or more, believing the fire could be snuffed out any time they wanted. Then it was too late.

Heat and smoke began to fill the shaft and the labyrinth of passageways that made up the mine. It stopped men from getting to the mule barns to attach a hose that had been sent down. Another attempt to attach a hose to a pipe near the main cage failed. The pipe was too small. The water too hot. By now smoke was rolling up the shaft and the word raced through town. The mine is on fire.

And there began contradictory, confusing efforts to stop the fire, to rescue the men that were to contribute to all these graves in all these cemeteries and all these inscriptions.

"Lost his life in the Cherry Mine."

There were to be 259 victims. It was the worst mine disaster in Illinois history, the third worst in the whole country. There would be 151 widows, 607 children left without fathers. And when it was over, those pathetic notes found with the bodies: "Good-bye wife and children . . . I wish you and our children to attend church and live good Christian lives."

"Dear Ermina am very sure that my last hour has struck and never will leave this grave. I beg of you not to think no longer of my death for I feel I will have an easy death. I have nothing more to say only that to educate my dear child the best you can and when he grows you may tell him that he had an honest father. Would like to say hoping to see you again, but must say

good bye forever. Last kisses from your Antenore."

Pete Donna, now 83, was 16 back in 1909 and had been working the mines for three years. Newspaper accounts claim Frank Zanarini, who died in 1955, was the last survivor of the Cherry Mine. Donna says he is.

"There was smoke coming through this canvas door and the word comes, tell the men in there to get out, so I did. It was a Saturday, you see. I started gathering tools. We had to climb a ladder. There was no light. We felt our way out by feeling the rail with our feet. When we got on top of the tipple the sun was shining we could could hardly see. My father got out, too. I can't tell you how many survivors there were, but there were over a thousand on the payroll. They worked two shifts. The night men took care of the roads, kept the timber up. We made a dollar and six cents a ton.

"It was a bunch of carelessness. Somebody reversed the fan. It drew the fire up instead of blowing the air out and that did it."

Reversing the fan also shut off the oxygen supply to those still trapped

below. And it drew the heat and fire to the fan house, which was destroyed, and the air shaft was cut off as an escape route.

The only way out was the main cage and there began a heroic rescue attempt by a dozen volunteers. Six times they went down in the cage and brought up survivors. How many nobody knows for sure. On the seventh trip, there was a mixup in signals and the hoist engineer refused to bring up the cage until he received the proper signal. Finally he did and up came the cage with the rescuers, all dead. They had been lowered directly into the flames on the seventh try. Rescue efforts were halted and at 8 that evening, company officials decided to seal the mine to smother the flames.

But with all those men inside, it was a decision that raised a torrent of protest. The women waiting outside pleaded that the mine be opened, but their pleas were not heard for a week. By Sunday morning rescue experts and fire-fighters from throughout the state were at the mine. They had come from Chicago, from Pittsburgh. Peoria's Bishop Dunne arrived to help comfort the stricken. And a woman insisted that the mine be opened again since she knew her husband and brother inside were not dead.

She was right. One week after the fire, rescuers slogging through the wet, black depths heard sounds. Twenty-one men and a mule were still alive. For the last four days they had stayed alive in complete blackness. They were the last to come up alive. The next day the fire began again.

On Wednesday, Nov. 24, 168 bodies were found on the third level. Nearby was a piece of wood with the message, "We all die here together." The mine was sealed again and the rest of the bodies were not brought out until the following year. March 4, 1910, 61 bodies were brought up and stacked up in a tent. Sometimes identification could be made only from a watch, a piece of clothing, a ring.

The mine reopened later that year and was worked until the late 1920s when competition from cheap southern coal put it permanently out of business. By then Cherry had declined to a small town of 500. And at the time of the disaster it had been a company town of 2,500, with 17 taverns and rows on rows of bleak, unpainted houses.

It is quiet these days. At the south edge of town is the cemetery with its classical tragic figure against the memorial erected by the United Mine Workers on Nov. 13, 1911, and its graves—Ossek and Bauer, the Germans, Fayen and Durand, the Frenchmen, the Polish, the Italians, the English, the Slavs. And at the other end are the twin slag heaps, reddish now from 50 years of rain and rust, but white when first piled up, they say. Shale, or soapstone, and it smoldered for years. Going down the street in his Oldsmobile, slowly, is Pete Donna, who quit the mine the day after the fire and ran a grocery store in town and later played 3-I baseball and soccer.

And there, in the Coal Dust Inn, is Dick Lord, now 71, an Englishman from Yorkshire, who worked in many of these old mines, including this one. He came later, and when they closed the St. Paul Mine, he would go to another one, finally ending up working in Peru and walking back and forth to work.

Retired now, but full of memories of the old mines, of his time during the war in Italy. He sits sipping his beer in the early afternoon. He has consented to put on his old miner's hat and carbide lamp. And from a plastic pouch he extracts a Hohner Marine Band harmonica and plays old songs with a kind of rhythm so accented that it sounds like a vague and distant memory. "Put Your Arms Around Me" and "Oh, Marie."

"In one row of thirty-three company houses, only three men came out alive," he says. "One guy said drinking saved his life. He stopped to have a drink of whiskey and never made it to work that day."

Now these deep mines are all gone and all that remains are the slag piles, looking faintly prehistoric, like Mayan temples. After the war the young men didn't want to work in the mines. People went to gas, or oil, or butane, and the mines disappeared one by one. Last one in this area was that at Peru. Somewhere down there where the spring wind never reaches, all that coal. Some miners, too, for there are those who were never accounted for. The crying is stilled now, the grief dissolved by the softening springs of three score and more years. But the memories will never pass, not as long as stone lasts, or life. There will be those tombstones, those words, "Lost his life in the Cherry Mine."

It is still down there, all that coal, in thick veins that run 200, 300, 500 feet deep from our own area down into the kills of Kentucky. Enough coal down there to boggle the mind and to cause, incidentally, a new look at this enormous source of energy which lies just a few hundred feet down. This story is only a footnote to the great age of coal, which may be dawning again soon.

Travels

There's Beauty Around the Bend

Were someone to pass out blue ribbons to the various states on the basis of their lack of scenic splendor, Iowa might well be rated near the top, right along with Kansas, Nebraska and the northern half of Indiana.

But somewhere amid all that wall-to-wall corn is one of the most overlooked pieces of terrain in all the Midwest, a spectacular stretch along the northeast corner of the state that runs along the Mississippi from the Minnesota border to Dubuque. And if one can tolerate the leisurely and archaic pleasures of second class travel along winding, two-lane and sometimes gravel byways that make up the Great River Road in this part of the world, the rewards are plenteous indeed, partly because they are so unexpected.

A year ago we came home from delivering a son to school in Winona, Minnesota, on Interstate 90. It was a harrowing, high-speed trip which screeched to a long, heated halt amid a 20-mile traffic jam comprised of red-faced, fist-shaking Chicagoans towing their boats and trailers back from a weekend at Wisconsin Dells. Dante's Inferno was never like this.

We have since stuck on this particular journey to the back roads and the only one left for us to explore was that winding along the west bank of the Mississippi. It alternates between Rt. 16, 76, and the kind of roads which are discovered only by asking the man at the gas station, "Which way is it to Millville?" The first problem, however, is finding the gas station.

Through much of its wandering way through this part of Iowa, the Great River Road brushes the Mississippi, which has, in this part of its course, a lonely, brooding grandeur. There is little barge traffic, there are few towns and the roads are so little travelled that people wave as one passes—not fists, as on I-90, but hands, in greeting. And litter is so scarce that the sight of a beer can or a paper cup along the roadside seems to be an unthinkable desecration.

For this type of travel, one must be prepared to tarry, not in sweaty, maddening traffic jams, but in peaceful and sometimes illuminating serenity. Our first startling and wholly unplanned stop came at the sudden site of a small country church with a graveyard out front and an adjacent shrine, which loomed up against the hillside so unexpectedly that the foot automatically stabbed for the brake pedal.

The sign by the church indicated that this was Wexford and there seemed to be none but Irish buried here, people named Murphy and Powers and Quigley and Fitzgerald, all of them Michaels or Patricks or Bridgets. The church was built in 1848 and most of the settlers came in 1850 on the Ticonderoga, bound from Liverpool to New Orleans. From there they scattered through the Mississippi Valley to become miners, canal workers, laborers, tavern keepers.

But one small group, most from County Limerick, gravitated to this corner of Iowa, to the church nestled against the hills, and they lie now beneath tombstones worn with age and darkened with lichen, their names growing fainter by the year. There are twin tablets in one spot—"Annie Russell, Died May 7, 1855, 30 years" and "Timothy Russell, Died March 26, 1883, 65 years" and the difference in ages has long dissolved. The only apparently non-Irish graves are those of a family named Martelle.

The little church of the Immaculate Conception with its shrine and cemetery is half-way between Lansing and Harpers Ferry along the Great River Road. There is only a single house across the way, plus the priest's house, and the rest of the area seems to be totally deserted, save for the Irishmen who sleep there. Peacefully, one hopes.

A few miles to the south is perhaps one of the better kept secrets of the upper Midwest—the Effigy Mounds National Monument, which is worth a long stop and the miles of walking it requires. One might easily look at the Indian mounds without being moved one way or the other, even though these are in the form of bears and birds and have enormous archeological value. Of more immediate appeal is the area itself, beautifully laid out and almost totally unspoiled.

There are cool gravel paths leading up to the high bluffs, deep, untouched forests of quaking aspen and oak and hickory, and a feeling, if one is willing, that nothing has really changed in the thousand or two thousand years since some of these mounds were created.

There are discreet markings identifying trees and wildflowers, stunning views of the river from the high palisades, and the feeling that children ought not really to be brought along because of the danger of falling. The paths wind for over six miles and they are virtually unlittered. The only exception on this day was a piece of tinfoil from a roll of film, so out of place that I bent and picked it up and presented it to the ranger with compliments.

A little farther to the south is, of all things, Pike's peak, a state park with a view of the Mississippi and its valley from such a height that the stomach contracts. Right below is the juncture of the Wisconsin River with the Mississippi, the spot where Father Marquette and Joliet first entered the great river in June of 1673 with an uncommon outpouring of joy. It must look almost the same now as it did then, save for the buildings of Prairie du Chein across the river and to the north.

There is a plaque set in a rock near the overlook commemorating the event. These days the few people who pass sit at picnic tables on the high cliff with the wooded hills falling away in the distance and the watergap of the Wisconsin River visible off toward the horizon where the green woods turn into blue hills. Fishermen may nose into the channel way down there in a motor-powered boat. Or a train will cross that far-off bridge, its Burlington and Northern green cars barely discernible. Otherwise it is the same, and one can almost see canoes coming, two of them, the paddles flashing in the sun, and the near great, profound stillness, which, too, is unchanged.

Somehow the detour signs near Gutenberg divert one, almost permanently, from the Great River Road, which runs southeast of Millville on decidedly second rate surface. But the terrain is magnificent, reminiscent of the foothills of the Alps at one point, and of the rich, rolling countryside of the old duchy of Burgundy the next.

Perhaps one of the most staggering views of the whole trip is just before Balltown, another unspoiled little town with its Catholic church, shrine, and the hills descending to such sweeping distance that it seems as if this must indeed be the top of the world. Terrapin Ridge near Galena suffers grievously by comparison, although its roads are better and its reputation wider.

Then there is Dubuque, with its old houses and steep hills—a story in itself, and this trip through a small part of Iowa has taken hours and many gal-

113

lons of gas. But we are much richer for it all. And this may be the way we will all travel in the future, when simply getting there will no longer be worth the expense.

Lake Superior Circle Route—Unspoiled, Unchanged

The old Royal Road to Romance has been pretty badly littered with beer cans these late days. Hardly anybody swims the Hellespont any more, as Leander once did, and then Byron, or treks across the Gobi or climbs the pyramids. Many of the folks clustered before the Acropolis are from Muscatine or South Chicago and wear loud sport shirts. Too often have the great attractions of the world been rendered almost uninhabitable by pollution and the dreadful roar of motorcycles.

And yet there remains one unspoiled and unchanging attraction, still so close, so cheap, so accessible that it requires nothing more than a car, a free week and at least a vestigal trace of adventure and romance. It is the Lake Superior Circle Route, best done out of season while the weather is still good and offering to those who follow it something of a spiritual retreat on one hand and a feast for the senses on the other.

As some unknown poet of the area put it,

Leave the city's din behind you,
Seek the peace ambition stole,
Look you closely as you wander,
You may find instead your soul.

We have dropped off one of our sons at college near Minneapolis and headed across Wisconsin, into the land of the vacationer near Rhinelander before turning north into the wilderness. Up through the Nicolet National Forest in Wisconsin and the Ottawa National Forest in Michigan's Upper Peninsula. Already there are the white and gray birches and aspens beyond number and pines and spruces and firs soar over the road like the endless arches of some Gothic cathedral. It is all deciduous in one area, then all coniferous, then a mixture. The forest changes and the sun sinks lower, sifting through stained glass. We play music from "Siegfried's Rhine Journey" and the "Elvira Madigan" theme on our portable tape player. And roll for miles and miles through the forest without seeing another car.

Nor is there anyone else at the Golden Lake campground that evening, save for an elderly man along the rocky shore, fishing by the light of a Coleman lantern. Open fires are forbidden because of the long drought, so we cook over a small propane burner. There is no litter here. Instead a clean, pristine, undiscovered feeling. At 8:20 a huge silver moon rises over the jagged tops of the pine trees, looking like some idealized scene from the Nick Adams stories, or something from Jack London. There is something staggering about this peace, this solitude, this beauty. We awake refreshed in the morning and hear waves lapping against the shore. It is a musical sound, like Mozart.

Our first view of Superior is from the hill leading into Baraga, across the Keweenaw Bay from L'Anse on our way to Copper Harbor. There are Finnish names hereabouts, and those curious meat pies called pasties. Old industries that once flourished are gone now, and there are ruined and abandoned docks and rusting mining gear. The copper and silver have largely ended and the major industry now is taconite, the attraction is recreation.

Halfway up the peninsula is Houghton, a long, busy town with the river running through, reminiscent of Prague with its steeples and old-town look. We arrive at last at Copper Harbor. Nothing much here but a couple of expensive grocery stores, motels and gift shops. To the north is Fort Wilkins, erected to protect the copper miners from the Indians and now a historic site of small interest. It is closed since the buildings are being fumigated to kill the borers.

But Rt. 26 to the south has made the drive worthwhile, for it skirts the lake here, offering sudden vistas of wide water and clean, sandy beaches. At Eagle Harbor, two elderly women sit on a bench on the sand dangling their feet in the water. Everywhere people complain about the heat. It has been this way all summer long, they say. And they worry, with good reason, about forest fires.

At Siskiwit Bay south of Duluth it is suddenly cold and windy. The lake is gray, its waves frosted with whitecaps. Presently a rain begins and in Duluth the businessmen are wearing their winter suits and topcoats. It is thriving and busy. Downtown is filled with people hurrying. Where? We pick up a brochure at the vistor's information bureau which recommends taking three to four days to circle the lake. It is possible if one drives pell mell and takes no time to stop and smell the flowers.

There are 1,500 miles of coastline to this lake, 31,800 square miles of water. Lake Superior is 350 miles long at its greatest length and 160 miles at its widest point. It is the largest expanse of fresh water in the world. And each mile, each gallon, each view offers something different.

After Labor Day it is off season and off season rates prevail. At the Silver Bay Motel north of Duluth, the proprietor gives us the key to a three-room suite with sleeping space for six, a living room, two color television sets (one with an FM that brings in classical music) and coffee maker, for $20. We have a late dinner at Beaver Bay, where we are alone in the spacious dining room, and we eat and drink well for $20 for the two of us. The waitress says the warm and lovely weather is not unusual for this time of year. Along the lake, September can be beautiful. October, too.

By morning the lake has changed again. It is calm and serene and the sky blue and deep. We stop at one link after another in that long chain of Minnesota state parks and waysides that offer spectacular views, one from high, rocky outcroppings, the next from a spot right along the lake. The lake is almost cerulean in places, looking like the Aegean. Always changing patterns of light and shadow, dusted here with a sudden ruffle of wind, glistening off there with a million diamonds from the late morning sun. And to the west, great towering clouds looming over the hills. Overhead a lone hawk is circling.

We hike into the woods to see the highest falls in Minnesota at Baptism River State Park. It is a remote and inviting path into pure wilderness. The sound of traffic fades quickly and there is that primitive, unspoiled beauty, untouched by the scrape of bulldozer, the clink of beer cans. One is drawn into deep contemplation, deep wonder here. Is there intelligent life in Gary, Indiana? One may spend days along this tip of the arrowhead in Minnesota with its parks, its inland trails leading to canoe country and countless lakes, and its fascinating towns, Grand Marais, Grand Portage.

But we pass into Canada and pause at the Middle Falls Provincial Campground along the Pigeon River. Fires are allowed at last, and needed, since the thermometer falls along with the sun. We wear two wool sweaters by night, T-shirts by 8 the next morning.

This country has a wild and lonely feel. There are soaring, fir-tipped peaks, distant wooded buttes and awesome cliffs. We look constantly for wild animals. There are signs along the road designating moose crossings. We see no moose. No bears. But there is in the road hereabouts what must be a red wolf. And a porcupine. And hundreds of chipmunks. And north of Thunder Bay we come across Ouimet Canyon, a breath-stopping gash in the earth, surely not so dramatic as the Grand Canyon, but fearsome in its abruptness. It is as if the earth had suddenly collapsed here in a cataclysmic roar and lay broken and twisted far beneath in the form of huge boulders. The area is posted to the effect that children ought to be closely watched. Adults, too. No such precautions are evident along the Minnesota shoreline.

Thunder Bay is made up of the two old towns of Fort William and Port Arthur. It has over 100,000 inhabitants and an air of being prosperous and industrious. The old fort is still here with its glorious echoes of the fur trade and the bearded northmen arriving in their great canoes. This is the largest fur trade reconstruction in North America, and it is operated now as it existed between 1816 and 1821.

But perhaps even more fascinating than the big towns are the quaint villages where Indians walk the streets and the post offices are also known as the bureau de poste. Some of these towns have small clusters of houses along the lake, sailboats riding in the bay, and the ever present gulls with their high, lonely cries.

White Lake Provincial Park is inland along Rt. 17 located along the beach of still another pristine lake. It is closed, but people camp here even off season. The silence at night is almost complete and once again the moon rises over the pines as if on cue. Some 50 miles to the southeast is Obatanga Provincial Park, which is not in the *Guide Michelin*, but ought to be. Its campsites are scattered discreetly through a thick evergreen forest, where the tree trunks rise heavenward in a profusion of columns, a green and scented roof arching far overhead. The earth is carpeted with pine needles and moss and there is a white beach curving around a lake with a clear sand bottom. All of it looks so clean and sparkling that it might be part of a world that was created only yesterday morning.

Few junctions exist along this Rt. 17 in Canada and coming upon one is a major event. Much of the area to the north is available only by foot, or by canoe, and it seems as if every second car has a canoe on its roof. At Obatanga there are large wooden maps with canoe routes marked, including rapids and portages. And the Ontario road map indicates that there are millions of square miles accessible only by canoe, by foot, by seaplane, or by railroad. There is, for instance, a rail line running almost to Hudson Bay, but no roads go quite so far.

And there are names hereabouts with a familiar ring: Father Marquette, of course, and the explorers Radisson and Grosseilliers. It seems remarkable now that they managed to travel so far and see so much, going so slow as they did. Even at 60 or 65 miles per hour by car, it takes hours and days to cross this wild and lonely land, so dotted with clean freshwater lakes that the temptation to tarry must have been irresistable then, as it is now.

But civilization begins again as one progresses to the southeast. Near Old Woman Bay and the Lake Superior Provincial Park there are more and more cars and motorcycles. The firs and balsams become mixed with deciduous

117

trees now and there are colors high in the hills. Along one cliff we find Indian pictographs, painted representations of primitive animals that have resisted time and the water. Steel catwalks once erected to provide a safe view have been washed away by the storms of winter and one must now venture onto a rocky ledge to view the ancient paintings.

More parks to the south, Pancake Bay and Batchawanna Bay, the one a Provincial park and the other a picnic area, both stretching along unlittered sand beaches. We pause to lunch beneath pine trees, the forest at our back and the beach and the lake in front. It is the best of both worlds. But summers here are short and sweet. Not a moment's sunlight to be wasted. Nor a chance to smell the flowers.

On Saturday, in the glare of the late afternoon sun, we stand beside the locks at Sault Ste. Marie and watch the Murray Bay from Toronto passing through, empty, on her way into Lake Superior. Waiting to the west is the John S. Patton out of Wilmington, riding low, her holds full of taconite. It is a symbolic exchange, somehow, for we too have come away from Lake Superior filled with a wonder, a reverence, a respect for this vast and unchanged wilderness that lies so close at hand and remains so clean, so unspoiled. We emerged laden with riches beyond measure.

Here Lie Custer's Men

Custer Battlefield, Montana—this is not one of those overwhelming battle-field-cemeteries, like Verdun, or Gettysberg, where so many thousands have fallen that one stands mute and helpless. It is rather the commemoration of a small but significant disaster that seems almost personal, almost family.

Something about the way the wind sighs out of the west, rolling those hot white clouds over the Bighorn Mountains and whispering through the dry grass of late summer, then playing among the tombstones which mark the places where the men of the Seventh Cavalry died. Something human, under-standable here which has to do with a miscalculation, vanity, perhaps, or over-confidence. For until this fateful battle in the waning days of June, 1876, just as the nation was celebrating its centennial, the Indians had always melted away at the appearance of the U.S. Cavalry, bugles blowing, the band perhaps playing "Garry Owen."

Not this time.

And too bad for us all. For the result was an aroused nation, so stunned by the defeat that it became committed to wiping out the "red devils" com-pletely in a genocidal vendetta whose repercussions are felt to this day. Here-after the Indians were relentlessly pursued, hunted down and either slaughter-ed as at Wounded Knee, or hounded onto reservations, like so many cattle.

The passing of a hundred years has softened some matters and made others more inflexible than ever. Custer's men have been gathered up from the places where they fell and died and placed in a common tomb, lying beneath an obelisk which bears their names. Many of them are Irish or English. Maho-ney and Butler, Burke, Cheever, McCarthy, Dugan, Graham, Burnham and Smith. A few Germans, Kolzbursher, Kiefer and Eisman.

The tablets on the hill read "U.S. Soldier, 7th Cavalry, Fell Here June 25, 1876" or simply "Unknown Soldier." They are empty now, serving to indicate the places the bodies were found by the stunned members of the relief battal-ion under Lt. Bradley. It is a most unlikely place to die, like Zinderneuf or Isandhlwana.

On the porch of the visitor center a guide delivers the prescribed lecture, showing on a relief map the location of the Northern Cheyenne and the Sioux and the lines of march of Custer and Reno. Hindsight makes extraordinary generals out of the least of men. The paths are marked with rattlesnake warn-ings, the headstones scattered across the dry and rolling hills. Two here. A dozen there. At the top of the hill, the evidence of the last stand, with Custer and the last survivors clustered together, dying beneath a hail of arrows and the Indians' warclubs. Custer is buried at West Point, but most of the others are still here.

The Bismark *Tribune* of July 6, 1876 reported that all of the brave men who followed Custer perished. "No one lives to tell the story of this battle. Those deployed as skirmishers lay as they fell, shot down from every side hav-ing been entirely surrounded in an open plain. The men in the companies fell in platoons and like those on the skirmish line, lay as they fell, with their of-ficers behind them in there (sic) proper positions. General Custer, who was shot through the head and body, seemed to have been among the last to fall, and around and near him lay the bodies of Col. Tom and Boston, his brothers, Col. Calhoun, his brother-in-law, and his nephew, young Reed, who insisted on accompanying the expedition for pleasure. Col. Cook and the members of the non-commissioned staff all dead—all stripped of their clothing and many of them with their bodies terribly mutilated."

Over a hundred years have passed. Off to the east, the roads unspool like faded typewriter ribbons, some so straight they might have been designed by engineers snapping stringlines over maps. Now the Northern Cheyennes live here on their reservation, many of them in two bedroom ranch houses set amid the salmon-colored hills. They drive old cars and some of them bear bumper-stickers, "Indian Pride on the Move." The yards are often littered with derelict autos and the most popular color for houses seems to be turquoise. The government has provided the Indians with craft and work centers and these descendants of Two Moon, Lame White Man and Dirty Moccasins are only now beginning to feel the stirrings of any pride whatsoever.

Somehow there are mixed sympathies here, for the Indians losing their land, their identity and their pride, and for the young troopers who lie in the mass grave atop the hill overlooking the Little Bighorn. All the sounds have died away, the rattle of the carbines, the screams of the wounded and dying, the yelling of the Indians, the dying notes of the last bugle call.

The tall prairie grass waves in the hot wind and the clouds sail endlessly across the mountain tops. Nature has a short memory and even the wind has forgotten. Only the gravestones remain, imbedded firmly in the earth, the legends growing fainter year by year. There is a new one on the side of the visitor center that is ascribed to Black Elk. It reads, in both English and Indian, "Know the Power That Is Peace."

Mississagi Provincial Park, Ontario

There are certain unique joys to out-of-season camping in these remote and silent Canadian provincial parks, not the least of them being the fact that the population is now so drastically reduced. In this splendid and scenic location in the Laurentian Uplands nearly 20 miles from civilization, there are 101 camping sites, out of which only a handful—six to 10 at any one time— are occupied. Some of them are live-in sites for miners who work near Elliott Lake, some 20 kilometers to the south.

Most of the Canadian parks close after Labor Day, which is to say that the gate houses are no longer manned, the water turned off and no fees are collected. And yet they remain open to all who venture in. The result is often a grand sense of isolation and peace that is a far cry from the carnival atmosphere which so often prevails in summertime.campgrounds with their strings of Japanese lanterns, barking dogs and the Johnny Carson Show sounding from dozens of crowded motor homes and campers.

We spent a week here in mid-September when the first gold and crimson of autumn was seeping into the distant hills. We canoed across limpid lakes at dusk, tented through nights of pelting rain and booming thunder and others when the wind was a mere whisper in the pines and the stars seemed to hang like lanterns just out of reach. And all at a cost of $107 for the two of us.

We had a canoe for four days, rented from the Elliott Lake Marina for $30 (in-season rental is $14 a day). We carried in a week's supply of groceries, which we would have bought had we stayed home. And our other major expense was the cost of getting there and back—$45 for gas, $5 for toll charges, a $4 fee for camping in Michigan's Manistee National Forest, $5 for ice and $18 for a motel in Oconto, Wisconsin on the way home.

We walked primeval wooded trails where lichen and mosses still go about their millenial work of turning granite into soil. We saw the birches shedding their first leaves onto the forest floor, looking like golden coins flung by some passing monarch.

So astonishing was the solitude it was almost as alarming to encounter other people along these still forest paths as it would have been to run across bear or moose. According to the entry in the registration book along one hiking trail, no other human had passed this way in two weeks.

We came across abandoned logging camps, one with pieces of iron stove and porcelain washpans still on the site, along with iron hasps and eyebolts, pieces of leather, the remains of a fireplace. Along one narrow path winding through the deep woods, some of the immense white pines, so prized by loggers of 60 years ago, still stand, rising well over 100 feet.

There also are remains of logs left where they fell when the last lumberjacks quit these woods, along with a rude log cabin without windows, the remains of a copper camp and evidences of the intricate logchute system used to carry logs down small streams, all in a forest that constantly changes from birches, aspens and maples to fragrant stands of pines and balsam fir. In some places are huge boulders, glacial erratics and signs of ripple rock caused by shallow, lapping seas so far back in antiquity that the mind can scarcely comprehend.

We explored distant shores in our canoe, finding a thin sliver of white beach, an isolated marsh where moose would feed on misty mornings, an al-

121

most hidden island covered with pines and shrubs, on which stood a picnic table and a trash barrel—empty. At dusk, gliding across a mirror-smooth lake, rustlings in the woods, the flash of a deer, the far-off bellow of a moose.

We watched the sun sink into the west, taking the light with it and draining the colors out of the clouds in a spectacular golden rush. The kind of evening the people doing the advertising for Molson beer and Canadian whiskey cherish. And later, from a lowering gray sky, came the sound of geese, like distant barking dogs, and a ragged line moving low over the trees, following those ancient urgings and beginning to head south once again down the long flyways.

Then the campfire with its welcome glow, smoke twisting toward a star-filled skies and later, flashes of the northern lights gleaming across the heavens in a long, icy beam. Muted voices, the glow of kerosene lanterns, quilted sleeping bags and the comforting feel of woolen blankets.

Some obvious disadvantages to this late season camping. None of the comforts of home. Cold noses. And weather that is, as one approaches the equinox, distressingly unpredictable. Languid breezes from the south one moment and wintry clouds boiling across the hills the next. Midday winds that howl through the forest and raise angry whitecaps on the lakes, then a cold, stringy rain from lowering skies that stubbornly refuse to clear.

But the bugs are mostly gone, save for a few hardy mosquitoes and the yellowjackets that we know too well. And the people are almost all gone, which may be an alarming loss for some and for others a most reassuring absence.

But there is in this living in the rough out-of-season some sense of challenge, of accomplishment, of survival. And there is, too, some elemental understanding of nature that helps to shuffle many of the things of this Earth—the material concerns, the petty conceits, the small worries and doubts—back into proper perspective.

As Robert Louis Stevenson wrote, "The world is so full of such wonderful things; I think we all should be happy as kings."

New Orleans, Quick and Cheap

I know now precisely what feelings must have beseiged Phileas Fogg as he walked in apparent defeat through the doors of the Reform Club of London that December evening of 1872.

Fatigue, yes, and despair and what we have come to call jet lag. And yet a sense of monumental personal triumph and achievement. Well, my own exploit is considerably less spectacular than his making it around the world in 80 days by a variety of bizarre conveyances in Jules Verne's novel of a hundred years ago, but hardly less hectic or foolhardy.

Consider a man at half century mark traveling 1,700 miles up and down Mid-America.

In 48 hours.

Alone.

By bus.

For $33.

This is one part of the travel bargain currently being offered by Greyhound and Trailways. The great travel sale, in effect through March and probably to be extended, has as its attractions one way fare anywhere in America for $50, a $99 nine-day Ameripass which gets you all the bus riding you can stand for nine days, or a $33, three-day round trip to anywhere.

I chose the latter and went from Peoria to New Orleans and back in just under 48 hours. In that span of time, I spent an hour and 25 minutes in Springfield, four hours in St. Louis, two hours and 20 minutes in Memphis, 55 minutes in Jackson, Mississippi, and three hours and 23 minutes in New Orleans. The other 38 hours all passed on the bus, including two anguished, sleepless nights, and the accumulated sensation of seeing more in that short space of time time than anybody reasonably ought to.

I had not been on an American intercity bus for 30 years, and that incident followed the demise of our family car in Champaign. The ghastly trip home that followed was distinguished chiefly by the fumes, heat and sweat and the certainty that we were never going to get anywhere because of all the stops.

The old highway bus ain't what she used to be , although the echoes are sometimes strong. These new buses are cool, roomy, smooth and quiet, reminiscent of jet airplanes in their modern decor, except that there are huge windows and something to see besides passing clouds. And they are, at least during this time of the slack travel season, comfortably underpopulated so that there are, on this trip, at least two seats for everybody.

This, following my weathered journal, is how it went:

We leave Peoria at 10:10 on a Tuesday morning. Eight people aboard, including two men heading back to their towboat at St. Louis to renew their 30-days-on, 30-days-off cycle. They are talking loudly, about women, the state of the world, television and what their kids are thinking. "It's entertainment, but they see it as a way of life."

Out past the taverns and used car lots of South Jefferson and across the Cedar Street Bridge. There are stops at Pekin, Green Valley, and Mason City and we are at Springfield on time, 11:52. This is a transfer point and there is a 45-minute layover before the Greyhound leaves for St. Louis, enough time for a short walk and a cold drink.

The Greyhound Americruiser, red, white and blue, is newer and slightly more luxurious than the Peoria-Springfield bus. Windows high above the road, eyeball to eyeball with truckers. The seats have backs of imitation wood and are richly upholstered. There are 17 people on this leg of the journey, most of them reading, talking softly, or sleeping. One elderly man croons tunelessly to himself, occasionally clapping his hands together.

At 2:20 we are across the McKinley Bridge and into St. Louis. I have the option of taking a local bus to Memphis within the hour or waiting until 5:20 and taking an express. I choose the later and spend a leisurely afternoon in St. Louis, walking along the riverfront, viewing the impressive new displays beneath the arch, walking slowly back to the bus depot. There are no matinee movies I care to see. The taverns are closed because it is election day. There is a Cadillac cruising the streets with a loud-speaker extolling the virtues of Cervantes for mayor.

We leave St. Louis at 5:20 in rush hour traffic, heading along the express-way into the setting sun before turning south. Soon it is dark and we are wind-ing through the Ozarks. There is little communication between these bus passengers. People fall asleep, or try to. But there is a strange feeling of deja vu in this lonely nighttime travel, reminiscent of those interminable wartime train journeys, of tired people in railroad stations waiting with vacant bore-dom, and the little towns floating past the window, unreal in their insulation. Now they have come to look alike, each with its own little shopping center and its franchise fast food stands, all stamped from the same mold.

We are on time at Sikeston, Mo., 9 p.m. and the passengers stumble into a garishly lighted depot for vending machine snacks and Cokes. I am hardly 12 hours outward bound, but already have begun to acquire that glazed look of fatigue and despair that afflicts travelers who would rather be someplace else.

Soon we are. In Memphis. It is midnight, and this is a clean, modern bus terminal, full of people. I manage to shave in the washroom and scrape away some of the glaze. But the city is so deserted that I think better of venturing into those empty streets and remain instead in the terminal with its polite and well dressed black people, waiting for the loudspeaker to summon us to Gate 9, or Gate 3, or whatever. Somebody strums a guitar. Somebody sleeps, mouth open. A middle-aged man and woman chain smoke cigarettes, trem-bling like palsied antiquarians.

At 1:15 a.m. we are outward bound again. Suddenly it is dawn, near McComb, Miss., and voila, there is a haze of spring green across the treetops and redbuds and dogwoods already in bloom. We are soon passing through piney woods and a thin, smoky mist clings to the ground. Jax Beer signs be-gin to sprout along the roadsides, although the beer is no longer being made, and houses with tin roofs, bearded live oak trees and palms.

There are several unexpected stops in such towns as Ponchatoula, where nobody gets on or off, except the driver, who perhaps pauses for coffee, or a rest room.

"We're running a few minutes late," says J.L.Moore, who is at the wheel during this final stretch. "Probably be about five minutes late in New Orleans."

He is right. We arrive at 9:37 a.m., instead of the scheduled 9:30, but it is not bad for 850 miles. We are near the Superdome, which looks like some vast thermonuclear tank, or a gigantic mushroom. But like most tourists, I

124

head for the French Quarter with its irresistible Gallic blend of decadence and sanctity. In the nearby Immaculate Conception Church, even the pew backs and sides are of delicate wrought iron.

Already in March, the quarter is throbbing with tourists. St. Charles Square, facing the St. Louis Cathedral, is thronged with artists and looks like the Place du Tertre in Montmartre with its touristy art and sidewalk profilists. Across Decatur Street is a river overlook and the steamboat Natchez is tuning up its calliope at the Toulouse Street Wharf. "Down on the Levee" erupts with an ear-piercing shriek and the music echoes along these crowded, narrow streets.

At noon, several blocks are barricaded and become long and colorful promenades, where people walk, drinking beer out of plastic cups and looking at one another. It is a very French thing to do. There are countless arcades that have been turned into art galleries, and others leading into courtyard cafes, like those of Parisian suburbs. And there is, along these streets, that curious blend of the sacred and the profane, churches on one hand and topless and bottomless nightclubs on the other, bars and ice cream shops, patisseries, hotels, more churches. There is chic sleaze and porn, but a sense of charm, too. It is an old and gracious slum that has been restored and made expensive. It echoes with the beat of jazz, the sound of steamboat whistles, a sense of Bohemianism that is almost gone from our plastic world, but not quite.

My three hours and 23 minutes are up. The bus leaves for home at 1:00 and not at 1:15 as previously announced. New schedules are suddenly in effect and it is advisable to check departure times on arrival. Across the bayous again, Lake Ponchartrain and part of the new road that rides above the unstable ground on its thousands of concrete legs.

At 4:10 p.m. we are in Jackson, Miss., a clean and prosperous looking big town. Fifty-five minutes on the ground and we are off for Memphis again. Scraps of conversation drift up from the passengers.

"You know what I think? I think this country's ripe for a military takeover."

There is a girl from Australia on her way to Calgary. There is another river worker on his way back to his boat at Philadelphia. And more talk.

"Pro hockey, hell, that ain't even worth watching any more. And bowling on television bores me to death."

Now, 8:35 and we are back in Memphis and it looks as if the same people are sitting and waiting in the same seats as the night before. Could that be the same nervous couple chain smoking and hacking away, the same guitar player? Probably not. My face in the mirror, when I shave, looks the same, only more tired. I am already the helpless traveler, at the mercy of other people and afflicted with that vague sense of futility and dejection.

It is not helped by the fact that the trip from Memphis to St. Louis is a local this time. Secondary roads, bumpy and curving. Countless stops. Brakes hissing. The driver has a nervous foot, racing away one moment and letting up the next so that the bus lurches in and out of its planetary gearing all the night through. Sleep is fitful at best, laying back with head against balled up raincoat, then with head wedged onto adjoining seat. Nothing works.

St. Louis again. It's 4:50 in the morning and we are 15 minutes late. We stand in line waiting for the bus to Springfield, soldiers and heroes, sinners and, hopefully, saints. The bus is ready but nothing happens. No call comes. Some people fall out of this queue and into adjacent chairs. Nobody talks. It seems a driver somewhere has overslept. Finally things stir and we leave at last, 50 minutes late, at 5:50.

We are in time for the Peoria connection at Springfield, with enough to spare, in fact, for another bus depot breakfast of sausages, eggs and toast. And onto the Peoria bus. "Hey, you been there and are on the way back already," says the driver, who has obviously slept since I last saw him. I nod wearily and we are off, arriving at Peoria at 9:55 a.m., which is right on time and just 15 minutes short of 48 hours since I left.

It is Thursday, the 10th of March. A touch of spring is in the air. No particular stir at the Reform Club that one can detect, and no one at the Creve Coeur Club has, in fact, the least inkling that this extraordinary adventure has been completed so brilliantly. Through the fatigue, through that disoriented sense of bus lag, the small glow of triumph. Around the Country in 48 Hours. By bus. Move over, Mr. Fogg.

Wilderness Train

Moosonee, Ontario—one of the last of the wilderness train trips stops here, an otherwise inaccessible by land slice of the frontier with lonely, desolate beauty and Monday night football on color T.V.

The train is not, as one might hope, the least bit reminiscent of anything out of Dr. Zhivago. It is rather a high speed, smooth and comfortable luxury train that hits nearly 70 miles per hour on its run through the deep forests of northern Ontario. It is 186 miles from Cochrane, where the highway ends, to Moosonee, at the southern end of James Bay. In summertime (June 21 to Sept. 5) the Polar Bear Express makes the trip in four and a half hours for $18 round trip, and most passengers elect to go up on the morning train and return on the evening.

But the rest of the year, the local covers the same route in roughly six and a half hours, and it stops at tiny villages with only a few houses, where hunters, trappers and a few railroad section hands live their lonely lives.

One hopes for glimpses of moose or bear out the window, but there are none on this particular trip, only miles and miles of forest, so many as to stagger the imagination. Fifty miles north of Cochrane, the train runs through part of the 30,000 acres burned out in June of 1976. The only sign of life is the small purple flowers growing along the forest floor, which look similar to our own Sweet William.

Occasionally there are glimpses of logging operations, at Gardiner, where the Ontario Paper Company cuts 35,000 cords of black spruce annually and keeps a 25,000 cord surplus on hand for emergencies. There are hydroelectric stations, like that at Otter Rapids, 93 miles north of Cochrane, where the fully automated power plant is operated by VHF and microwave signals. But mostly there is that green forest rushing past in its changing pattern of spruce, tamarack and birch, dark and cool and seeming so endless that one speculates wildly on the energy potential of those countless trees.

As the train approaches Moosonee, there is a gradual thinning, a hint of the flat and arid tundra that lies so near to the north. Already there is the unsettling awareness of vast, empty space. The clouds rolling in from Hudson Bay and beyond have an epic grandeur, as if they had been painted for some Wagnerian drama. The tree-lined horizons are as jagged as the teeth of a Swedish bow saw, and there is that lingering suspicion that one's next step might be the first to fall on that particular spot.

Moose Factory Island is one of the two oldest settlements in Ontario. It was founded in 1673 as a Hudson's Bay Company fort by Governor Charles Bayley, the same year that Comte de Frontenac established Kingston as part of New France. The company's staff house, built 150 years ago, remains intact, as does the post manager's trim stucco house, surrounded by a flower garden ablaze with color and a small vegetable plot with its cabbages, carrots and potatoes.

The old St. Thomas Church nearby is a wooden relic from 1860 with elaborate moosehide altar cloths and curious wooden floor plugs. In the past, ice coming down the river in the springtime would pile up along the sandbars, creating a natural dam. Eventually the pressure caused by the backup resulted in avalanches which swept everything in their path, including, on one occasion,

127

the church. Parishoners managed to tow it back into place before the water went down. But to prevent old St. Thomas's from floating away again, the ingenious Anglicans bored holes in the floor. Now, in case of flood, they pull the plugs and let the water in. The church has not left its moorings since.

Out back, in the crowded cemetery, are scores of wooden crosses, many of them unmarked. Among those who sleep here are Capt. George Moore, who spent 40 years in the service of the Hudson's Bay Company, and his son, a sapper with the Canadian Expeditionary Force in World War I, along with McLeods by the dozens and a beloved Indian, Sarah Cheechoo.

In the small museum just down the road, the visitor's log records the presence of people from Wisconsin, Illinois, Frankfurt, Germany, Delaware and California.

But once away from the few tourist attractions, there is, both on Moose Factory Island and on the mainland at Moosonee, a grinding feel of listless poverty and an appalling accumulation of litter and soda cans lining the streets. It is an ironic footnote on the Advertising Council of America's commercial in which the Indian landing his canoe finds a littered land and turns his face, tear running down his cheek, to the camera.

This is Cree Indian land and Crees form more than two thirds the population of the two towns, with their total of about 1,500 people. Some of them work at the 126-bed hospital on Moose Factory, which serves the entire James Bay-Hudson Bay area. Others are fishermen or trappers or guides. A few are section hands on the Ontario Northland Railroad. But many of them do little or nothing.

During the short tourist season and the autumn goose hunting season, some of the Crees make a living running passengers to and from the Moosonee riverfront to Moose Factory Island. They use long Rupert House canoes, which carry surprising amounts of freight, or as many as a dozen passengers. They are the modern version of the great canot du nord, but are powered by 20-hp Johnsons. When nearly empty, they knife across the shallow Moose River, bows high, trailing rooster tails in their wakes. But with Labor Day, the tourist traffic slows to a trickle, revives briefly during goose season, then dies away with the coming of the ice age.

There are two modern lodges in Moosonee. The Moosonee Lodge is owned by the railroad, and there is also the Polar Bear Lodge. Doubles in both are $28 with bath (television is in the lounge overlooking the river, and telephones are in the hall), and dinner prices range from $4.70 for Salisbury steak to $9.50 for sirloin. They are clean and attractive and have more the air of those small European family hotels than American motels.

Both Moosonee and Moose Factory have Hudson's Bay stores, which sell everything from heavy woolen trousers and Levis to groceries and hunting knives. There is a state liquor store at Moosonee, a Chinese restaurant, a general store, a handful of buildings that look like frontier movie sets and a school complex that resembles a prize-winning architectural project. There is also at Moosonee the seat of what may be one of the world's largest Roman Catholic diocese.

It is presided over by Bishop Jules Leguerrier, who was himself a mission priest at Fort Albany, on James Bay to the north, 34 years ago. "We traveled by dogsled then," he said. "And we were elated when we got regular mail service—four times a year." Now his 15 priests cover the wilderness diocese by seaplane, hitching rides with the bush pilots who fly into such outposts as Winish and Fort Severn. The Bishop said his diocese is roughly 900 miles across and 600 miles deep—half a million square miles—covering all of Northern Ontario and parts of Eastern Manitoba and Western Quebec. The area is thinly populated by Cree and Ojibway Indians, all of them, he said, Catholic.

His 7:30 p.m. daily Mass is mostly in Cree, with a little English. The eight or nine women in attendance sing the old Lourdes pilgrim hymn, "Immaculate Mary," in Cree. In their nylon jackets, boots and headscarves, they look like parishoners in almost any ethnic neighborhood. Along the walls, the stations of the cross are in French—"Jesus muert sur la croix"—and the Cree women sing and pray the rosary in a simple chant, like that of Cistercians.

The Bishop is proud of his people. "You know, the explorers got all the credit, Marquette, Raddisson and the others. But everybody forgets it was the Indians, the Crees, who showed them where to go and told them where they were when they got there. All those names, Mississippi, Illinois, Milwaukee, are all Cree names. You know what Chicago means? The place of the skunk."

His church, Christ the King, stands on one of the few streets with sidewalks. They run, conveniently, from the train station to the river-front lodges, roughly six blocks. The Crees often get off to let white visitors pass. They are not unfriendly or subservient, but rather remote. One occasionally finds scrawled anti-white slogans, but there is little overt hostility and even less violence. The Lodge, however, locks its doors at 11 nightly. Only when the Indians get too much to drink do they cause trouble.

Visitors are invariably greeted by what seems to be a puzzling and plaintive query from the small Indian boys along the riverfront. "You goin' over?" they will ask. "You goin' over?" For some it is all the English they know, or will admit to knowing. "Goin' over" refers to the trip to Moose Factory Island in the outboard powered canoes. It costs $2 per person, each way, in the comfortable Rupert House canoes. And the most persistent or most appealing boy inevitably attracts the most passengers to his father's canoe, and the most money.

But September's song signals the end of the passenger business. When the first ice thickens over the river, government helicopters ferry the Indians back and forth from Moose Factory Island to the school, the church, the railroad station. And later, the people of Moosonee and Moose Factory drive back and forth across the ice in their cars, which are limited by lack of roads to local travel only. And winter here comes with a rush.

But the railroad continues. They say it has never been stopped yet by the snow. It has, out of season, some of the characteristics of the old milk train. Two bearded voyagers load their canoe into the baggage car. They have paddled down the Moose River (rivers this far up run to the north) and are returning to their car, parked at Fraserdale or Cochrane. A lady across the aisle with Germanic accent and figure (she is Finnish) is reading *Anna Karenina*. The trees rush past the windows again as we head south, past cold little streams and majestic fast flowing rivers. Something plaintive, unforgettable remains, a combination of that lonely wilderness and desolation, that clean and bracing air, those stunning skies, that appalling litter along the streets, that defeated poverty. It is profound and unsettling and it seems to ask again and again as we head back to our comfortable car, our comfortable life, "You goin' over?"

Larger Places

Galesburg

No place in Galesburg is ever far from Carl Sandburg or the railroads. They still dominate the city, even though the one is reduced to ashes that lie beneath Remembrance Rock and the other so diminished that the old C.B. & Q. depot slumbers through most of the day, its rows of waiting chairs empty, its shoe shine man idle.

You still hear the trains in Galesburg, one of the few towns on two main lines with passenger service on both, but they are mostly freights. There is something about the air or the space that gives to their whistling the sound of distant horns, those of hunters or coachmen. Both lines bisect Main Street and hardly a Galesburger is now alive who has not sat as enormous freights clacked past with suffocating slowness. It is an inescapable fact of life, even for the visitor.

Mornings and evenings bring back some of the excitement of the old days of railroading. Voices echo in the cavernous depot and there is the loud hiss of steam. A train looms out of the distance and Mrs. Florence Skeen's voice announces, "Eastbound Denver Zephyr for Aurora and Chicago on Track 5."

A young man in a tan raincoat pushes an iron-wheeled baggage cart with one suitcase. People on the train sit eating their breakfast staring out at the depot. Then it is gone, fading into the mist and fog to the east, stopping traffic on Main Street only briefly.

Despite the trains and Interstate 74, which bends around to the east, Galesburg has an air of being deep-rooted and somehow changeless. There are miles of brick sidewalks, all laid in herringbone pattern, and the monuments and markers have the long ring of history.

On the lawn beneath the Swedish-Lutheran tower of the Courthouse, is a marker honoring the dead buried in Knox County from the Blackhawk and Seminole Indian Wars, from the Revolution, the War of 1812 and the Mexican War. Nearby a huge statue of Mother Bickerdyke props up a wounded soldier and holds a cup to his lips. Engraved beneath is the quotation "She outranks me," which is attributed to General Sherman. There is an antique French cannon aimed at the north wing of old Whiting Hall, and at the corner, nearly hidden beneath the blossoming bushes, a small plaque, "Tompkins Street. Names for Samuel Tompkins, member of the committee that purchased the site of Galesburg in 1835 and who carried the surveyor's chain while the town was laid out."

Old men sit with canes at their sides in the lobby of the Hotel Custer. On the magazine rack are copies of *Oui, Penthouse,* and *Playboy.* A sign says, "Ask to see the Carl Sandburg suite." The lady at the desk says it is permanently rented. "I don't know why they don't take that sign down." Most of the hotel is rented out now on a permanent basis. It is the last hotel in town. The Arlington is deserted. The Broadview burned years ago.

The sidewalks are long and almost empty. Follow the signs far enough and there is Carl Sandburg's birthplace. A ring of the front doorbell will bring Lauren Goff from his house next door with endless stories about Sandburg and his family and how the house was saved and restored.

"His mother came from Sweden and went to work in Bushnell. His father was a railroad helper and the two met in Bushnell. She followed him back and they got married.

Goff said he was raised in the same neighborhoods as Sandburg and went to the same schools, although at different times.

"This is a unique place, this town. Before Caterpillar settled in Peoria, they tried their best to get in here—on account of the railroads. But the business people were opposed. They knew it would raise the wage scale. Ford wanted to build a big assembly plant, but it was turned down for the same reason. You know, this is one of the few towns in the United States that did not have a bank failure during the Depression."

On the walls are copies of Sandburg's poems. "Look at six eggs, in a mockingbird's nest . . . Look at songs, hidden in eggs." And pictures. Sandburg with the Crown Prince of Sweden. Sandburg in uniform, with Co. C, 6th Illinois Volunteer Infantry during the Spanish American War. The famous heads of Sandburg, photo by Steichen.

"The town was founded in 1837 by the Rev. George Washington Gale from Oneida, New York," Goff said. "Bought thirty thousand acres for a dollar and a quarter an acre. He started Knox and Knox owned the whole town. Yes, and the Ferris wheel was invented by a Galesburg man. Built it for the Columbian Exposition of 1893."

Goff is president of the Sandburg Assn. He talks about how Sandburg studied, how his father thought it was such a waste of time, how the house came to be preserved. A man from St. Louis comes in. There are more stories. Out in back, flanked by evergreens that whisper softly in the spring wind, is the rock under which Sandburg's ashes lie. ". . . for it could be a place to come and remember."

Half a dozen blocks north, the Burlington and Northern Depot is deserted. There are trains morning and evening. In the early afternoon there are only memories. Steam hoses hiss and the long silver tracks stretch into the distance. There are two trains a day in either direction. The board shows the Denver Zephyr arriving at 7:50 a.m. daily, and the Illinois in from Quincy at 7:40, both going east, and the Zephyr at 7:10 p.m. and the Illinois at 8:40, westbound.

Bob Robinson sits by his shoeshine stand, alone. He is the only shoeshine man in town. He has just turned 71 and has been shining shoes pretty close to 50 years, 15 of them at the station. "I come in about nine and stay for about five hours. I do mostly railroad men. Sometimes I do two shines a day, or more. Sometimes none."

Once there were 30 trains a day. Once the New Arlington Hotel across the street was booming. It is no longer a hotel. Its choice corner rooms, with rounded cupolas and three-way view, are vacant and dusty. Bricks are falling away and an old sign advertises telephone services—local and long distance. Its main floor is now a sheet-metal shop and a sign shop.

At the Santa Fe's depot there also are two trains a day in either direction. The depot was dedicated in 1964 and a plaque on the building salutes the city and the cordial relationship between Galesburg and the Santa Fe, dating from the line's first service on Dec. 17, 1887.

Main Street is incredibly wide and clean and has some of the charm of a big small town. There are Swedish names on the stores, some dating back to the 1850s when the colony at Bishop Hill failed and the Swedes moved to Galesburg or Galva. No longer is there diagonal parking, with backing cars that cause traffic to pile up. Only the trains do that now.

You can park for six minutes for a penny. In the Chamber of Commerce's bright new office, executive vice-president George Warren radiates optimism. "We're into a big building program of economic development, working with the Fantus Company of Chicago on a program for the city. There will be a new motel on the square and Sandburg Mall, 350,000 square feet on Henderson south of the Holiday Inn with fifty, sixty small stores. We have an instrument landing system going in at the airport. The sanitary district has completed a seven-million-dollar program. There's a trauma center at St. Mary's Hospital. But the population has stayed about the same in the last ten years. A number of our young people go elsewhere."

Ken Schleifer has been in business at Ken's Coney Island since 1952 and says it's the oldest restaurant in town. From behind the long counter, he pulls a packet of pictures, one showing the corner about 1909 when it was the old Gaiety Theater—"High class vaudeville. Afternoons at 2:30. Evenings at 8." Along one wall is a row of heavy oak school-type chairs with large table-arms. They are part of the original equipment, installed when a Greek family first opened the place around 1921. There are high tin ceilings, a beam that marks the place where the Gaiety lobby used to be. People drink coffee out of thick white mugs. And eat hundreds of hot dogs—600 to 700 on a good day.

In the Hong Lee Chinese Laundry, Lee Au says he wants "noo picture." Neat rows of neatly packaged laundry lie on the shelves. There are few Chinese laundries left in any town. He says he has been there about 30 years or so. He will say no more.

Along Kellogg and Prairie are massive old homes that look like a set from some turn-of-the-century movie. There are ornamental street lamps, wide brick streets and some have hitching posts out front. Not fakes from knick-knack shops, but the real thing.

Henderson Street, known as "The Strip," is a long trail of discount stores and franchise food shops that looks no different from the sprawling, garish streets in scores of towns and cities. But the rest of Galesburg has a uniqueness to it, a big-small town or a small-big one, with a deep sense of stability and long roots.

Huge churches ring the downtown area, old, well kept and obviously well supported. One that goes back a long way is the massive Central Congregational Church, built on land donated by Knox in 1838. The structure today dates from 1895. It towers over the square, solid and ageless. In its cornerstone is a 75-year-old letter by Charles A. Webster, first clerk of the church:

"I have touched hands and talked with soldiers of the wars of the Revolution, 1812 and Mexico. I have lived through the excitement and anguish of 1861-65 in which my brother and my older companions bore arms. I have toiled and suffered in the heroic struggles of my time and my weary eyes turn longingly toward the golden age of the future. God grant that it may soon come, and that you may be living in a better, purer and happier constitution of society than the present; that legislators may be patriotic and incorruptible; business men honest and humane; church members religious when your eyes rest upon these pages, and that poverty, oppression and drunkenness may have long passed from the earth."

In Corpus Christi Church a few blocks away, the candles flicker softly and the doors have anti-abortion posters. On one is the picture of a baby and the words, "Never to laugh or love or taste the summertime . . .?" Another says, "That aborted child could have been you."

Away from Main and Henderson streets, the town seems strangely quiet, and even on the campus at Knox there is no rush nor hurry. From the courts comes the soft thunk of tennis balls. Students cross the wide grassy campus slowly. Mother Bickerdyke holds the cup to the soldier's lips for as long as statues last. From far off the sound of a freight whistle floats across the spring air. Red lights wink on and the traffic begins to back up along Main Street.

Atop Old Main, where Lincoln debated Douglas and where Carl Sandburg once looked down a line of old elms raised like a Gothic arch, the bell marks the passing of another hour.

Schaumburg

On the maps that detail the great urban spread north and west of Chicago, Schaumburg is another pale orange spot, looking vaguely like a computer chip wired onto a line running between Evanston and Elgin. It is not to be found on the big Illinois highway map, wedged as it is into what is called the "Golden Corridor," that booming panhandle of Cook County. And in a curiously ominous way it seems to be a glimpse into the future.

On the surface, Schaumburg would seem to have everything a progressive urban community could possibly desire. Here is Woodfield, the world's biggest mall, bigger than Vatican City and mecca for hundreds of thousands of shoppers from a vast circle stretching half a day's journey away.

This is an area of such growth and prosperity that the population signs at the edge of town not only do not agree (one reads 47,000, another 50,000) but have special bolt-on sections so that numbers may be updated more easily. Its progress has become legendary.

It has been predicted that Schaumburg will become the second largest city in Illinois by the turn of the century—far earlier if what one sees is to be believed. For as far as the eye can reach there is new construction—homes, townhouses, condominiums, apartment buildings, more shopping centers and office buildings rising on the good black earth once tilled by German farmers.

Schaumberg and its neighbor, Hoffman Estates (37,500) have 10 village shopping centers, four swimming pools, three golf courses, two skateboard parks and a median family income of nearly $27,000.

Schaumburg has 28,000 registered vehicles—a car for every 1.8 citizens, and land sells for as much as $2 per square foot. And virtually everything is new: schools, homes, streets, office buildings, sewers, even the trees, straight and orderly saplings planted in neat rows along the winding curbing. This, clearly, is what growth is all about.

So, too, it might be noted, is cancer, although this is almost perfectly planned and controlled. The vision of the computer chip will not go away. For what one seeks vainly here is a past, a heritage, a sense of roots, of continuity. There is almost none. It has been wiped away, paved over, obliterated.

Schaumburg seems to have sprung full blown from the brow of the same designer who created Mattel toys and Ken and Barbie houses. There is no downtown as such—Woodfield Mall is downtown—nor are there slums. The historic center of town is at the intersection of Schaumburg and Roselle Roads, site of such relentless traffic that it is hardly possible to appreciate its significance. Nor is it worth it. There is a real estate office in an old building at the corner. There are a few old houses and a 1930s vintage gas station. Down the street is St. Peter's Lutheran Church, the one genuine landmark, with a building dating from 1863 and a peaceful cemetery along side where the founders and early parishioners sleep into another clamorous spring.

These came from Schaumburg-Lippe in Saxony in the 1830s, refugees from Prince Metternich's repressive policies, and they founded what was to become an all-German community. English was almost unknown. As recently as the turn of the century it was called the only exclusive German settlement in the United States. By 1965 there were about 150 farm families living here and they incorporated their village in order to protect it from the encroachment of the newly developed Hoffman Estates.

Then came the boom times. Slowly at first. Country singing star Bob Atcher (Smilin' Bob Atcher from the WGN National Barn Dance) moved to Schaumburg in 1965 seeking the legendary peace and quiet of the country. He soon realized he was too late. It couldn't last.

There was O'Hare Field to the east. Then came the Northwest Tollway and Interstate 90, right past Schaumburg's front door. People were sure to follow, and they did, fleeing to the suburbs from the crime and deterioration of their old Chicago neighborhoods.

Atcher as mayor was the formulator of Schaumburg's master plan, an urban wonder, which allotted specific percentages to residential, retail, industry. The town's 25 square miles were cut as carefully as a Thanksgiving pie—20 percent for commerce and industry, 60 percent for single family homes, the rest for apartments, townhouses and condominiums.

The plan was all inclusive, right down to the prescribed size for storm and sewer pipes, and it provided that the developers should build and maintain the streets. In exchange for tax breaks, developers also gave the village its school sites, three fire stations and the municipal and public service buildings.

Schaumburg has no municipal taxes, only a $7 annual car sticker fee. Residents pay property taxes to county, schools and park districts, but Schaumburg's major income is from the sales tax, which amounts to $7 million a year. (Peoria's sales tax, for 1978, was $8.6 million.)

There is a rare self-sufficiency at work here. Mayor Ray Kessell has been quoted as saying that the village has become self-generating, for with more people there is more disposable income and with more disposable income there is a need for more retail stores where the money can be spent, and the more money that is spent, the more money comes back to the village. It is a theory that would seem not to work on paper, but it does in reality.

If there is a single reason for it to work, it lies in the presence of Woodfield Mall, which brings some 50,000 shoppers a day (150,000 on weekends) into its 2.2 million square feet to account for much of the $1.3 million daily retail sales.

The mall was the brainchild of A. Alfred Taubman of the Taubman Co. in Troy, Michigan (potential developers of Peoria's downtown mall). Taubman decided after detailed and prolonged studies that the mall in Schaumburg would come at the right place and at the right time. It was named for General Robert E. Wood, former chairman of Sears, and Marshall Field, and it has become one of the wonders of the merchandising world.

It covers 191 acres. Vatican City, by comparison, covers 108.7, the Louvre a mere 40 acres. Its parking lot has space for almost 11,000 cars. There are 235 stores, anchored at the four corners by Penney's, Lord & Taylor, Sears, and Marshall Field. Inside are shops and stores which range from the Boudin Bakery, which sells a heavy, San Francisco sourdough French bread, to Frederick's of Hollywood with its exotic lingerie, from the Magic Pan Creperie to F.A.O. Schwartz toys, an ice rink, and the kind of shops that are found in hundreds of malls—Just Pants, B. Dalton, Jean Nicole, Thom McAn . . .

The Chicago Sympjony Orchestra played here and drew a crowd estimated at 40,000. Christmas shopping brings up to 150,000 in a day. More than a hundred tour buses draw up each morning and leave women shoppers for the day. People want to come here not because it is the grandaddy of malls, but because it is the biggest, the champion.

137

But for all its sculpture, waterfalls, ramps, rest areas, restaurants, specialty shops and people watching opportunities, it does not differ essentially from the basic suburban mall, except that it is admirably designed and does not seem to be quite so large as the figures would imply.

Meanwhile, the Woodfield area, just off the expressway, has become a centerpiece for future growth. There are still cornfields to be seen and here and there a silo, a barn. But they are passing. Among the new projects, new buildings planned is Woodfield 76, a $300 million urban development to be completed around 1995. It will include a cultural center which will, it is claimed, rival Lincoln Center.

Perhaps.

Meanwhile, Schaumburg, with all its excellent schools, tax advantages, new homes and constant growth, is like the Tinman from *The Wizard of Oz*, desperately in need of a heart, a soul. It is a suburb in search of a center, 50,000 characters in search of an author, an instant city in search of a past. There are moves to preserve what is left, although it is precious little, and to keep a portion of field, trees, woods—some evidence of heritage and continuity.

For now it is as if the surface has been peeled back, the past stripped away, and everything paved over, sodded, neatly landscaped, clean, prosperous, secure, healthy . . . and sterile.

If Schaumburg is, in this respect, a glimpse of the urban future, it ought perhaps to be observed, not as a model, but as a warning.

Springfield: Abe Lincoln Sleeps Here

Springfield—one quickly reaches the conclusion here that Lincoln and the state government dominate the city, that without them it would be another town out on the prairie, and that the two have converged in a unique and permanent fusion, even though the one is past and the other always present.

Lincoln's presence is that of a hallowed martyr, a secular saint, and his myths and legends go straight to bedrock. The government is, by contrast, a simple and powerful economic and political reality, the major employer, which gives to the city much of its vitality, its drive, its sense of purpose.

"Take the government out of here and what have you got?" said one long-time Springfielder. "You've got just another country town, that's what."

Could be. But what other town is so uniquely Lincoln's and still a state capital? This rare combination of historical presence and governmental power makes Springfield in its way like a small Washington, and yet with a distinctive character all its own. No one can adequately appraise how much money and power and influence flow in and out of this governmental seat of the fifth most populous state, but it is easier perhaps to assess the continuing impact of Lincoln.

The grand and ornate capitol, to be sure, draws its hordes of school children, lobbyists, demonstrators, newsmen, influence peddlers, senators and more, all contributing to a heady and exciting ferment. But there remains to this an intrastate nature, whereas the Lincoln presence draws visitors from everywhere.

For there are, on this April morning, in the parking lot before Lincoln's tomb in Oak Ridge, one Illinois car, two from Indiana and one each from Utah, Iowa, Wisconsin and Michigan. It is long before the travel season, but a good time to be here, before the crowds, before that awful heat of summer. And now the flowering trees of another springtime add their soft perfume to the air and soften the sting of death.

People stand silently inside this dark marble tomb, staring at the flag-draped marble slab where Lincoln lies. Over a million visitors a year, they say. And many of them inevitably rub parts of the statues here for good luck. The nose of the famous Gutzon Borglum head outside is worn smooth and bright. So is the head of the Circuit Rider's horse, the feet of the replica of Daniel Chester French's famous work from the Lincoln Memorial in Washington.

And in that cool tomb is the inscription, "Now he belongs to the ages." The words are those of Lincoln's Secretary of War Edwin W. Stanton. Prophetic words, indeed, for the ages so far have accepted Springfield's Mr. Lincoln with wide open arms.

Outside the redbuds are open and drift like smoke from a spring campfire across the greening valleys and hillsides. Already some of the graves of the Union dead who lie nearby are sprinkled with fallen blossoms, as if from passing bridesmaids. This was, for better or worse, Mr. Lincoln's war, and his troops are sown thickly hereabouts, and at nearby Camp Butler. All of these, too, belong to the ages.

But Lincoln belongs to the people in a multitude of ways, not all of them expected. It seems that virtually everything that does not walk or breathe here is named after Lincoln, and lots of things which do move and breathe.

Hardly does one clear the iron gates of Oak Ridge when there is the Lincoln Souvenir Shop and the Ann Rutledge Pancake House. Lincoln's name is everywhere, on banks and offices, churches, car lots, taverns . . .

And yet Lincoln is honored much more fittingly with an honest and careful preservation and restoration of the places where he lived and worked. There is a walking tour which leads visitors to such points as the Ninian Edwards Home where Lincoln and Mary Todd were married, to the Lincoln Wax Museum, the Lincoln Depot, and so on. But the best of these are Lincoln's Home at 8th and Jackson, and the old state capitol.

The home, a still handsome Greek Revival wooden building, is the only one Lincoln ever owned. Half a million people a year troop through here. They stare at the room where Lincoln slept and at the adjoining one where Mary occupied her smaller bed, at the maid's room, the kitchen. Some of the furnishings are original, but most of them were in a Chicago museum and were destroyed in the great fire. The carpeting is replaced every two years and the house is closed only at Christmas and New Year. It is in an area where there are brick sidewalks, board walks and flickering gas lanterns and no cars.

The old capitol, recently remodeled, is a marvel of historic restoration, so detailed and authentic that even the wax drippings of the candles seem to have come from some long session which dragged on yesterday evening. It all seems ready to come back to life as it was a hundred and more years ago. There are ashes beneath the stoves. There are papers of the era on the legislators' desks, eyeglasses, steel nibbed pens. They are, it appears, merely out for a short recess.

The guides are helpful, taciturn, witty. "Ought to give these modern legislators two dollars a day like they used to here," says one. "Then cut it to a dollar a day after forty-four days. Then we'd sure as hell get something done."

The modern lawmakers are paid considerably more. And during this opening period of the spring session in the newly refurnished capitol, not a great deal is getting done. Each desk in the impressive Senate chamber

blooms with a potted boquet of flowers from the Illinois State Flourists' Association ("We Care"). A lady senator is eating huge wedges of watermelon at her desk and another senator twirls a long cigar and stares intently high up at the wall. Someone is speaking about keeping employees in Illinois . . . "or we're going to have a desert here. We have been so good to the workingman we kill him with kindness."

Impassioned as the oratory is, it elicits little interest or attention. Senators laugh and clap one another on the back. One wears sunglasses beneath the new lighting system. The chairs, which reportedly cost $480 each, have not yet arrived, but the chamber is otherwise resplendent, beautifully decorated, tastefully restored, firm and solid.

Outside, the school buses wait while a class poses with their elected representatives on the capitol steps. The session ends and senators and secretaries stream toward the State Office Building, many of them carrying their flowers from the Florists Association.

There is a tunnel leading from the capitol to the office building and it symbolizes, in a way, the narrowly circumscribed lives many legislators live while here. Many of them have a kind of tunnel vision about Springfield itself, for they are bounded by chambers and offices by day and a few selected nearby spots at night. Most of them see little more of it than do the motorists who sweep past on Interstate 55 to the east—the soaring silver dome that towers high above the empirical splendor of the capitol and the tall, thin shaft of Forum 30.

But Springfield has its other side. It is a city of just under 100,000, and there are no great surprises to be found out there. The state employs most of the people—16,275, according to the Greater Springfield Chamber of Commerce. Fiat-Allis employs 3,900, more or less, Illinois Bell just under 2,000, Sangamo Electric about 1,350 and Franklin Life Insurance another 1,160. Employment elsewhere is numbered in the hundreds or in the dozens.

But out there away from the shopping centers and fast franchise food operations are some most gracious and appealing areas. Near Washington Park, some of the brick streets are lined with high old trees, big homes from the 20s and 30s and a look reminiscent of an Andy Hardy set. Inside the park, joggers plod slowly in their grim and searing run for life. Nearby is the tall slab of the Thomas Rees Memorial Carillon, third largest in the world.

The bridge across Spaulding Dam at the end of Lake Springfield looks faintly like one of those triumphal bridges that span the Tiber at Rome. The eastern shore is dotted with private clubs and golf courses and the headquarters of the summer Municipal Opera. Along the western edges of the lake is a road lined with tall sycamores and cool pines. There are large homes with immense lawns and sudden glimpses of sparkling water in the sunlight, like that of some distant and exclusive Wisconsin resort.

As the original Rt. 66 has been replaced by 66 bypass and now by I-55, there has been growth that is almost archeological, and one passes from one to the next with the feeling of encountering various civilizations, or at least decades.

Out on I-55 there are glimpses of the clean, glittering and familiar chain motels, the sweeping ribbons of concrete, the graceful Department of Transportation Building with its pond, and the small piece of Lake Springfield, all of it looking modern, functional, high speed. Only a few blocks to the west, along U.S. 66, are the 40s and 50s again, little family-owned motels such as the Shamrock and the Shady Rest, the truck stops from another time, the used car lots.

One of these is the Top $ Value Motors, which deals exclusively in used state equipment, selling dump trucks, state cars, tractors, acquired at auction and rehabilitated. Not much of their business is from Springfield, say owners Mitchell and Dave Brown, but they have a lot of customers in Peoria.

Farther on at the state fairgrounds are 300 cars, most of them former state police cruisers, that will be auctioned off May 5—as is. There are 366 acres here and this is said to be the largest state fair in the country. For 10 days. The rest of the year it is largely empty. Now there is windblown dust from the large oval track, a few horses whinnying in the stables. The rest of these acres and these buildings are deathly silent.

"Mary Hartman, Mary Hartman" is on at noon in a nearby tavern and bearded workers sit at the crowded tables watching. Only April, but already hot. An air conditioner purrs away nearby and the workers lean forward to hear what Mary is saying. Springfield, like Washington and St. Louis, has a reputation for being a hot and humid town. July's daily humidity is 80 at 6 a.m. and 82 at 6 p.m. and the maximum average daily temperature for July is 82.5.

Used to be hot here in different ways. Jack Maloney remembers the days when bootlegging was big and the slots were in. He says he had five different places in town over a period of years, all known as Jack Maloney's Shamrock. He remembers shaking hands with King Albert of Belgium at 4th and Jefferson, right near the St. Nicholas Hotel. That was in the 1920s. He remembers his father, a huge man, whipping the famous Jack Johnson in a fight at the fairgrounds. "Nearly killed him," he says.

The slot machines are gone and so is prohibition. Only memories now and a few trappings, such as those in the Chicago Speakeasy of Forum 30, a 20s type bar reached either throuth a telephone booth or past a reconstructed alley filled with 55-gallon gin and rye drums.

Downtown tends to die at night, almost as much as Peoria's, But in the daytime, it is pleasant, particularly along the Old Capitol Mall, with its shady brick walks and shops, the lobby of the Illinois National Bank with its exquisite hanging gardens, around the new capitol with its fountains and statues, even within the Illinois State Museum and its unique combination of art, science and history. Vachel Lindsay's home is nearby and the restored governor's mansion, and there persists that sense of vitality, of old things being saved and remodeled and new ones rising, the one complementing the other.

There is now a new four-lane road that sweeps into town from Capital Airport (spelled "Capitol" on the maps) with elaborate pole-type lamps down the median and extensive planting going on. The route leads past Oak Ridge where the soul of Springfield lies beneath the ballustrades and obolisk of that ornate tomb of Lincoln's, to the soaring capitol of Piquenard with its curious combination of classical and Parisian architecture, which is the heart of Springfield.

Lincoln left on Feb. 11, 1861, bidding his townspeople an affectionate farewell, and returned in the black draped funeral train four years later. Since then, Springfield has never been the same.

St. Louis

The lights of St. Louis are burning with uncommon brilliance these summertime days of 1977. Probably not since 1904, when Andrew B. Sterling
helped celebrate the St. Louis Exposition by writing "Meet Me in St. Louis,"
has there been such a glow of optimism hereabouts.

The city is booming, renewing itself, prospering. It draws more conventioners than New York City. Its downtown is safe, friendly and clean. And
while the building boom that started with the Gateway Arch and Busch Stadium goes on and on, there is a new attention to old neighborhoods. The rush
to the suburbs that left the town empty and dispirited has slowed, and St.
Louis is back in business.

It is not precisely a miracle, but a good omen. For what has happened
here represents what countless other cities are waiting for even yet. Something to save the town.

St. Louis was badly in need of saving. It was grimy and inert back in the
40s and 50s, slowly decaying in the haze and heat of long, watermelon summers. Something of a feeling of despair here then, that particularly urban depression articulated by Tennessee Williams in *The Glass Menagerie,* with all
those hot brick houses and bleak streets, neon lights blinking through muggy,
restless nights, saxaphones wailing, and, somewhere, a far off train whistle. It
seemed a dead town.

From 1931 to 1958 it was pretty much downhill. The city seemed to
empty out and the lights were down to a mere flicker.

No longer. The city's Gateway Arch has become not only a logo, almost
as readily identifiable with St. Louis as the Eiffel Tower is with Paris, but a
sign of hope, a symbol of the renaissance. With it and Busch Stadium, the new
I-55 bridge that sweeps traffic in from Illinois almost as easy as pie, it all began
to come together. Parking decks arose, hotels, insurance buildings, modern,
mirrored and glassy, and then a convention center and a soaring sense of con-
fidence and pride. St. Louis is back on the map in ways the 1904 exhibitors
never imagined.

It has not all been down with the old and up with the new, either. Ancient
neighborhoods have been reclaimed, lost, reclaimed again. A dozen years ago,
Gaslight Square blossomed briefly as one of the earlier redevelopment projects with its turn-of-the-century motif. And while it faded, the idea remained
so much alive that the newest of the redeveloped commercial areas is the oldest part of the city, that which lies along the waterfront just north of the Arch
and is known as Laclede's Landing.

It is named after Pierre Laclede Liquest, founder of St. Louis. The landing grew up around Laclede's trading post around 1764. It now contains the
last group of buildings surviving in St. Louis from the post-Civil War period.

In one of them is the Lounsbury-Donohue gallery with its interiors and
fine arts. It is reminiscent of one of New York's Soho lofts, but finished better, with impeccable taste. "This is the only thing left of old St. Louis," says
Barbara Lounsbury, who cleaned out what had been a warehouse to make
room for the gallery. The city has offered her and other tenants a tax defer-
ment for refurbishing these old buildings. Her windows, she said, were so
blackened with soot of the years that they had to be cleaned with acid. It was
unoccupied for a year and a half, and a mess.

The gallery is one of the first new businesses to locate in Laclede's Landing. Also moving in is the Bi-State Development Agency, which operates the transit system of Greater St. Louis as well as the unique train-type elevators in the Gateway Arch. Also new is the Old Spaghetti Factory, an elaborately baroque restaurant filled with old wood, stained glass and magnificent junk. The most expensive item on its menu is a dish of tenderloin slices with a side order of spaghetti for $4.50. Beer comes by the pitcher for $1.25 and wine by the carafe at $1.65. It is located in a cast iron fronted factory that was completed in 1874, same year as the famous Eads Bridge, and is now a national historic landmark.

This is an appealing area. Some sidewalks are tree-lined and have lantern style streetlamps. The blacktopping has been peeled away and the streets are now the way they used to be, roughly cobblestoned. The scent of anise drifts down like a bracing perfume from the Switzer Candy Co., nearby. Many of the old buildings still have fading remnants of signs advertising cotton, burlap bags, hides—echoes of the great riverfront days that pulsed with the hooting of steam whistles and the thrashing of paddlewheels.

A mile to the south is a different type of salvage operation. The St. Louis Redevelopment Authority has fenced off 55 houses in nine blocks and designated it an urban preservation area. These are old townhouses, built by merchants when St. Louis was still young. Solid red brick, most of them, with high ceilings and elaborately carved woodwork. Some of them have mansard roofs and chimney pots, like some older section of Paris, the rue de Faubourg Saint-Denis, or the Marais. They were all condemned back in the 40s, but indoor plumbing was installed and the area fought back for a while, but fell again. Now the houses are being offered to private buyers for as little as $1,500 with the stipulation that they must be restored.

Dean Pruitt and his father Charles are in the process of rebuilding one of these buildings. It is a long and painful job, for they are, in many cases, little more than shells. Pruitt figures when he is finished he will have a home and apartment worth $80,000 in an area that could become as exclusive and attractive as the Georgetown section of Washington.

For now it is still a dream. Most of the houses are still boarded up, the alleys empty, the yards overgrown, the alianthus trees drooping in the hot wind. Traffic drones past on the freeway, but one can almost hear in these ghostly streets the cries of peddlers, umbrella menders, knife sharpeners.

"Renew, Save, Rebuild," the apparent motto of the St. Louis Redevelopment Authority, seems to have fallen on receptive ears through much of the town. Nine years ago, the St. Louis Symphony—second oldest in the nation—elected to move out of Keil Auditorium because of the noise from basketball or bowling on the other side of the partition. Instead of building a new hall, it settled into the remodeled St. Louis Theater on Grand Avenue. It became Powell Hall, 2,690 seats, and a magnificent European type concert hall with superb acoustics and a high baroque decor that can no longer be duplicated.

Also being preserved, although its ultimate fate remains in question, is the Union Station, called one of the most beautiful buildings in the world when it was completed in 1894. It was supposedly copied after the architecture of Carcassone in Southern France, and looks, even now, like some enormous chateau dropped smack in the middle of an American city. It is filled with stained glass and French renaissance splendor, much of it crumbling now.

The floor of the King Louis Room is littered with fallen plaster. The great waiting room is empty and silent. There are few ticket buyers in the downstairs Amtrak area, desecrated by an ill-advised modernization project in the 1940s. A lady behind the ticket counter points out pillars that have been covered with wood, walls that have been altered, the floor. "The original is still underneath," she says. "And they're going to put it back the way it was."

Once there were 175 trains a day in and out of here. In 1945, 71,444 trains cleared the terminal and one sixth of the world's population passed through the depot. At least it is still here. And it is best seen from the front, at night, through the Carl Milles soaring and triumphant fountain which depicts the wedding of the Mississippi and Missouri Rivers. It remains a magic, splendid sight.

The old is here ecclesiastically, too, and the new. The old is represented by the original St. Louis Cathedral near the Arch, with its simple, honest, New Englandish looks, and the new by the St. Louis Cathedral, halfway out Lindell Boulevard. It is the second largest Byzantine dome in the world. Inside it is glittering and splendid with its gold mosaics and jewel-like windows glowing with the fire of the morning sun.

Farther west, along the perimeters of Forest Park, are the private streets, some with gates that were closed and locked at night. Solid and entrenched wealth here, a feeling of the ancienne regime. The streets are cool, remote and shaded, the houses stunning in their magnificence and even the coach houses, now garages, reflect a bygone style now almost out of reach.

Forest Park is an urban treasure, 1,700 acres of rolling green woods and field, bisected by winding roads that accomodate cars, bicyclists, joggers. They lead from areas of primeval wilderness to the Art Museum, where a Claes Oldenburg three-way electric plug stands hard by St. Louis himself, triumphant on his charger. Here, too, is the St. Louis Zoo, famous long before Marlin Perkins's "Wild Kingdom" and boasting the longest miniature railway in America, the Jefferson Memorial with its history of St. Louis and the westward expansion, the McDonnell Planetarium, and the Municipal Opera.

The Opera grew famous doing grand, schmaltzy operettas, "Naughty Marietta," "The Student Prince" and "The Song of Norway." It veered for a time into an outdoor concert format, but is now back to musicals. This summer it opens with "Hello Dolly" with Carol Channing, followed by "Finian's Rainbow," "Meet Me in St. Louis," "The Sound of Music," "Kismet," "Porgy and Bess" and "Sweet Charity."

People come here in summertime for the opera, for the baseball Cardinals in Busch Stadium, for the amusement park Six Flags Over Mid-America with its Screamin' Eagle rollercoaster, the world's longest and fastest (a 92-foot drop and 62-miles-per-hour speeds). But there is another reason for the attraction of St. Louis, and it may have to do with a certain warmth and friendliness that makes the city less oppressive and hostile than many of our big cities. People here have a slower approach to things that is part southern, and they are willing to stop and talk.

Here is Sam Westbrook, sitting on the coping of the abandoned downtown post office. His face has the look of polished ebony. He is smoking the stump of a cigar. His voice is high and reedy, almost flutelike. "Married? Oh, no. Married life is sweet, but single life can't be beat," he says. He comes down to sit and watch the people. Summer and winter. Summer is better.

He used to be a porter at a tavern and bookie joint and is now retired. People call out to him as they pass, white and black, and he waves back. Over his head the flagpoles of the abandoned building are empty. Nobody seems to know what will become of it. To some it is an eyesore, to others a historic treasure. It will keep. Sam says it is a good place to sit. He says he learned the secret of getting along years ago in Mississippi. "Yes, sir, Yes m'am and Yes, please."

On a nearby corner Ollie May and Jim Morris, selling the *Post-Dispatch*. "We sell about two hundred and fifty-five papers a day," Morris says. He makes six cents a paper, plus tip. He has been working the same corner since last December, cold weather and hot. Summer is better.

More friendly people at the Crown Candy Kitchen at 14th and St. Louis Avenue, a 1940 era soda fountain which sells homemade ice cream for $1.60 a quart and where the toppings are made by the 85-year-old Greek grandfather. People are willing to stop what they are doing and talk, here, at the Lounsbury-Donohue gallery, at the Spaghetti Factory, at the old home the Pruitts are re-modeling.

Summertime. The school buses pour into town for baseball games, for Six Flags, the zoo, the riverfront. The steamboat Admiral heads the riverfront flotilla. It is the largest steel-hull sightseeing boat on the river, gleaming and silver in its modern shell. Nearby are two smaller sightseeing boats, with lines of schoolchildren stretching from their bus to the gangplank, like a long hawser, and there is a Mississippi River Showboat, a World War II minesweeper, a helicopter pad and a steamboat restaurant.

And at night, at the baseball game, the crowd seems different, more relaxed. This is not the old-fashioned umpire-baiting crowd from Wrigley Field or Yankee Stadium, but more genial and goodnatured. Even the policeman outside agrees to tear up a parking ticket since we have parked just inside a no parking zone. "I'll take it back after the game," he says. "Otherwise some other cop will come along and give you another one."

Inside, an usher keeps moving people out of reserved seats into the general admission area, accomplished without hostility or resentment. There are people eating sunflower seeds and drinking wine out of a goatskin. A policeman says he has worked the stadium for four years and remembers only two incidents. "Most of the trouble is when the Cubs are in town," he says. It is possible to buy a pound and half of beer (on draft) at the stadium for $1.50.

Afterwards the policeman who has removed the ticket from the car waves as if we are old friends. The hotel is just across the street from the stadium, the Breckenridge Plaza, where a double costs $47 for two and a buffet style breakfast (sausages, bacon, eggs, rolls, milk, coffee, juice, prunes, melon, grapefruit, etc.) is $3.95.

Early afternoon at the Missouri Botanical Garden. Elderly women in summer dresses climb slowly into a jeep-pulled train, pass the sculpture of Henry Moore and Alexander Calder, and wind through these 79 acres of exquisitely tended plantings, including the newly opened Japanese Garden with its 4-acre lake, three islands and two waterfalls. Known as Shaw's Garden, it is the legacy of Henry Shaw, a hardware dealer who retired at 39 a century ago and spent the rest of his life developing his country home and botanical garden.

Bellefontaine Cemetery is a different kind of garden, although nearly as well maintained. Whole fleets of Kubota tractors with mowers hum across its rich turf and trimmers by the score work around its trees and monuments. It is imposing, immaculate. Here are the great names of St. Louis and those unknown outside their own families, the Lindell obolisk, the doctor for whom the Barnes medical complex is named, a gem of a mausoleum with a fleche like that of Ste. Chapelle in which Adolphus and Lilly Busch, brewer and wife, repose with the words "Veni—Vide—Vici"—I came, I saw, I conquered.

Far overhead, a jet floats in toward the Lambert-St. Louis International Airport. More conventioners arriving. Traffic flows steadily across the I-55 Bridge and its maze of ramps, bringing in more people for baseball, the zoo, the opera. School buses. Trucks. Cars. The good old summertime and good old St. Louis sounds here. A mighty blast from the steam whistle of the Admiral. The crack of a bat and the roar of the crowd and the voice of Jack Buck rising in excitement from thousands of transistor radios. "Hello, Dolly, well hello, Dolly" in Forest Park. The trumpeting of elephants. Girls on the Screamin' Eagle shrieking. The little steam train at Six Flags huffing into the recreated 1904 depot. "Meet Me in St. Louis, Louis" they are singing, and the lights are up again. Best in summertime. The livin' is easy. And for most people in St. Louis, it is very good this summer of '77.

Peoria East Bluff: We Thought It Was the Best Place in Town

We thought this was the best place in town.

This East Bluff.

There were the hills and playing fields of Glen Oak Park where we practiced football in the autumns and skated on the lagoon in the wintertime, clumping into the coal stove heat of the warming house on our tubular hockey skates. There were woods along the bluffs, intriguing and mysterious with their narrow footpaths and their vague and nameless fears about the gangs from down in the valley. There were a hundred alleys to explore where we sometimes unearthed such spectacular treasures as an ironing board, a brass lamp, a broken wagon with ball bearing wheels.

And all those little stores, one every few blocks, one across from every school, where the storekeeper or his wife would pluck boxes of Grape Nuts or Quaker Oats off high shelves with long hooks. And where we bought penny packs of firecrackers in the summertime when that sporadic, explosive rattle swelled toward its magnificent July crescendo. We thought the Argonne must have sounded like this. And we worked long and hard in our basements, fashioning bits of balsa and tissue paper into Spads and Fokkers, checking the dihedral carefully against the plans, then winding them up and letting them fly for what was a pathetically short existence, like that of Mayflies, like that of children.

We thought this was the best place in town.

The East Bluff looks almost the same these days as it always has. A little older, a little more faded, but not appreciably changed. Wisconsin is still its Main Street, and Wisconsin and Kansas its center, fixed there immutably by St. Bernard's on the one hand, and Glen Oak School on the other. True, the big Kroger and Super X complex, farther out, does more business and has all the parking, but it is a miniature version of what happens to the city and its downtown and the far out malls and shopping centers. The one has tradition, the other parking.

"No, I don't think the neighborhood has gone to hell," says Joe Weber, who has his barbershop on Wisconsin, just across from what used to be the No. 10 Firehouse, and has been there 38 years. "I'd say it's held its own. Sure, all the little stores have gone right along here—the Royal Blue, Larry's market, Leo Gorenz's Market and the Kroger store where Thills are now—but some of the people are still here."

Some of them are fixtures, firm, unchanging. One is the Wisconsin Tap, run by Eddie and Joe Bartolo since 1938. Joe remembers that the place across the street, later Green's Drug Store, used to be the Boerckle Garage, where they sold Kissel cars. "Yes, and George Welzenbach ran the Glen Oak Bakery. He got out and moved to California and Tilton had it for a while. Then a laundromat moved in there. A lot of old timers have left. You know, I don't think we ever had to call the police once in all these years."

Fixtures. Another is George Pople, tapping his way along Wisconsin outside Haddad's Market. He has been blind since birth and has lived at 1010 E. Nebraska for years, in a house he was able to buy following an accident settlement.

"I was standing out on the street waiting for the streetcar when I got hit

by this car and was thrown fifty feet," he says. "Broke my arms and legs."
He says he worked at Caterpillar repairing safety equipment, retiring after 30
years and seven months. He still sings in the Orpheus Club.

Down Kansas is St. Bernard's, its oddly Burgundian bell tower dominating the area, rising green and weathered above the treetops like a sceptre, a
magnet. Father Maurice Sammon (known as Baggy) built this church out on
the cornfields and ruled it for years like some ecclesiastical feifdom, creating
enormous affection and abiding faith with his blend of iron hard discipline and
powerful concern. Rich and memorable smells here yet, of incense and beeswax candles and altar wine. Memories of early mornings, slipping into cassock and surplice, the Hinners organ peeling forth, of tall candles guttering
beside burnished coffins, ancient chants, ancient words.

*"Qui pridie quam pateretur, accepit panem in sanctas ac venerabiles
manus suas . . ."*

And the smells at the school are the same as they always have been, that
timeless blend of children and Crayolas and Carter's paste which creates its
own distinctive memory-provoking essence. Mine are of heavy corduroy and
dropping woolen socks, of the janitor we all knew as Pop Scurry, yelling at us
to get out of the basement, of a sister asking who won the playground fight
and then rewarding me with a swift kick in the rear, the Filipinos coming in
the green of springtime with their Duncan Yo-Yo's and their techniques,
which must have derived from some Oriental wizardry.

And playing marbles after school on mud driveways with aggies, steelies,
glassies and the cheapest marbles of all, which appeared to be made from fired
clay. Crouched, one knee down, eyeing and aiming, letting fly, and sometimes
making one of those dead center hits in which one marble would replace another. Then dusk and mothers calling us from the deepening shadows: "Time
for supper. Supper."

"Just one more game, huh?"

Roller skating, too, down the sidewalks on iron wheels and on the
smooth asphalt surface of LaSalle Street, where I lived and where there were
hardly any cars. Scabby knees in the springtime from the falls, and later
from summer evening games of kick the can. Always a proper time for skates
and another for bouncing tennis balls off the front porch steps. A special
time for water pistols and rubber gun wars, marbles and soap box racers, making
lead soldiers, for model airplanes and the Wheaties boxtop premiums. Nothing
said so on the calendar. We knew.

We thought it was the best place in town.

A small world, this, and for many it encompassed two or three square
blocks, church, school, and one of those neighborhood stores. There were cisterns in the back yards and the garbage men came down the alley driving horses before gondola-like trailers. People put ICE signs in their windows, turning
them one way for 50 pounds and the other for 25, or fathers brought home
huge blocks of ice on the bumpers of cars. There were often open air rooms
in schools and the fear of tuberculosis. Girls played jacks, jumped rope, collected Dionne Quintuplet and Shirley Temple paper dolls. Every kid had his
Orphan Annie Ovaltine mug, which led to endless youthful contemplations
over infinity, for there, on every blue Orphan Annie mug, was a picture of Orphan Annie holding an Orphan Annie mug . . . ad infinitum. At dusk, Jack

Armstrong came on the radio, or the Kellogg Singing Lady. We played with sturdy iron cars and Lionel trains, which seemed to last almost forever.

We played in the streets on long summer evenings. Families sat on the porches and called back and forth to one another. The mailman knew everybody by name. And there were peddlers selling vacuum cleaners, brushes, Watkins products, and in the summertime, corn and beans off the backs of their trucks. There was a sense here almost of the village, tight and insular, bounded in by Glen Oak, Prospect, Knoxville and maybe McClure, unique, all its own.

Here, still, along Frye, is one of the longest blocks in town, running in an unbroken sweep from Wisconsin to Peoria. There is a public walkway near Indiana through which generations of schoolchildren trooped from St. Bernard's onto Republic and Thrush, into an area of neat 1920s-style bungalows and two-story homes. And farther down Peoria, to us, at least, the hated White School, which seemed to call forth rivalries as deep and unbridgeable as southern mountain feuds.

Little did I know the girl I would marry was there when I was within the sanctified precincts of St. Bernard's. *Quelle horreur.* But no Catholic-Public wars ever erupted in the area, so far as I know, although there seemed to be an imminent threat of some kind of childish crusade on both sides. It remained a peaceable kingdom.

Once the war veteran lived over here. He was a silent and polite man, turned into a semi-invalid by the mustard gas. A house old, but gracious and meticulously maintained, falling into disrepair only after the veteran and his family all died and people with motorcycles moved in and kicked the slats out of the porch railing and stopped painting. Over there, the house of the newspaper editor, still presentable, but old and tired now, like these streets, like this East Bluff.

But not too much changed. Still predominately middle class. No one ethnic class presides. Irish and Swedish, German, Polish, English. Miners, clerks, politicians, plumbers, factory workers. Changing slowly, slowly. Jack's Market at Ravine and Wisconsin is now a Vietnamese food store. There is no longer a sign down the street singling out the house of Hedley Waycott, artist. The brick streets are covered, the streetcar tracks gone. So, too, are the elms that once made high arches here in the summertime, cool and leafy, muffling sounds so that the streetcars going up Indiana sounded muffled and far off. And muffled, too, the voices of mothers calling in the growing shadows.

"Time for supper. Supper."

"One more game, huh?"

Still distinctive, not quite like the West Bluff, not quite like the North Side. Different in the ways the boroughs of New York are, those rigid districts of Vienna, the arrondissements of Paris.

This East Bluff.

We thought this was the best place in town.

Las Vegas: a Desert Disneyland for Adults

Las Vegas—various people call this sin city, the entertainment capital of the world, the most exciting city in America, the town which claims to have no clocks. Here the late show starts at 2:30 a.m. and the snick of cards at the blackjack tables, the rattle of dice, the discreet ticking of the roulette wheels and the clatter of bars, oranges and lemons falling into place in the slots goes on day and night, day and night.

There are more slot machines in these few square miles of desert than any place on earth. Las Vegas has so many blinking lights and racing electrical signs that Paris and New York seem gloomy by comparison. It has more air passenger travelers per capita than any city on earth, all of them rushing pell-mell to the gambling tables and shows. And it has more glitz, tinsel and sheer excess than any community in history. By comparison, the great days of Hollywood in the 30s were marked by baroque restraint, Pigalle at its gaudiest a mere shadow and Times Square at any time positively anemic.

This may not be Gomorrah revisited, for there obviously are 10 or more good and just men and women among its 350,000 inhabitants. But it is perhaps the most awesome example of the materialistic world gone wild, and probably the kind of place many cities in America would like to be, admit it or not.

For here is every town's commercial strip area raised to such a level that it becomes a staggering, grotesque parody lacking taste, reason. Much of it seems to have been designed by light bulb salesmen, stupefying enough by day, but by night a veritable orgasm of electrical madness.

Downtown Casino Center, a two block section along Fremont Street, is so bright sunglasses are obligatory at midnight. From beneath the lights there is an endless rumble of thousands of slots being pulled, punctuated occasionally by a tinkly rush of coins and wild, sybaritic shrieks. It seems, to the eye unafflicted with gambling fever, to be some ghastly danse macabre, some purgatorial scene as envisioned by Heironymus Bosch.

The strip itself is positively restrained by comparison, even with its own eye-popping marquees, gigantic billboards, dancing lights, girlie shows, wedding chapels and those incandescent resort hotels where the money flows in, and, sometimes, out.

What makes this such an adult playground is the unique combination of gambling and show biz that is found nowhere else in such profusion. It is, as every ancient knew, enormous fun to spend money, to scatter coins before peasants, or to be one of those receiving the scattering. Las Vegas capitalized on the deep-seated get-rich-quick dream with a vengeance.

Not only are those tempting slots everywhere, but nearly everyone's hand is extended as well. Perhaps nowhere else is one expected to cross so many palms so liberally with silver, or, preferably, paper. Everybody from the doormen who must summon cabs (there is a $200 fine if a cabbie takes a passenger along the street), the maitre'd who will, if sufficiently recompensed, find a better seat for a dinner show, the towel boy in the men's room, the porters who check baggage, along with bellhops, keno runners, bar girls, others, such a horde of recipients that it seemed almost natural to tip the usher at church.

Here the one-armed bandit is king and the show girl queen. Largely because of the former, and because of the take of such games as faro, keno, roulette, baccarat and the like, Nevada raked in $1.8 billion dollars last year, which translates readily into sports terminology: Nevada $1.8 billion, Gamblers 0.

What keeps this from disintegrating into an outright fleece and a simple con game is the fact that so much show biz and sheer luxury go along with it. The combination has been brilliantly exploited. There are so many big names and big shows here that it would take weeks, and a considerable outlay of cash, to cover them all. There is some restraint to the shows and spectacles, many of them rely heavily on the so-called T and A attraction, the letters implying bosoms and derrieres. And they are on display endlessly and abundantly, be everyone from the waitresses with their cheeky skirts to the topless showgirls, whose obligatory presence and astonishing uniformity strike a note of absurdity.

But the quality of the shows is extremely high. Seeing at least one big show is a necessity and our choice was the Lido. After standing in a long line that snaked through a rather dismal casino, an attendant announced that the show was full up and even those with reservations were simply out of luck. We saw instead the 2:30 a.m. show of "Hallelujah Hollywood" at the MGM Grand Hotel, which is the kind of thing one ought to experience once, and perhaps never again.

It is mostly one elaborate spectacle after another, extravagant settings, flying backdrops, gilded and feathered dancers floating down from above in cages or rising up from beneath the stage on elevators. It seemed like the climactic moment of some Ziegfield Follies show, with S. Z. Sakall beaming in the wings. The problem is that it is all a full-out assault on the senses, with not the slightest nuance, or crescendo. One out and out blast from beginning to end and even the pirate scene with ship sinking and nearly naked chorines being assaulted by crazed pirates was almost lost amid the excess of it all. Oddly the most memorable parts came with the appearance of Tanya, the elephant, and the orangutans and chimps of the Berosinis, one of whose orangutans is presently in Clint Eastwood's *Every Which Way But Lose*.

The other side of show biz here has considerably more impact, and that is the appearance of the individual star. Wayne Newton has managed to attract such a following that people will almost kill for the privilege of attending. We saw the two-person show of Anthony Newley and Juliet Prowse. In it he sings songs he wrote with Leslie Bricusse and others: "What Kind of Fool Am I," "Goldfinger," "Candy Man" and more, all done persuasively and elegantly. Miss Prowse follows with a display of dancing feats that is supurb. She remains, at 43, a stunning beauty, able to flatten an audience not only with her physical and athletic abilities, but with her personality. Best of all was the futuristic piece, with fog pouring off the stage, and the dazzling climax done to Gershwin.

The shows can run fairly high. The bill for two at the Newley/Prowse show, including dinner ($17 to $30) runs to about $50, including taxes, tips, and wine, and the MGM's "Hallelujah Hollywood" extravaganza is $18 plus tax (total $42 for two) including three drinks each. Again a few bills slipped discreetly to the maitre'd does help get one a better position.

Seating is crowded, but there are compensations. At one dinner show there were people from San Diego, New York City, Connecticut and Florida, all trading stories about the weather and their problems in getting to Las

Vegas. One woman, obviously a New Yorker, kept repeating the story of how she sat next to Frank Sinatra's wife at a show.

The MGM Grand Hotel is one of the newer and better available. Its rates are, by most big city standards, a bargain. The special charter rate for our room is $44 ($50 regular) and it has two double beds and a modified sitting room area with couch, two upholstered chairs and round table, all done in Mediterrannean, and scrupulously clean. The prints on the wall are from *Ben Hur*. Hedy Lamar's photo is on the wall outside and around the corner is Ava Gardner. Each door is embossed with the kind of star that goes on backstage dressing rooms, plus a symbol of the MGM lion, but the bath is so filled with mirrors as to be almost obscene. Because of the infinity of mirror effect, it is difficult to tell whether one is shaving his own face or that of some person three doors down the hall.

Throughout the hotel and grounds a continuous paging system drones on. "Telephone call for George Schotzke. Telephone call for William Brady. Telephone call for Marie Sanderson." It goes day and night and one occasionally sees a person presumably of some importance, racing for a house phone.

And everywhere are the ladies, gray-haired in their polyester doubleknit pantsuits, playing the dollar slots and doing extremely well, judging from the excited shouts and the cardboard cartons they utilize to carry their winnings. They seem to know which machines are paying off and they guard them with a fierce, proprietary interest.

These are the ladies, Midwestern, Texan, Californian, who seem to typify the Las Vegas gambler rather than the gaunt and lonely beauties one normally associates with casinos. Now and then one of these will linger around some elegant baccarat table, but the suspicion arises that she is part of the decor, perhaps an MGM extra hired to look ruined and hopeless, like deposed royalty at Monte Carlo. More obvious are the prostitutes, whose work brings them into contact with the pant-suited ladies, like bumblebees in clover, preying upon the appetites Las Vegas both nurtures and heightens.

This city exists these days not on gambling and show business, but on conventions, which are pouring in at a record rate. One of the bigger, the National Automobile Dealers Association drew 13,000 delegates during our stay. Conventions have become the second industry and the revenue generated has neared the billion mark over the past 20 years. This is now one of the country's top five convention locations with an average of 330 conventions a year and anywhere from 9 to 10 million people involved.

But whatever else Las Vegas has, its attraction is essentially the slot machine, the gambling table. Las Vegas—the name means The Meadows—lies in an area with little more fertility than the surface of the moon. The first settlement here was by a group of Brigham Young's Mormons in 1850, and it did not become a city until 1905 when the railroad made this a major division point. After World War II, it began to develop into a resort area.

Perhaps only by driving away from town for a few hours can one regain some kind of perspective into the curious phenomenon that has turned this into such a mecca. The desert, the mountains are wild and inhospitable and scarcely any life can survive, save for rattlesnakes, lizards, tarantulas, cactus and Joshua trees. There once were rich mines here, filled with silver and gold, the kind of places where grizzled men fought and sometimes died over a few parched acres. One of the few places remaining is Nelson, a ghost town south of Hoover Dam, mostly abandoned now, and an area of grinding poverty, but somehow symbolizing the wealth that has gone out of here.

These days it comes from gambling, shows, conventions, girls. And there are the little wedding chapels, looking like little churches, and named "Wee Kirk o' the Heather," "Silver Bells," "Cupid's" and "We've Only Just Begun," which arrange everything from "a beautiful wedding and a lasting marriage" to adjacent motels, some with waterbeds and other carnal attractions. Most honor Visa or Master Charge.

It all begins to seem after a few days like some mirage that will vanish if one alters his perspective. It is as insubstantial as a bubble, this mind-boggling display of ostentatiousness, wealth, vulgarity, glitter that remains unrivaled in the western world. It is perhaps not Gomorrah, not yet, for there is something peculiarly single-minded about the day and night hustle that goes on. It seems unconscious, almost innocent, as if it is a logical response to the barren and hostile environment. It has become the biggest gold mine of all time, inexhaustible, in fact, since it draws on the rest of the country.

But as the airplane leaves, curving up over these barren, rippled peaks, there is a reluctance to look back. There is that awful story about Lot's wife being turned into a pillar of salt and it remains in the mind, a lurking warning. Having survived the one-armed banditry, it is hardly the time to risk this kind of gamble.

Chicago

Morning and there is the traffic.   It booms and shakes, clangorous and terrible in its hell-bent intensity.

The huge trucks that rumble along outside the car windows have an almost obscene motion about them.   Their head-high wheels are a blur.   Air hoses sway menacingly.   Tires pound.   Universal joints spin madly.   The cabs sway.   Up there somewhere sit the drivers, who one fervently hopes are aware of their immense destructive capacity.

And from higher up come the voices from the sky, like a rush-hour litany:

"And inbound Elston is backed up three blocks at Montrose. The Kennedy is bumper-to-bumper and moving very slowly with some stop-and-go activity. Coming up on the Dan Ryan at 57th Street, the leftbound lane is blocked by a stalled car."

Up ahead the long line slows, shudders, lurches.   Brakes hiss, and this part of Chicago slows to an agonizing crawl.

There is a terrible paradox at work here, for this is a city with the biggest and the best of everything and perhaps the meanest and the worst.

It has the world's finest symphony orchestra, the biggest hotel, the busiest corner, the highest building, the biggest convention center, the most active airport, one of the best collections of Impressionistic art.   It has areas of such opulence as to excite the envy of a shah: elegant town houses along the Gold Coast where black limousines and fur-clad matrons whisper and rustle in moneyed splendor; high black towers with stunning views of Lake Michigan and sailboats bending under summer winds.   Solomon in all his glory did not live as one of these.

But its worst is almost unliveable.   It is crowded, deteriorating, violent, dull and gray, depressing and morally and culturally deadening.   For there is a gulf of such yawning infinity between the rich and the poor, between the haves and the have-nots, between those who live amid pneumatic playgirls and those who are surrounded by cockroaches, that there comes at times the sudden realization that this is what it might have been like before the holocaust of the Revolution—the French one.

And yet it remains a mecca.   Young people are drawn by its excitement.   Bigger pay.   Better jobs.   All those people.   All that vitality.   The city of big shoulders, they call it.   But for others it has become a prison from which they joyfully flee at retirement, or sooner.

And in between are all kinds.   There are people who would live nowhere else.   There are people who would if they could but can't.   There are people who know nowhere else.   There are those who do and want to go back.

There are those, too, who remember it as it once was.

Here was a city that gleamed like a beacon.   Everything else in the whole Midwest was second rate, minor league.   Many of us who never lived here felt incredibly gauche and small-town when we were exposed to Chicagoans. They seemed bigger, taller.   They came from what was, after all, the center of the world then.   It had to be.   Why else would so many people gather in one place?

Who remembers that glorious Century of Progress in 1933?   I was too little to go, but there were the pictures in the rotogravure sections of the unique articulated buses, of the gingerbread buildings, of the incredible rides, of Sally Rand and her fans. Chicago.

Nearly everybody in those days read *Studs Lonigan*. Almost every other nun in our school came from Chicago and couldn't wait to go back. Everybody else was some kind of deprived outlander.

This was the magical city where the wind blew in the summertime, where those clean green-blue waves of Lake Michigan rolled in foaming curls up near the Edgewater Beach, where a Scotch and soda at the Saddle & Cycle Club was the epitome of sheer chic.

Never mind all those steamy tenements, all those people who had never passed through the doors of the Edgewater Beach or the Palmer House. That was the other Chicago. Somehow that seems to have changed and the other Chicago has become the real Chicago and the rest might be only a facade. Too early to tell, perhaps, for the city is a mere infant as great cities go.

It has been barely more than 100 years since the fire. But in many ways this has become the quintessence of the American megapolis, embodying the best and the worst of what this country has been, of what it is coming to: the extremes of splendor and squalor, hope and despair, sanctity and corruption.

From south on I-55, the city appears to be all smoke and storage tanks, power lines and factories and black bridges. The red and white stacks of a power plant are lined up like rockets poised for a launch. Through the haze, the Sears Tower rises in the distance, looking oddly like one of those grain elevators that loom high above the small towns out there on the prairie.

Up close it is an immense black pylon, like some child's domino tower, surprisingly thin, breathtakingly tall. Past the cold plastic ballet of Calder's electrified mobiles in the lobby is an elevator that goes from Jackson Street to the 103rd floor, 1,353 feet above the ground, in 59 seconds. McCormick Place from here looks like the deck of an aircraft carrier, the Federal Correctional Center like an IBM punch card, the Lake Point Tower like some modernistic chess piece, Tribune Tower like the top layer of a wedding cake.

The old LaSalle Street Station is quiet and nearly empty. A man sits in a well worn bench reading his *Sun-Times*. "This used to be the real place," he says. "You should have seen it in the old days." Full of soldiers and sailors once. Throngs of people at those ticket windows. Wives and girls crying at the gates and the young men heading off on those long trains that rolled endlessly across the fields of Nebraska. Short hair. Frightened half to death. Listening to the long mournful cries of the whistle. The conductor coming through like something out of Norman Rockwell. The incredible loneliness of places like Needles, Calif. Then coming back one day, much older, through the LaSalle Street Station again. Most of them anyway.

"Now it's a landmark," says the man. "That's all. A landmark."

So, too, is the Dearborn Station. Even the clocks of its quaint crenelated towers show different times to the world, none of them right. These days electronically controlled lights blink out the time, the temperature (both in Farenheit and Celsius) and the date on the cold and functional new building.

The El still screeches and rumbles as it always has—45 cents a ride. The signs read "No smoking" and "No se permite fumar." The cars are newer. Otherwise it is the same. One somehow expects James T. Farrell to be lounging there somewhere on the iron platform, looking wisely out of those deep Irish eyes, sad somehow at the way things have changed. They say this is dangerous and one hears and reads stories about violence. All kinds of stories.

The Civic Center Plaza at noon seems to be part of some carefully put together movie set that says "Chicago." Throngs of people hurry past the Picasso, which has rusted to a dark mocha shade.

Traffic is at a standstill, and there is a rolling counterpoint of car horns and police whistles, the latter trilling like bosun's pipes.

A beefy Irish cop stands talking through a car window to a girl, and from overhead, descending like a tranquil prayer from the carillon of the Chicago Temple Church are the sounds of "Rock of Ages." The marquee of the McVickers advertises a triple bill of violent black films and a magazine stand on the corner displays a ghastly array of pornography, including *High School Masturbation* with an indescribable cover.

Mayor Daley's office is impregnable. "No appointments for interviews," says one of his public relations spokesmen. "Hell, there are eighty guys in line in front of you. Why don't you come back for one of his press conferences if you want to see him?"

No thanks. Instead we look at the pictures of the old mayors staring down from the wall in the mayor's outer office. William Dever. Anton Cermak. Edward Kelly. Martin H. Kennelly. On another wall is a massive seal with the city motto, "Urbs in Horto"—City in a Garden.

It seems a strangely inappropriate motto for a city that has been so relentlessly paved over. Only along the Outer Drive coming up past the Field Museum is there anything remotely resembling a garden. That is, without a question, one of the world's most beautiful city avenues. It is, unfortunately, almost impossible to appreciate fully, not being made for walking and hardly suited these days to the leisurely sightseeing type of driving.

Standing on the steps of the Field and looking north presents a staggering view. Also a continuing awareness that the automobile has made the city almost uncivilized and that the street's beauty, at least in this part, has to be glimpsed at 50 miles per hour or from the momentary safety of a stoplight.

The Loop empties out quickly at night. No more throngs. Nothing like it used to be. Only at noon. The crowds along the street are still something to see. All kinds of people.

"I'm not as concerned about downtown Chicago as I was a few years ago," says Daryl Fenton, manager of The Berghoff. "The Loop used to be a fun place. Now it's all business. But it's culturally stronger now than ever. The symphony is great and there is more theater than ever."

His is one of the city's most famous German restaurants. It serves 3,000 people a day. Friday, Fenton says, is belly-to-back day in the men's bar. The restaurant's special beer used to be made here. It is now brewed by Huber in Wisconsin from the same formula the grandfather brought over in 1887. The restaurant seats 750 in several rooms. Among its employees are representatives of 34 different nationalities, including 14 Greeks and a Persian. Two are German.

There are still lingering memories of Ralph Ginsburg at the Palmer House. The Empire Room has just been closed, except for lunch and private parties. "The entertainers just want too much money," says Anthony McNicholas, who has been a bellman here for 47 years.

He remembers it all, those great days when Potter Palmer II was still alive, when the exhibits from the Century of Progress filled the lobby. He escorts us to some rooms that have recently been redecorated. $69 a night. In that opulent lobby, he points to the ceiling which was originally painted by an Italian lying on his back on a scaffold, as did Michelangelo at the Sistine Chapel.

"Twelve years ago a man from Austria came to redo it, you know, and he fell and killed himself right here."

Now in the quiet of Graceland Cemetery, Potter Palmer lies in Elysian splendor in his magnificent, columned tomb. It has a noble Roman look and in back the ground slopes to a small pool, serene and lovely, even in winter.

Nearby, in the kind of crypts one sees at Pere Lachaise in Paris, are other great names of Chicago. Ryerson and Pullman. Kimball and Pinkerton of the Pinkerton detectives.

One mausoleum is like a pyramid, another like a small Romanesque church. The cemetery is surrounded by a massive wall with barbed wire strung along the top, obviously to keep out vandals. No one inside is trying to leave. Not yet.

Beyond that wall there are still dozens of Chicagos. Some of them have emptied out, draining the Irishmen and Greeks and Poles and Germans into the suburbs which swell with whites as the old neighborhoods become increasingly black or Puerto Rican.

But not all of them. There are still those unique ethnic areas which so distinguished this city for years. This one is German. Hansa's Inn and Delicatessen at 3356-58 N. Southport, half a dozen blocks from Wrigley Field, has the look of a Rhineland bierstube. There is a picture on the wall of von Richthofen's 80th and final victory, another Sopwith Camel falling beneath his blazing guns. There is a coat of arms from the Saar and a discreet nude. "I don't care if she's Irish or Chinese," cries one of the regular patrons. "I like her."

There are more than 10,000 Germans in the area, they say. The proprietor is Hans Mechenbier, who plays soccer with the Hansa Club and has often played in Peoria. Two kinds of imported beer on tap, Pschorr from Munich and Dab from Dortmunder, and an American brand. "Used to be good," says one of the patrons, "until the kikes took over."

The neighborhood itself looks like a hundred others. Chicago architecture may be justifiably famous, but it does not extend to the houses. There is a grim sameness about them and they seem to have a look of solidity, of permanence. Above those tiny backyards are patterns of stairways and porches in latticework and in the fronts, the stoops lead almost to the sidewalk, leaving hardly room for a tree or bush or more than two blades of grass.

Chinatown is a gay facade, an elaborate arch at one end and a score or more of Chinese restaurants. It looks like Shanghai or Tientsin in the old days. There are street signs in Chinese and American. Hardly a block away the look is the same again. Chicago.

The afternoon traffic is beginning to pile up. From far off are police whistles, horns.

"The easterly Stevenson is dense and slow from Central Avenue to Damen, then stretching out nicely from Damen to the Dan Ryan and Lakeshore Drive . . ."

All kinds of things going on out there. People phoning in their complaints, their ideas, their weird opinions to Bill Berg at WGN. The incomparably good music of WFMT. A matinee of *Mourning Becomes Electra* letting out at the Goodman. A new exhibition of French painting at the Art Institute. Another group of children emerging from the U-505 at the Museum of Science and Industry. Dick Butkus growling, someplace. Saul Bellow here, too, writing, and Harry Mark Petrakis and somewhere here, even now, is James T. Farrell.

159

There is a lone skater on the long pond of the Midway Plaisance at the University of Chicago. Acres of college Gothic buildings. This was once a Big Ten power. The Maroons. Some people worry now about sending their sons and daughters here.

The university is separated from downtown by an immense stretch of what used to be moderately fashionable apartments and townhouses. Many are boarded up now. Broken windows and an awful sense of desolation and despair hangs over the area. It is a kind of urban purgatory, especially on a late February afternoon when the snow has turned to gray slush and the core of the city is far to the north, looking in the gathering dusk like some far off, unattainable Xanadu.

"Outbound Kennedy is compact. Kimball to Irving Park is the scene of an accident, but beyond Irving Park you'll do quite well . . ."

The lights are coming on again. Downtown is deserted. The action is farther north, along Michigan and those little streets around Ontario where restaurants proliferate and the little clubs are crowded. In the Loop, one has a hard time finding a cup of coffee. Most people know better and do not try.

A postman who has carried this route says he is going to retire next year and get out. To Tucson. He carried mail in what he calls "The Jungle" to the south and was robbed half a dozen times while on his route. And once in a Loop theater. He will not go there anymore after dark.

Along Rush Street, the marquees blaze around the clip joints. "Live Nude Dancers." Is there any other kind?

"I wouldn't go in there," says a young man selling a magazine called *Foundation—For the Glory of God—Visions of the Millenium.* He is Brother Jethro and his concern seems to be not so much moral as economic. "Everybody gets ripped off in those places." Members of the Foundation Church of the Millenium serve with the kind of zeal and dedication and asceticism that once distinguished members of the established church.

Overhead, another jet comes floating in across the evening sky. From London? Cleveland? Luxembourg? Another 200 or 300 people. Then another jet. And another.

Soon the passengers will be pouring into the cabs, hotels, nightclubs and restaurants. And they will pay for accomodations and meals that can be superb. A double at the new Ritz-Carleton in Water Tower Place starts at $69, which is not out of line for the area, insists the smooth young lady at the desk. She is right. Far lesser hotels ask—and get—$59 for the smallest doubles.

We are the privileged ones for now and we do not live in those gray and depressing rows of flats. We have dinner at a moderately priced French restaurant, La Cheminee, for $13,50 prix fixe. With wine, special desert, tax, and tip, the bill is $48 for two.

Down the street we find the Chess and Backgammon Shop, where people pay 50 cents an hour to play and where one can buy a hand-carved Indian-style ivory chess set for $3,000. There are eight or ten games going on, mostly young men, black and white, hunched over their boards. Beethoven drifts from the stereo. This is the biggest chess shop in the city and one may buy all kinds of sets, those which resemble Rhenish castles to designs by Max Ernst.

Scores of churches raise their spires against the gathering dusk. Some look like Prague or Cracow. Corner taverns by the thousands out here. Strange little shops. Even a tattoo parlor, where a man who does not want to be identified talks about running away with the circus 30 years ago. He looks like Ray Bradbury's illustrated man.

He says that earlier in the day he tattoed flowers on the breasts of two girls. A mark of some kind. A cab driver says the real mark of influence these days is brand new bills, 50s preferably. A sign says, "Visit the Gaboon Viper. Animal of the Month at the Lincoln Park Zoo."

Old buildings are torn down and new ones put up with such speed that much of the architectural heritage has vanished. One hotel goes down and another goes up. Huge ornate theaters are empty and the new small ones with draperied walls overflow with people.

One of the biggest boom areas now is around the John Hancock Building, near north, around the water tower. The grand atrium of Water Tower Place has a futuristic look. Triple elevators rise in a high, exposed core to the seventh floor of Marshall Field, reminiscent of some fantastic city from an old Flash Gordon strip. And everywhere there are shrubs and indoor trees, blooming and leafy all year long, even when that cold, cold wind turns the forehead to stone and seems never to be at one's back.

Urbs in Horto. The Great Seal indicates the city was incorporated on the 4th of March, 1837. There is a ship under full sail, an Indian staring out in the classic cigar store pose, a sheaf of wheat and an angel or a child overhead in a sea shell.

And there is that sound that is incomparably Chicago. J.F. Powers wrote in his novel *Morte d'Urban* of the Chicago cops calling to each other like nightingales:

"The most beautiful sound I know is the sound of whistles on Michigan Avenue at dusk, especially in the fall . . . I like to come out of the Blackstone or the Drake at dusk, especially in the fall, with two or three good ones in me, and hear those whistles, the mush and whine of rubber, the distant roar—it always seems to be centered over LaSalle Street, to the south, but it's like a haze you can see and never touch . . ."

There are millions who love this city and would live nowhere else in the whole world. There are those who leave and wonder why they remained for so long. There are those who would not go back for anything, not even to visit.

I would do that. To visit the Gaboon Viper. To watch the Cubs play in the gathering shade of Wrigley Field on a summer afternoon. To see all those magnificent Monets and Renoirs left by the Palmers and the Ryersons. To hear that symphony again. But not to stay. Never to stay. When traffic is moving very slowly across Peoria's McCluggage Bridge and the people courteously let every other car in, I listen to flying officers Jim Cavanagh or Ed Peterson with humility and thanksgiving.

"The inbound Kennedy express lanes are clear sailing. Northbound Damen has a block backup at Fullerton and the northbound Dan Ryan is congested and creeping from 96th to 71st. Remember, cutting in too fast can cut off your future."

I think they should follow those reports with a song. "Oh How I Wish I Was in Peoria."

There's Still Something to Like in New York in June

I like New York in June, how about you?
I like a Gershwin tune, how about you?
Holding hands in a movie show
When all the lights are low
May not be new,
But I like it, how about you?

from "Babes on Broadway," Leo Feist, Inc. Corp. 1941

It is still possible to like New York in June, although there have been some changes in 30 years . . .

The babes on Broadway these days are called hookers and hang out night after night on the same corners. Up in Central Park once was a gay musical, when gay meant happy and carefree, but now the park means trouble and gay means queer. On one Sunday in June, several bicyclists in the park were attacked and beaten and their bicycles stolen.

Along 58th Street, where one might expect to see ladies with blue hair walking poodles or Gene Kelly dancing in the rain, a lady in a store specializing in imports from India keeps her door locked all day long, unlatching it only for customers, who look safe. "They keep saying it's better, but it really isn't," she says as we leave, and the door locks behind us.

There are blocks over on Eighth Avenue near the theater district where one hesitates to breathe too deeply for fear of contracting some social disease. The movie house marquees blaze with all sorts of odious matter, much of it homosexual. Some houses have closed-screen TV out front, where men stand and stare with impassive faces at the tamer action.

It is easily seen, easily condemned. There are compensations. Despite the legendary rudeness of people in crowded cities, most notably New York, it is seldom encountered. "Have a nice day" is a greeting one often hears from cab drivers and others, offered with sincerity. Standing in a subway station a couple of times with an open map invariably brought some good underground Samaritan with an offer of help, both times from black people.

There is a bewildering variety, constant, unexpected. On some Sundays Fifth Avenue becomes a gigantic parade route, this time a celebration of Puerto Rican independence and traffic backs up for miles. The cab driver laments the idiocy of it all as bands and phalanxes of uniformed troops sweep past and suggest that they ought to close up Central Park and let them parade there. On his sun visor is a newspaper clipping telling how he returned a wedding veil to a girl who had left it in the cab and won immortality in print. "They invited me to the wedding," he said. "And it cost me fifteen dollars for a present."

There is a break in the parade and the traffic moves, but only for a few minutes.

The town is filled with French sailors, thousands of them from the aircraft carrier Foch, the cruiser Colbert and the destroyer Bouvet. They earn $10 a month and complain about high prices in New York—$1 for a beer. One sailor said the subway was disgusting, although they had been warned not to ride it, or to go north of 72nd Street on the west side or 96th Street on the east side.

Five p.m. brings horn-blasting traffic jams with cars and trucks backed up across intersections and nothing moving. It becomes in the summertime a daily inferno and somehow in the midst of it the old visions of Judy Garland dancing, Gershwin tunes and the romance of the city and its bright lights fade and die.

There are oases. Far down on lower Broadway is St. Paul's Church, which Washington attended, and its little graveyard out in back where people with names like Purdy and Bowcott still sleep after 200 years. The weathered gravestones stand shoulder to shoulder, insulated faintly from the outside world by feathery trees, green grass and flowers. The subway rumbles past underneath, stirring the dust faintly, and the long thin spire of the church steeple rises almost unseen amid the tall buildings and the World Trade Center nearby.

At the other end of the island is The Cloisters, reached from 200th Street subway stop and standing high on a hill over the Hudson. It is the 12th century, assembled from monasteries and abbeys in Europe and reassembled into a Romanesque and early Gothic wonder. It houses not only architectural treasures, but liturgical ones as well, along with medieval art, carvings from crypts, the unicorn tapestries, paintings and old chapels, with vaulted ceilings that still must ring somehow with ghostly chants, and steps and stones worn by centuries of footsteps, most of them stilled. It is not Manhattan at all, but Poitiers, or Gascony, and in the gardens there is an almost unearthy and certainly unurban serenity and peace. At 12:30 there is a concert of recorded music, medieval chants, the Obrecht Kyrie, the New York Pro Musica, and one can almost visualize into being a file of monks on their way to chapel, and lose track of what century he is in.

Down the hill, the city resumes. The subway roars through the underground blackness and the light bulbs in the tunnel flick past the windows like tracer bullets. The trains have become a kind of moveable art form, scrawled inside and out with spray paint graffiti, most of it symbolic and unreadable.

At the other end of the island near the old Fulton Fish Market, is the South Street Seaport Museum, a long wharf surrounded by ships of the past, one of the old Day Line Hudson River sidewheelers, a light ship and the sailing vessel Wavertree. Students sit on the wharf with the Brooklyn Bridge in the the background, sketching the pilings, old ships, and each other.

On MacDougal Street in Greenwich Village, the old brick buildings are covered with ornate fire escapes, a colorful wrought iron lichen, and on warm days women lean out their windows and call to one another or holler at their children in the streets below. There are little shops at street level, apartments higher up in the old seven-story buildings, and an air along the street that is decidedly continental. People live here. They have lived here a long time and their imprint is unmistakable.

There is art everywhere in the city, from the rude scrawlings on the subways to the massive Dubuffet exhibit on the spiral ramps of the Guggenheim, some of it looking like a set from The Flintstones. It also flourishes in Soho, street talk for South of Houston, an area of old brick factory buildings and low rent that now is dotted with little galleries and workshops where lights burn late into the night. Painters live and work side by side with little factories. A flat truck of newly made corrugated boxes may rest beneath a larger banner indicating the presence of a gallery.

Some are reached by climbing three stories of rickety stairs lighted only by a single naked bulb. In one is a sign, "In case of anything call Jerry" and another sign advertises a 10-day summer Yoga retreat by Sri Swami Satchidananda, and on a wall is the plea "Free the Watergate 500."

Fourteenth Street on a dry day is an outdoor bazaar, lined with racks of remnants, polyesters, slacks, fabrics and tops. The creak of hangers as shoppers sift through bargains sounds faintly above the noise of traffic. Farther on are boxes of electrical appliances, cords, plugs, motors, tools, which give way to a bewildering array of unclassified bric-a-brac.

There are bargains here, but most prices in midtown Manhattan are out of sight. Coffee runs from 35 cents to 65 cents a cup. A dinner for two is $20 up, usually up. One of the best bargains in town is a long subway ride at 35 cents.

"Striptease. Topless. Girls'" cry the signs. "Best Play of the Season." "Canadian Club." "Sony." "Coke." "One Way." "Mature Adults Only."

The man in the delicatessen says a six-pack of beer is $2.40—"any kind" —$2.54 including tax. The same Eurasian girl stands at the corner near Carnegie Hall. Along Central Park South the doormen linger in evening clothes, and long black Cadillacs whisper to the curb. The elevator glides upward and down below is the darkness of Central Park where tiny pinpoints of light gleam through the trees like stars through a partly cloudy sky. The red lights of a police car blink through the night and somehow it seems to be 30 years too late for Gershwin tunes and holding hands in movie shows. But perhaps not, for the echo keeps sounding over and over . . . "I like New York in June, how about you?"

Colonial New York

The echoes of this Colonial town of about 16,000 are nearly all drowned out these days by a ceaseless clamor: new buildings rising, honking horns, buses, trucks, subways, "Walk," "Wait," jack-hammers and the mingled sounds of millions of people.

But they are still there is one listens, in the sudden silence that comes at the Fraunces Tavern, among battle flags, dress swords, regimental bunting and prints of Washington bidding farewell to his troops; at the Morris-Jumel Mansion, then so far out that people referred to it as "the place beyond Mrs. Watkins," or farther up the Hudson at Van Cortlandt Manor, where the initials scratched into the mantelpiece are said to be those of Hessian mercenaries.

The Jumel Mansion these days sits in a decaying area of Washington Heights at West 160th St. and Edgecome Ave. It is a white Georgian home, built in 1765, which seems to have pollinated history rather than simply witnessed it.

It was built by Col. Roger Morris, a retired British Army officer and his wife, Mary Philipse, as a summer home. Morris had served with General Braddock during the French and Indian War, where he became a friend of George Washington. He later took part with Wolfe in the expedition against Quebec on the Plains of Abraham.

But when the War for Independence began, the Morris family left the mansion. Washington established headquarters in the home in September, 1776. After the British captured New York, the mansion was used as summer headquarters first by Sir Henry Clinton and the British and later by General Knyphausen and the Hessians.

A French wine merchant, Stephen Jumel and his wife, Eliza, restored the mansion in 1810, and after Jumel's death in 1832, Madam Jumel married Aaron Burr in the house's reception room. The marriage lasted six months and they were divorced, the decree coming just at the time of Burr's death. Madam Jumel remained until her death in 1865 and the city of New York bought the mansion in 1903 and turned it into a free museum.

There are few visitors these days, probably because of its location, and the guest book on a Tuesday in April showed pitifully few entries. In her upstairs office amid the echoes Natalie Bunting talked about the house and the room in which Washington planned the battle of Harlem Heights. She walks to work daily and advances the inarguable logic that her chances of getting mugged are infinitesmal.

The Philipse name surfaces again farther up the Hudson, at Tarrytown, in the heart of Sleepy Hollow Country. Philipsburg Manor is one of the most impressive of the Sleepy Hollow Restorations. This was, in the early 1700s, the seat of a 200-square mile estate presided over by a powerful Dutch landholding family. Flour and meal from the mill and biscuits from the Philipse ovens were shipped down the Hudson and on to worldwide ports. During the Revolution, the Philipse family backed the English. Afterwards the lands were sold at public auction and the holdings passed on to tenants.

There are elaborate tours conducted by well trained guides in period costume. Included is a demonstration of the waterpowered mill and the sale of stone-ground corn meal.

Washington Irving's Sunnyside near Tarrytown has nothing to do with the Revolutionary War, but is an obligatory stop on the Sleepy Hollow Tour. It is a strangely whimsical house, overlooking the Hudson, all gabled and festooned with ivy and seemingly something out of a story rather than life. There is, about the area itself, something somber and remote, brooding old pines and plane trees and a feeling that one might at any moment hear the thud of hoofbeats and see some mysterious cloaked rider along yon ridge.

A tour of kindergarten children was decamping from school buses. If we hurried, the ticket seller said, we could go on ahead and be out of their way. The guides, she said, would be expecting us.

But there are no guides as we knock at the door and then go in. There is the rich smell of ginger spice cookies coming from the kitchen. The cookies had just been taken out of the oven, a huge black iron wood-burning affair, and they lie cooling in cookie sheets on the table. No one in sight. For the moment. It is a mutual surprise when a girl dressed as a colonial farmwife arrives. She says the cookies are served as part of the tour. The guides have been in another room, girding themselves for the onslaught of kindergarteners.

They pass visitors along from one room to the other as if they are guests. Just inside the front door is Irving's study. His walking stick hangs on the chair. His cloak is in the hallway and all seems ready for one of his more famous guests, Holmes, Thackery or Louis Napoleon. But on this day it is kindergarten children.

The Van Cortlandt Manor, farther north at Croton-on-Hudson, is considered to be one of the most authentic restorations of early America. Its visitors included Lafayette, Franklin and Rochambeau in the manor house, which has a curiously southern look with its verandah-like porch. The Albany Post Road ran past here and part of the restoration includes an inn, or ferry house. At its common room tables are pewter plates, tankards, clay pipes and it is the kind of place where fiery young patriots might have helped fuel the Revolution.

The main house was once a hunting lodge and the guide in her early Dutch garb points to the scrawlings over a fireplace, crude initials and markings believed to be that of the Hessians. In the lower kitchen a young girl removed a stuffed goose from the wood-burning oven and the house fills with the scents of a colonial recipe as might have whetted the appetite of Lafayette.

Washington's echoes are, however, more centered in Manhattan. His pew remains discreetly roped off in St. Paul's Church, whose spire these days is dwarfed by the twin towers of the New York Trade Center nearby. There is to be a concert by the choir from William and Mary, which has its own historical antecedants. And out back, thinly insulated from the noises of the street by an iron fence and greening trees, the English dead, the Purdys and the Bowcotts and others sleep into their own bicentennial beneath blackened tombstones.

Washington was inaugurated president at Federal Hall at the corner of Broad and Wall Streets in 1789. His statue stands today outside that Greek revival structure in the heart of the financial district and beneath is that constant, bewildering street procession: taxicabs, street vendors selling roasted chestnuts and hot pretzels, honking horns, buses, trucks, "Walk," "Wait," men with briefcases, the solid boom of Wall Street.

And they are serving lunch at the Fraunces Tavern at the corner of Broad and Pearl in lower Manhattan. The restaurant is on the first floor and the museum is upstairs with the battle flags, swords, uniforms, decorations and paintings of the Continental Army and the Redcoats in massive battle, of Molly Pitcher at her cannon. This was a recruiting station for the Continental Army. And at the end of the war, Gov. George Clinton honored Washington here at a great public dinner. But its most notable date was Thursday, Dec. 4, 1783, when Washington bid farewell to his officers at the tavern.

Col. Talmadge witnessed the event, describing how Washington drank a glass of wine with his officers and embraced each in farewell. "Such a scene of sorrow and weeping I had never before witnessed, and I hope may never be called upon to witness again. It was indeed too affecting to be of long continuance, for tears of deep sensibility filled every eye and the heart seemed so full it was ready to burst from its wonted abode."

"Not a word was uttered to break the solemn silence that prevailed, or to interrupt the tenderness of the interesting scene. The simple thought that we were then about to part from the man who had conducted us through a long and bloody war and under whose conduct the glory and independence of our country had been achieved, and that we should see his face no more in this world, seemed to me utterly insupportable . . ."

Amid all the glass and steel and concrete and noise, the echoes still remain.

Paris Anytime

One never really leaves Paris, once here. It is a moveable feast, a portable one even. It is a city, yes, like other cities with its traffic, its crowding, its noise. But Paris is like a beautiful woman, strange, fascinating, unpredictable. This is a feminine city, as Chicago is masculine, but so much older, so much more beguiling, so much more easy to love.

It is a Sunday morning and we are at a crowded Mass at Notre Dame, sung in Latin, with the great organ pealing forth as if heaven's gates were about to open in a shower of gold. A bewildering spectacle of tourists and faithful, of sacred and profane.

A strange man wearing a red apron over his blue suit and one white glove approaches the altar in an elaborate pantomime, saluting and posing, reverent and insulting. Another jongleur of Notre Dame, perhaps. But no. He is finally led away by a patient priest who has probably seen worse. A young man in blue jeans and long hair leans against a vaulting Gothic pillar chewing a hot dog with studied insolence. Candles blaze like tiny suns. The ancient hymns ring again off these ancient stones and the unchanging sacrifice goes on.

Afterwards the square outside is a teeming mass. People photograph one another, although many are from Stuttgart or Brighton. A small band of Krishna followers bang away at their tambourines and gongs and chant their sing-songery. There is a street mime in the Place du Parvis, a flute player and always the platoons of German tourists tramping on and off their great Deutz buses.

We reach the Jeu de Paume at the far end of the Louvre, passing through swarms of pretty young men. This Tuileries Gardens area on Sundays seems to be their favorite showplace. Entrance to the Louvre's impressionistic museum is half price on Sundays and almost everyone who can takes advantage of its rich and popular collection of Monets, Renoirs, Morisots, Cezannes, Van Goghs, The Orangerie across the way is closed and we cannot see the great Monet Nymphiaedes. Some other time, perhaps.

But there is never enough time here. People come for a single day and do Paris by sightseeing bus and river cruise. "And over here is the obolisk of Luxor . . . Notre Dame . . . St. Chapelle. Everyone be back on the bus in five minutes." Others spend their lives here and never see it all.

The best way is by foot. We walk. And look. On Monday the printers are demonstrating high atop Notre Dame and the tough riot police have sealed off the area. A man in the crowd complains loudly in English that he came all the way from Brussels for the day just to see Notre Dame. Crazy Frenchmen. He is from Joliet, Ill., visiting his son, who works for Caterpillar in Brussels. Seeing Paris for the day. He will look at St. Chapelle instead, St. Louis's little chapel with its magnificent jewel box look. He will not be disappointed.

The bookstalls along the Seine display everything from *Mein Kampf* to *The Kama Sutra.* Always there are the fishermen along the river, old men who sit patiently and watch the water. A hopeless quest, really, for the river yields little, but it is a pleasant one. And always there are the silent black Africans, selling their carvings and leatherwork. They are like the fishermen. It is a patient wait, seldom rewarded, it seems, but a scenic one.

We stop at a small cafe for beer. Pelican Beer from Lille, about 75 cents for a 25 centiliter bottle (7 ounces). Madame, who minds the place, pays us little heed, but goes about ironing petticoats at an adjacent table. Traffic thunders past on the Boulevard Henry IV and then around the Place de la Bastille. It is possible to climb to the top of the monument. What seems impossible is reaching it across the mad traffic circle.

This is in some ways a strange independence day that is celebrated here. The mob that tore down the hated monarchy also martyred many, destroyed churches, left thousands headless and much of the country in ruins. The oppression here was no doubt more severe than our own, and the gap between the rich and the poor was a festering chasm, but one has the feeling that our own Revolution was handled with somewhat more intelligence. And restraint.

One sees signs of our own fight for independence here, of course, since the French played so large a role. At Versailles, in one vast room of massive paintings of the great French battles, is a scene from Yorktown showing Rochambeau with General Washington. Franklin has always been revered, having had a particularly French outlook on life and love. His statue is in the Square Yorktown near the Palais Chaillot. He sits holding a sheaf of papers in his hand, staring pensively across the endless Paris traffic at Marshal Foch on his horse. And Foch, in turn, stares toward the Eiffel Tower, from where the gaze falls across all of Paris.

There are countless treasures in these streets that lie hidden to all but the walker. They are along the broad boulevards of Baron Haussmann and in narrow and winding streets so old one expects to be struck by the contents of a chamber pot.

Along the Rue Francois Mirou, near the church of St. Gervais, is the house where Mozart lived. A massive doorway stands open. Cobblestones lead into a small courtyard. Mozart. Beaumarchais. "The Marriage of Figaro." The Couperin family lived nearby. Elegant harpsichords. The discreet sound of woodwinds. The clatter of horses' hooves and a fiacre drawing up before the door. All drowned out now in the boom of traffic, the roar of motorcycles. But not really.

Victor Hugo's house in the Place des Vosges is closed. But in the antique square, once so popular for dueling that Cardinal Richelieu issued an edict against it, the people sit on iron chairs in the late afternoon sun, the old ones talking animatedly, the younger ones running and playing. There is a policeman who shouts at the children to stay off the grass. They do. For a while. The children have high thin voices, like reed instruments. There are tides of pigeons swooping down on crumbs of bread, or on a magnificent pastry someone has dropped.

More surprises. The Parisian hot dogs, known as a sandwich saucisse, comes in a long piece of wonderfully crusty bread—a baguette—and contains two hot dogs laid end to end. It normally costs about 55 cents. Wine is absurdly cheap, about $1.10 for a fifth-sized bottle of St. Emilon, less for Cote du Rhone, which can be had for as little as 75 cents a liter.

There is a McDonald's in a noisy arcade on the Champs Elysees, where people order a "Beeg Mock et frites." It is the same rush, the same smell, the same taste. In the same arcade is a Brasserie Lowenbrau Munich, the Club Mediterainne headquarters, a record shop. The Big Mac is about $1.10.

Streets bloom in the daytime with incredible displays. The sidewalks fill up with everything from shirts and coats outside the big department stores, to the bizarre markets along the Seine, where one can buy Holland bulbs, strawberry plants, rabbits, dogs, garden utensils, exotic birds. One shop along the

Rue de Rivoli is full of nothing but antique armor. Another deals exclusively in Tiffany type shades. In another is nothing but fishing tackle.

At noon at St. Germain de Pres in the student quarter there is an organ concert. At 12:14 seven priests emerge from a side door and celebrate Mass. The reader is a young man who has left his motorcycle helmet in his chair. Afterwards, the priests change into business clothes and hurry into the busy Boulevard St. Germain, briefcases in hand, looking like insurance salesmen.

The cemeteries of Paris are like small cities of tiny churches, so crowded together there is hardly room to squeeze between the tombs. There are, in the little cemetery of Passy near Foch's statue, counts and dukes and the very rich dead. Among them are Edouard Manet and Berthe Morisot, a young aviator who died two months before The Great War ended and an immense orthodox crypt containing the remains of sculptor Marie Bashkirtseff (1860-1884) which includes inside an overstuffed chair, paintings on the wall, pieces of sculpture.

In Pere Lachaise are the graves of Chopin, Sarah Bernhardt, Bizet, Enesco, Edith Piaf, Abelard and Heloise. A golden late afternoon sun slants through the horse chestnut trees, a sudden wind, an autumn shower and the chestnuts rattle on the cobblestones. We pass the tomb of a young man who has been cast larger than life in bronze in his death pose, top hat beside him.

High above the steps at Montmarte where the young people gather is Sacre Coeur, massive, white and domed, looking like some confection atop a wedding cake. A plaque notes that people have been praying here night and day before the Blessed Sacrament since Aug. 1, 1885. It is the world's center of perpetual prayer. A man in church asks a group of loud tourists to be more discreet. They ignore him and go on talking in their metallic voices. There is another plaque which shows the points where 13 American bombs fell in the closing years of the war. There were people in church then. None were injured.

Far below is the Metro, or subway, which goes everywhere. It is cheap— 19 cents a ride if one buys a book of 10 tickets—and fast. Many of the trains are rubber-tired. They are clean and safe. Sometimes in the long underground tunnels leading into the station one runs across folk singers, singing plaintive songs about Oklahoma or the Shenandoah and the sound is pure and sweet, oddly amplified and projected in those tiled corridors.

From afar the Eiffel tower may resemble an enormous heap of scrap, but close up it is surprisingly lovely, soaring and delicate in its way as Alencon lace. The famous Army Museum at Les Invalides is about to close this day, so we remain outside and save five francs each. There is a World War I Renault tank, one of the taxis of the Marne, a Rommel fieldpiece from Bir Hakim, General de Tassigny's jeep, which has a flat tire. Only a few old veterans remain in this enormous complex, built to house Louis XIV's wounded and maimed troops. Its greatest attraction remains the tomb of Napoleon, who is almost universally revered here.

Always there are the reminders of past glory. After feasting on the spectacular view from atop the Arc de Triomphe, visitors browse through a room high above the eternal flame which depicts the great moments in the history of the Arc. Napoleon's remains being returned to Paris. The Unknown Soldier being interred. The flame kindled. The liberation by the Allies. Notably absent are pictures of the German occupying Paris in 1940.

To the west, a new kind of Paris is arising at la Defense. There are 40 and 50 story buildings, broad esplanades, fountains, sculpture. In the underground station of the regional Metro is a huge shopping center. Among the many pieces of new sculpture is a Calder, still being welded and bolted together. In a brand new underground gallery we come upon a display of tapestry, including several works by Calder. The Arc de Triomphe glows in the distance, brushed in the evening light with gold. Most Parisians hate this new area, which looks like a sparkling clean Chicago. But not all.

And there are the people of Paris, insular and remote as most big city people. And yet there is something different. It may not be hospitality or friendliness. But there is still respect, some vestige of the amenities we all used to display.

There is, too, a noticeable lack of the rage, the hostility that has infected so many American cities. When people bump into one another on the crowded sidewalks, there is invariably a mumbled "pardon" or "excuse." Even the traditionally wild drivers show respect for the rights of pedestrians.

These are not necessarily the cold and rude people of myth and story. One night on a crowded street we stood bags in hand looking for a hotel which seemed to have vanished in the midst of an excavation for the Metro. A man stopped and asked if he could help. He spoke no English, we little French, but he spent ten minutes finding the hotel and insisted on escorting us to the door. In a student restaurant one evening, the red wine we ordered did not come and the young bearded man who shared our table poured us some of his own. Perhaps one finds in Paris what he is looking for, what he wants to find, what he takes with him.

There are young people kissing in the Tuileries Gardens. And in the Luxembourg Gardens. Older people, too. Men play their games of boules near the Louvre. The streets are crowded. And safe.

At night there are the floodlights on the monuments and the city takes on a different kind of beauty. Do not drive in Paris is the universal recommendation. We try. On a Saturday night. Twice around the Arc de Triomphe Through the Place de la Concorde. Past Norte Dame, lovely and silvery white against the night. To Sacre Coeur, which is also lighted.

And along Pigalle, where there is a fungicidal flowering of porno and "le hard core." Posters and pictures of formidable depravity for all to see. *Le Figaro* warns that pornography breeds violence. Cardinal Marty thunders against a growing tide. President Giscard is supposed to be considering action, so intense is the pressure. Porno, one recalls, was not allowed under the hand of General and Madame DeGaulle.

The city does not sleep. Another Bateau Mouche glides along the Seine, beneath the Pont d'Alexandre. Notre Dame raises her spires against the soft sky. There is a burst of music from an open door, the red glow of wine by candlelight, eyes shining, people kissing. There is the endless roar of traffic, a gendarme stopping cars with a raised white glove, the trees rustling with their dry October sound, the sharp smell of roasting chestnuts, a siren off somewhere "Eee-aw, eee-aw."

This Paris.

The Japanese come in droves. With cameras. And the Germans. Always there are Germans. Hitler ordered the city blown up before the Allies arrived. His orders were disobeyed, for the Germans, too, love Paris. Almost, perhaps, as much as the French. Or the Americans. In the springtime. In the fall. In the winter.

This Paris.

End Piece

All Quiet on the Western Front

The 11th hour of the 11th day of the 11th month. That meant some-thing special back in the days when people of my generation were growing up between wars. Armistice Day was not so big as Christmas or July 4th, but big, even though most of us had come no closer to the war than reading about it in such books as *The Army Boys in France* or in the Collier's *Illustrated History of the Great War.*

And the moment the armistice had been signed in the forest at Compeigne the bells would peal out from church steeples, factory whistles would blow and there would come a moment of suspended stillness when we would face the east in tribute to all who had died in the Great War. And feel a soft wind on the cheek.

Wars have come and gone since then, and Armistice Day has lost much of its meaning. To the young, it is a date quite as remote as that of Agincourt. But to anyone traveling through France today, World War I and its armistice are inescapable reality. The fallen dead still lie here—at Verdun, where the earth is a massive graveyard; in scores of neatly trimmed cemeteries with row on row of orderly white crosses; in cool ossuaries, silent as churches.

And there are thousands of Americans here, many of them forgotten now. More than 36,000 in all. Another 4,000 missing. One finds occasionally a wreath before one of these eloquent white crosses, but not often. They are rather quiet, ghostly parks, symmetrical and orderly and sadly desolate.

The American Cemetery at Belleau Wood is as neatly kept as a country club. Crosses fan out like a formal garden around a small chapel nestled a-gainst a thick wood. Each one just so. The grass is a short, bent variety, like that surrounding the putting greens of better golf courses, thick and cushiony as a costly shag carpet.

There are men here from New York State, Arizona, Illinois, Ohio—2,288 in all. Another 250 are unknown and a thousand were never found. Most of them died during the final months of the Great War when American strength in the Chateau-Thierry sector helped turn back Ludendorff's last drive to Paris.

Tourists used to come here in droves. Now the cemetery is deserted. The battlefield at Belleau Wood is empty, too. There is a ring of artillery pieces, a stack of shells, an American flag slowly unfurling in the breeze. The woods have grown over now, hiding the scars that made the ground useless, but it remains hillocked and lumpy from shellfire in the midst of these silent trees.

And those who lie here are forever young. They never knew those glor-ious football weekends, those great beery Legion conventions, their children crying in the night, winter vacations in Florida, the joys of grandchildren. They missed the Depression, house payments, the new cars with the shift levers on the steering column, the coming of television.

The survivors are going now, like the Civil War veterans did in the 1920s, scattered by wind and time into thousands of cemeteries. But many of them keep the same memories, of the way horses died, screaming, in the shellfire, of men blown to pieces, of glistening, severed arms and legs, of the sound of shells going overhead like express trains, of the dreadful chatter of machine guns, of men going mad and sitting empty-eyed for years in asylums.

174

The French, the British, the Germans are here almost beyond numbering. One recalls that on the first day of the Battle of the Somme, in June 1916, 60,000 British troops—a whole football stadium full—were killed or wounded. They went walking across no-man's land in neat rows, led by an officer kicking a football. And they died and are buried in the same neat rows.

At Verdun there is that deathly silent ossuary that contains the bones of more than 130,000 men. The whole population of Peoria, Illinois. There are orange-stained windows that throw a fiery light on the walls and on the names of all these men, all these regiments. The pile of bones keeps growing. Even now old mines, old shells explode and there are more bones for the ossuary.

The scale is overpowering and poignant, vast fields of crosses and small memorials. Off one roadside, down a well-tramped path, are two graves and the sign, *Deux heros parmi tant d'autres* ("two heroes among so many others"). There are faded flowers on the graves. Verdun. People cry even today when they leave here.

The poppies still grow in Flanders Field. In Belleau Wood the wind sighs softly through the rows and rows of crosses. It is a gentle wind these late autumn days along the road to Paris. For the guns that blazed so relentlessly across these scenic and wooded hills and valleys are stilled. Forever, we hope. As another Armistice Day comes, all is quiet on the western front.

Photo Credits